A Thoreau Profile

An 1856 daguerreotype of Thoreau made in Worcester, Massachusetts, by B. D. Maxham. The white area over the breast is not a handkerchief but a blemish in the print.

A Thoreau Profile

By *Milton Meltzer*
and Walter Harding

▼

THOMAS Y. CROWELL COMPANY
New York   Established 1834

To Anna Shaughnessy and E. C. Prime

Grateful acknowledgment is made to the authors and publishers for permission to quote from the following copyrighted publications:

The Correspondence of Henry David Thoreau, edited by Walter Harding and Carl Bode, copyright 1958 by New York University Press.

Alcott Memoirs, edited by Frederick L. H. Willis, Badger, 1915. (By permission of Bruce Humphries, Inc., Publishers.)

The American Notebooks of Nathaniel Hawthorne, edited by Randall Stewart, copyright 1932 and 1960 by the Harvard University Press.

Henry Thoreau as Remembered by a Young Friend, by Edward Emerson. Houghton, Mifflin Co., 1917. (By permission of Raymond Emerson.)

Journals, Bronson Alcott, edited by Odell Shepard. Little, Brown & Company, 1938.

The late Francis Sanborn, for permission to quote from copyrighted works of Frank Sanborn.

Preface

A Thoreau Profile presents the life of one of our major American literary artists. It includes not only every known portrait of Thoreau made from life, but a full array of daguerreotypes, photographs, paintings, drawings, cartoons, broadsides, news clippings, maps, and charts of his Concord contemporaries, his friends, and their times. Although there have been many biographies of Thoreau, this is the first to portray his life graphically; the text is derived for the most part from Thoreau's own autobiographical writings, supplemented on occasion by the writings of his friends and contemporaries.

Thoreau in his own lifetime and for many years thereafter was usually dismissed as a minor disciple or imitator of his Concord neighbor Emerson. Within the last several decades there has been a revaluation of his position, his contribution, and his worth and he is now generally recognized as one of the few American literary figures of world-wide significance and stature. What is more, it is now realized that he has made contributions not only as a writer but also as a naturalist, a philosopher, a political theorist, and a scientist. *A Thoreau Profile* presents all these facets of Thoreau's life— and more besides. In general, the movement of the book is chronological, but now and then gaps in time are leaped to bring together allied material —such as that on Thoreau as a lecturer, as a surveyor, as an abolitionist, and as an "excursionist."

In the texts of letters written by and to Thoreau that are quoted in this book, identification of individuals, places, and events mentioned is set off in brackets. Oddities of spelling, punctuation, and paragraphing follow the original. The arrowhead symbol [►] is used to set off quotations from Thoreau.

We owe thanks to many persons for permitting us to use material from their collections, private and public, and for their advice in the editorial work. We are especially indebted to the librarians of Abernethy Library at Middlebury College; the American Antiquarian Society; the Berg Collection of the New York Public Library; the Boston Athenaeum; the Brooklyn Mu-

PREFACE

seum; the Concord Antiquarian Society; the Concord Free Public Library; the Essex Institute of Salem, Massachusetts; the Fruitlands Museum; the Harvard College Library; the Library of Congress; the Minnesota Historical Society; the Morgan Library; the New Jersey Historical Society; the New-York Historical Society; the New York Public Library; and the Ohio Historical Society.

We wish to express our appreciation for the very generous assistance offered by Mrs. Herbert B. Hosmer, Mrs. Howard W. Kent, Mrs. Marcia E. Moss, Mr. Robert F. Needham, Mrs. Dorothy E. Nyren, Mr. Roland W. Robbins, and Mrs. Caleb H. Wheeler, of Concord, Massachusetts; Joseph P. Templeton of the Joseph Dixon Crucible Company, Jersey City, New Jersey; Mr. Elliott S. Allison, Dublin, New Hampshire; Leonard Kleinfeld, Forest Hills, Long Island; Clayton Hoagland, Rutherford, New Jersey; Kenneth W. Cameron, chairman of The Emerson Society; Mrs. Hilda Wheelwright, Bangor, Maine.

For typing of the final manuscript we are indebted to Miss Anne Coldewey and Mrs. Helen Falconio. Bernard Cole, Bernard Hoffman, Keith Martin, and Toms Smith are due special thanks for photography.

Contents

CONTENTS

A Thoreau Profile

The leaf crystals on the ice of Walden Pond, on the preceding page, were observed and drawn by Thoreau on New Year's Day, 1856.

1

If I Forget Thee,
O Concord...

HENRY DAVID THOREAU was born on July 12, 1817, in Concord, Massachusetts. Because his father had recently suffered financial reverses, Thoreau was born in the home of his paternal grandmother, a plain New England farmhouse on Virginia Road on the outskirts of Concord village, where his family was temporarily weathering their storms.

Thoreau's father was a quiet, reserved man of whom Thoreau said:

▶ Father first came to this town to live with his father about the end of the last century, when he was about twelve years old. (His father died in 1801.) Afterward he went to the Lexington Academy (Parker's?) a short time, perhaps a year, then into Deacon White's store as clerk; then learned the dry-goods business in a store in Salem. (Aunt J. shows me a letter from him directly after his going there, dated 1807.) Was with a Hathaway. When about twenty-one, opened a store for himself on the corner where the town house stands of late years, a yellow building, now moved and altered into John Keyes's house. He did so well there that Isaac Hurd went into partnership with him, to his injury. They soon dissolved, but could not settle without going to law, when my father gained the case, bringing his books into court. Then, I think, he went to Bangor and set up with Billings, selling to Indians (among others); married; lived in Boston; writes thence to aunts at Bangor in 1815 with John on his knee; moved to Concord (where I was born), then to Chelmsford, to Boston, to Concord again, and here remained. Mother first came to Concord about the same age that father did, but a little before him.

As far as I know, Father, when he died, was not only one of the oldest men in the middle of Concord, but the one perhaps best acquainted with the inhabitants, and the local, social, and street history of the middle of the town, for the last fifty years. He belonged in a peculiar sense to the village street; loved to sit in the shops or at the post-office and read the daily papers. I think that he remembered more about the worthies (and unworthies) of Concord village forty years ago, both from dealing as a trader and from familiar intercourse with them, than any one else. Our other neighbors, now living or very recently dead, have either come to the town more recently than he, or have lived more aloof from the mass of the inhabitants.

Thoreau's mother, the former Cynthia Dunbar, on the other hand, was forthright and outspoken. She is best described in the words of one of her neighbors, Jean Munro LeBrun, in a letter to the *Boston Advertiser* of February 14, 1883:

I think the characteristics which chiefly impressed those of us who knew Mrs. Thoreau best, were the activity of her mind and the wideness of her sympathy. The first quality Henry inherited. She was also an ex-

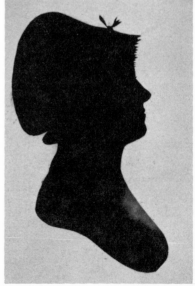

Their third child was born to John and Cynthia Thoreau of Concord on July 12, 1817. The records of the First Parish Church (at top) show "David Henry," as he was then called, was baptized on October 12.

The center of Concord village, as drawn by J. W. Barber and published in 1841. Thoreau was baptized in the church at the center rear. In 1817 the village population was about 2000.

cellent mother and housewife. In the midst of poverty she brought up her children to all the amenities of life, and, if she had but a crust of bread for dinner, would see that it was properly served. . . . Year after year, on Christmas and Thanksgiving days, she invited to her table, not the rich who would return her hospitality, but her poorer neighbors from whom she could expect no return. She was never so poor or so busy that she did not find ways of helping those poorer than herself.

And yet she did not confine her hospitality to the poor; people of every kind and degree were welcomed under her roof.

Her efforts in the anti-slavery cause are well known. She was unsparing in her denunciation of the fugitive slave law, and was one of the first to give aid and comfort to fugitives.

She had her faults, as which of us has not? but her aim was high. She expressed herself frankly at all times, and she sometimes told disagreeable truths; perhaps she felt it a duty to do so. She had the courage of her convictions, and she certainly never hesitated to condemn a fault. It was done in all honesty to bring about a reform. She was much more likely to say severe things to people than of them. This does not make a person popular. She was a great talker, and she occasionally said sharp things; but what was this in comparison to her virtues? She was quick-witted and observing, and naturally had more to say than some of her neighbors. She was never guilty of mean and petty gossip. She was not uncharitable,

[*3*]

and could readily forgive a fault if she saw any signs of repentance. On the whole, I think few women have done more good and less harm in the world than Mrs. Thoreau.

Thoreau had an older sister—Helen—quiet, retiring, a school-mistress much of her brief adult life. She died of the family scourge, tuberculosis, in 1849. John, born between Helen and Henry, was vivacious and outgoing, the leader of the childhood activities, and the idol of his younger brother. But John too died at an early age, in 1842—a blow from which Henry never fully recovered. Sophia, the fourth child, was two years younger than Henry. She in turn worshipped Henry, sharing his interest in nature, accompanying him occasionally on his hikes and boat rides, and in the years after his death, devoting herself to editing his manuscripts for publication.

The Thoreau household was always filled to overflowing with relatives, friends, and in later years, boarders. Among them were various aunts:

▶ Aunt Jane says that she was born on Christmas Day, and they called her a Christmas gift, and she remembers hearing that her Aunt Hannah Orrock was so disconcerted by the event that she threw all the spoons outdoors, when she had washed them, or with the dishwater.

Father says that he and his sisters (except Elizabeth) were born in Richmond Street, Boston, between Salem and Hanover Streets, on the spot where a bethel now stands, on the left hand going from Hanover Street. They had milk of a neighbor, who used to drive his cows to and from the Common every day.

But favorite of them all, so far as Thoreau was concerned, was his bachelor uncle, Charlie Dunbar. "Uncle Charles buried," he recorded in his Journal on March 28, 1856. "He was born in February, 1780, the winter of the Great Snow, and he dies in the winter of another great snow,— a life bounded by great snows."

A few days later:

▶ People are talking about my Uncle Charles. Minott tells how he heard Tilly Brown once asking him to show him a peculiar (inside?) lock in wrestling. "Now, don't hurt me, don't throw me hard." He struck his antagonist inside his knees with his feet, and so deprived him of his legs. Hosmer remembers his tricks in the barroom, shuffling cards, etc. He could do anything with cards, yet he did not gamble. He would toss up his hat, twirling it over and over, and catch it on his head invariably. Once wanted to live at Hosmer's, but the latter was afraid of him. "Can't we study up something?" he asked. H. asked him into the house and brought out apples and cider, and Charles talked. "You!" said he, "I burst the bully of Lowell" (or Haverhill?). He wanted to wrestle; would not be put off. "Well, we won't wrestle in the house." So they went out to the yard, and a crowd got round. "Come spread some straw here," said C. "I don't want to hurt him." He threw him at once. They tried again. He told them to spread more straw and he "burst" him.

He had a strong head and never got drunk; would drink gin sometimes, but not to excess. Did not use tobacco, except snuff out of another's box sometimes. Was very neat in his person. Was not profane, though vulgar.

Uncle Charles used to say that he hadn't a single tooth in his head. The fact was they were all double, and I have heard that he lost about all of them by the time he was twenty-one. Ever since I knew him he could swallow his nose.

Of his childhood in Concord Thoreau reminisced:

▶ Mother tried to milk the cow which Father took on trial, but she kicked at her and spilt the milk. (They say a dog had bitten her teats.) Proctor laughed at her as a city girl, and then he tried, but the cow kicked him over, and he finished by beating her with his cowhide shoe. Captain Richardson milked her warily, standing up. Father came home, and thought he would "bustle right up to her," for she needed much to be milked, but suddenly she lifted her leg and "struck him fair and square right in the muns," knocked him flat, and broke the bridge of his nose, which shows it yet. He distinctly heard her hoof rattle on his nose. This "started the claret," and, without stanching the blood, he at once drove her home to the man he had her of. She ran at some young women by the way, who saved themselves by getting over the wall in haste.

Father complained of the powder in the meeting-house garret at town meeting, but it did not get moved while we lived there. Here he painted over his old signs for guideboards, and got a fall when painting Hale's (?) factory. Here the bladder John was playing with burst on the hearth. The cow came into the entry after pumpkins. I cut my toe, and was knocked over by a hen with chickens, etc., etc.

Mother tells how, at the brick house, we each had a little garden a few feet square, and I came in one day, having found a potato just sprouted, which by her advice I planted in my garden. Ere long John came in with a potato which he had found and had it planted in his garden,—"Oh, mother, I have found a potato all sprouted. I mean to put it in my garden," etc. Even Helen is said to have found one. But next I came crying that somebody had got my potato, etc., etc., but it was restored to me as the youngest and original discoverer, if not inventor, of the potato, and it grew in my garden, and finally its crop was dug by myself and yielded a dinner for the family.

[5]

Helen (left), Henry's older sister, was born in 1812. She died in 1849, of the tuberculosis that was to take Henry, too. Sophia (right), youngest of the Thoreau children, was born in 1819. She became Henry's literary executor, publishing several articles and books extracted from the vast mass of manuscript he left. She died in 1876. None of the Thoreau children ever married.

Thoreau's two maiden aunts, Jane (left) and Maria (right), boarded with the family from time to time. Jane was quite deaf, and a steady talker. Maria's chatty letters reveal she thought Henry was putting things into *Walden* "that never ought to be there"; parts of it sounded "very much like blasphemy" to her. These Transcendentalists, she once said, "do so transmogrophy."

The regulars at Mrs. Thoreau's boarding table were women. "Here at my elbow," Thoreau's 1838 Journal notes, "sit five notable, or at least noteworthy, representatives of this nineteenth century—of the gender feminine." Among them were the widow (left) of Col. Joseph Ward, a Revolutionary soldier, and her daughter Prudence (in old age) (center). Mrs. Ward and Aunt Maria were old Boston friends, and staunch abolitionists. Prudence was an amateur botanist and flower painter. Aunt Louisa Dunbar (right), sister of Thoreau's mother, was a pretty steady boarder.

I was kicked down by a passing ox. Had a chicken given me by Lidy— Hannah—and peeped through the keyhole at it. Caught an eel with John. Went to bed with new boots on, and after with cap. "Rasselas" given me, etc., etc. Asked P. Wheeler, "Who owns all the land?" Asked Mother, having got the medal for geography, "Is Boston in Concord?" If I had gone to Miss Wheeler a little longer, should have received the chief prize book, "Henry Lord Mayor," etc., etc.

In his early years, Thoreau's family rarely remained settled in any one house for any length of time. In 1855 he noted down these wanderings:

▶ Recalled this evening, with the aid of Mother, the various houses (and towns) in which I have lived and some events of my life.

Born, July 12, 1817, in the

Minott House,	on the Virginia Road, where Father occupied Grandmother's thirds, carrying on the farm. The Catherines the other half of the house. Bob Catherines and John threw up the turkeys. Lived there about eight months. Si Merriam next neighbor. Uncle David died when I was six weeks old. I was baptized in old M. H. [Meeting House] by Dr. Ripley, when I was three months, and did not cry.
The Red House,	where Grandmother lived, we the west side till October, 1818, hiring of Josiah Davis, agent for Woodwards. (There were Cousin Charles and Uncle C. more or less.) According to day-book. Father hired of Proctor, October 16, 1818, and shop of Spaulding, November 10, 1818. Day-book first used by Grandfather, dated 1797. His part cut out and used by Father in Concord in 1808-9, and in Chelmsford, 1818-19-20-21.
Chelmsford,	till March, 1821. (Last charge in Chelmsford about middle of March, 1821.) Aunt Sarah taught me to walk there when fourteen months old. Lived next the meeting-house, where they kept the powder in the garret. Father kept shop and painted signs, etc.
Pope's House,	at South End in Boston, five or six (?) months, a ten-footer. Moved from Chelmsford through Concord, and may have tarried in Concord a little while. Day-book says, "Moved to Pinkney Street Sep 10th 1821 on Monday."

Whitwell's House, Pinckney Street, Boston, to March, 1823 (?).

Brick House, Concord, to spring of 1826.

Davis's House, (next to S. Hoar's) to May 7th, 1827.

Shattuck House (now William Monroe's) to spring of 1835.
  (Hollis Hall,
    Cambridge) (Hollis, Cambridge, 1833.)

Aunt's House, to spring of 1837. At Brownson's while teaching
  (Hollis Hall and in winter of 1835. Went to New York with Father,
    Canton) peddling, in 1836.

Parkman House, to fall of 1844. Was graduated in 1837. Kept town
  (Hollis, school a fortnight in 1837 (?). Began the big Red
    Cambridge) Journal, October, 1837. Wrote a lecture (my first) on Society, March 14, 1838, and read it before the Lyceum in the Masons' Hall, April 11th, 1838. Went to Maine for a school in May, 1838. Commenced school in the house in summer of 1838. Wrote an essay on Sound and Silence, December, 1838. Fall of 1839 up Merrimack to White Mountains. "Aulus Persius Flaccus," first printed paper of consequence, February 10th, 1840. The Red Journal of 546 pages ended, June, 1840. Journal of 396 pages ended January 31st, 1841.

An old drawing of the Concord building which is now the Colonial Inn. In 1789 Deacon John White bought the central part for a variety store, and moved his family into the left end. Henry's father John Thoreau, at 14, for a time worked as a clerk in White's store. In 1799, Henry's grandfather bought the right or northeast end as a home. While Henry was in his last two years at Harvard in 1835-37 his family lived here with aunts.

(R. W. E.'s)	Went to R. W. E.'s in spring of 1841 and stayed there to summer of 1843.
(William Emerson's Staten Island	Went to Staten Island, June, 1843, and returned in December, 1843, or to Thanksgiving. Made pencils in 1844.
Texas House, (Walden) (R.W.E.'s)	to August 29th, 1850. At Walden, July, 1845, to fall of 1847, then at R. W. E.'s to fall of 1848, or while he was in Europe.
Yellow House,	reformed, till present.

And in the Yellow House he remained until his death in 1862. But no matter where he lived, so long as it was in Concord, he was happy.

"I have never got over my surprise that I should have been born into the most estimable place in all the world, and in the very nick of time, too," he wrote in 1856. And the next year: "Almost I believe the Concord would not rise and overflow its banks again, were I not here."

Concord, to him, was the center of the universe. And no matter what the time of year, he found the beauty of nature all around him:

▶ WINTER

What a contrast between the village street now and last summer! The leafy elms then resounding with the warbling vireo, robins, bluebirds, and the fiery hangbird, etc., to which the villagers, kept indoors by the heat, listen through open lattices. Now it is like a street in Nova Zembla, —if they were to have any there. I wade to the post-office as solitary a traveller as ordinarily in a wood-path in winter. The snow is mid-leg deep, while drifts as high as one's head are heaped against the houses and fences, and here and there range across the street like snowy mountains. You descend from this, relieved, into capacious valleys with a harder bottom, or more fordable. The track of one large sleigh alone is visible, nearly snowed up. There is not a track leading from any door to indicate that the inhabitants have been forth to-day, any more than there is track of any quadruped by the wood-paths. It is all pure untrodden snow, banked up against the houses now at 4 P.M., and no evidence that a villager has been abroad to-day. In one place the drift covers the front-yard fence and stretches thence upward to the top of the front door, shutting all in, and frequently the snow lies banked up three or four feet high against the front doors, and the windows are all snowed up, and there is a drift over each window, and the clapboards are all hoary with it. It is as if the inhabitants were all frozen to death, and now you threaded the desolate streets weeks after that calamity. There is not a sleigh or vehicle of any kind on the Mill-Dam, but one saddled horse on which a farmer has come into town. The cars are nowhere. Yet they are warmer, merrier than ever there within. At the post-office they ask each traveller news of the cars,—"Is there any train up or down?"—or how deep the snow is on a level.

As you go down the street, you see on either hand, where erst were front yards with their parterres, rolling pastures of snow, unspotted blankness swelling into drifts. All along the path lies a huge barrow of snow raised by the arctic mound-builder. It is like a pass through the Wind River Mountains or the Sierra Nevada,—a spotless expanse of drifted snow, sloping upward over fences to the houses, deep banks all along their fronts closing the doors. It lies in and before Holbrook's piazza, dwarfing its columns, like the sand about Egyptian temples.

The windows are all sealed up, so that the traveller sees no face of inhabitant looking out upon him. The housekeeper thinks with pleasure or pain of what he has in his larder. No shovel is put to the snow this day. To-morrow we shall see them digging out. The farmer considers how much pork he has in his barrel, how much meal in his bin, how much wood in his shed. Each family, perchance, sends forth one representative before night, who makes his way with difficulty to the grocery or post-office to learn the news; i.e., to hear what others say to it, who can give the best account of it, best can name it, has waded farthest in it, has been farthest out and can tell the biggest and most adequate story; and hastens back with the news.

The town and country are now so still, there being no rattle of wagons nor even jingle of sleigh-bells, every tread being as with woolen feet, I hear very distinctly from the railroad causeway the whistle of the locomotive on the Lowell road. For the same reason, in such a day as this the crowing of a cock is heard very far and distinctly.

Two years later, early in 1856:

▶   The coldest morning this winter. Our thermometer stands at −14° at 9 A.M.; others, we hear, at 6 A.M. stood at −18°, at Gorham, N.H., −30°. There are no loiterers in the street, and the wheels of wood wagons squeak as they have not for a long time—actually shriek. Frostwork keeps its place on the window within three feet of the stove all day in my chamber. At 4 P.M. the thermometer is at −10°; at six it is at −14°.

I was walking at five, and found it stinging cold. It stung the face. When I look out at the chimneys, I see that the cold and hungry air snaps up the smoke at once. The smoke is clear and light-colored and does not get far into the air before it is dissipated (?), condensed. The setting sun no sooner leaves our west windows than a solid but beautiful crystallization coats them, except perhaps a triangularish bare spot at one corner, which perhaps the sun has warmed and dried. (I believe the saying is that by the 1st of February the meal and grain for a horse are half out.) A solid sparkling field in the midst of each pane, with broad, flowing sheaves surrounding it. It has been a very mild as well as open winter up to this. At 9 o'clock P.M., thermometer at —16°. They say it did not rise above — 6° to-day.

The next day:

▸ The coldest night for a long, long time was last. Sheets froze stiff about the faces. Cat mewed to have the door opened, but was at first disinclined to go out. When she came in at nine she smelt of meadow-hay. We all took her up and smelled of her, it was so fragrant. Had cuddled in some barn. People dreaded to go to bed. The ground cracked in the night as if a powder-mill had blown up, and the timbers of the house also. My pail of water was frozen in the morning so that I could not break it. Must leave many buttons unbuttoned, owing to numb fingers. Iron was like fire in the hands. Thermometer at about 7.30 A.M. gone into the bulb, —19° at least. The cold has stopped the clock. Every bearded man in the street is a graybeard. Bread, meat, milk, cheese, etc., etc., all frozen. See the inside of your cellar door all covered and sparkling with frost like Golconda. Pity the poor who have not a large wood-pile. The latches are white with frost, and every nail-head in entries, etc., has a white cap. The chopper hesitates to go to the woods. Yet I see S. W——— stumping past, three quarters of a mile, for his morning's dram. Neighbor Smith's thermometer stood at —26° early this morning. But this day is at length more moderate than yesterday.

Though the cold has been moderate to-day compared with yesterday, it has got more into the houses and barns, and the farmers complain more of it while attending to their cattle. This, i.e. yesterday, the 6th, will be remembered as the cold Tuesday. The old folks still refer to the Cold Friday, when they sat before great fires of wood four feet long, with a fence of blankets behind them, and water froze on the mantelpiece. But they say this is as cold as that was.

▸ SPRING

Every incident connected with the breaking up of the rivers and ponds and the settling of the weather is particularly interesting to us who live in a climate of so great extremes. When the warmer days come, they who dwell near the river hear the ice crack at night with a startling whoop as loud as artillery, as if its icy fetters were rent from end to end, and within a few days see it rapidly going out. So the alligator comes out of the mud with quakings of the earth. One old man, who has been a close

Henry Thoreau's maternal grandmother, Mary Jones Dunbar Minot. Thoreau was born in the house of her second husband, Captain Jonas Minot. She died at 82, in 1830.

observer of Nature, and seems as thoroughly wise in regard to all her operations as if she had been put upon the stocks when he was a boy, and he had helped to lay her keel,—who has come to his growth, and can hardly acquire more of natural lore if he should live to the age of Methuselah,—told me—and I was surprised to hear him express wonder at any of Nature's operations, for I thought that there were no secrets between them—that one spring day he took his gun and boat, and thought that he would have a little sport with the ducks. There was ice still on the meadows, but it was all gone out of the river, and he dropped down without obstruction from Sudbury, where he lived, to Fair Haven Pond, which he found, unexpectedly, covered for the most part with a firm field of ice. It was a warm day, and he was surprised to see so great a body of ice remaining. Not seeing any ducks, he hid his boat on the north or back side of an island in the pond, and then concealed himself in the bushes on the south side, to await them. The ice was melted for three or four rods from the shore, and there was a smooth and warm sheet of water, with a muddy bottom, such as the ducks love, within, and he thought it likely that some would be along pretty soon. After he had lain still there about an hour he heard a low and seemingly very distant sound, but singularly grand and impressive, unlike anything he had ever heard, gradually swelling and increasing as if it would have a universal and memorable ending, a sullen rush and roar, which seemed to him all at once like the sound of a vast body of fowl coming in to settle there, and, seizing his gun, he started up in haste and excited; but he found, to his surprise, that the whole body of the ice had started while he lay there, and drifted in to the shore, and the sound he had heard was made by its edge grating on the shore,—at first gently nibbled and crumbled off, but at length heaving up and scattering its wrecks along the island to a considerable height before it came to a standstill.

At length the sun's rays have attained the right angle, and warm winds blow up mist and rain and melt the snowbanks, and the sun, dispersing the mist, smiles on a checkered landscape of russet and white smoking with incense, through which the traveller picks his way from islet to islet, cheered by the music of a thousand tinkling rills and rivulets whose veins are filled with the blood of winter which they are bearing off.

Few phenomena gave me more delight than to observe the forms which thawing sand and clay assume in flowing down the sides of a deep cut on the railroad through which I passed on my way to the village, a phenomenon not very common on so large a scale, though the number of freshly exposed banks of the right material must have been greatly multiplied since railroads were invented. The material was sand of every degree of fineness and of various rich colors, commonly mixed with a little clay. When the frost comes out in the spring, and even in a thawing day in the winter, the sand begins to flow down the slopes like lava, sometimes bursting out through the snow and overflowing it where no sand was to be seen before. Innumerable little streams overlap and interlace one with another, exhibiting a sort of hybrid product, which obeys half way the law of currents, and half way that of vegetation. As it flows it takes the forms of sappy leaves or vines, making heaps of pulpy sprays a foot or more in depth, and resembling, as you look down on them, the laciniated, lobed, and imbricated thalluses of some lichens; or you are reminded of coral, of leopards' paws or birds' feet, of brains or lungs or bowels, and excrements of all kinds. It is a truly grotesque vegetation, whose forms and color we see imitated in bronze, a sort of architectural foliage more ancient and typical than acanthus, chiccory, ivy, vine, or any vegetable leaves; destined perhaps, under some circumstances, to become a puzzle to future geologists. The whole cut impressed me as if it were a cave with its stalactites laid open to the light. The various shades of the sand are singularly rich and agreeable, embracing the different iron colors, brown, gray, yellowish, and reddish. When the flowing mass reaches the drain at the foot of the bank it spreads out flatter into strands, the separate streams losing their semi-cylindrical form and gradually becoming more flat and broad, running together as they are more moist, till they form an almost flat sand, still variously and beautifully shaded, but in which you can trace the original forms of vegetation; till at length, in the water itself, they are converted into banks, like those formed off the mouths of rivers, and the forms of vegetation are lost in the ripple-marks on the bottom.

The whole bank, which is from twenty to forty feet high, is sometimes overlaid with a mass of this kind of foliage, or sandy rupture, for a quarter of a mile on one or both sides, the produce of one spring day. What makes this sand foliage remarkable is its springing into existence thus suddenly. When I see on the one side the inert bank,—for the sun acts on one side first,—and on the other this luxuriant foliage, the creation of an hour, I am affected as if in a peculiar sense I stood in the laboratory of the Artist who made the world and me,—had come to where he was still at work, sporting on this bank, and with excess of energy strewing his fresh designs about. I feel as if I were nearer to the vitals of the globe, for this sandy overflow is something such a foliaceous mass as the vitals of the animal body.

At the approach of spring the red squirrels got under my house, two at a time, directly under my feet as I sat reading or writing, and kept up the queerest chuckling and chirruping and vocal pirouetting and gurgling sounds that ever were heard; and when I stamped they only chirruped the louder, as if past all fear and respect in their mad pranks, defying humanity to stop them. No, you don't—chickaree—chickaree. They were wholly deaf to my arguments, or failed to perceive their force, and fell into a strain of invective that was irresistible.

The first sparrow of spring! The year beginning with younger hope than ever! The faint silvery warblings heard over the partially bare and moist fields from the bluebird, the song sparrow, and the red-wing, as if the last flakes of winter tinkled as they fell! What at such a time are histories,

Thoreau's birthplace on the old Virginia Road, in Concord. He was born in the easternmost of the upper rooms. Another family lived at the other end of the house. The Thoreaus stayed there only eight months while Henry's father tried to farm widow Minot's land. The house was later moved eastward down the road, where it still stands.

An old photo of Concord's Main Street, with the Brick House visible at the far end. Thoreau lived here from March, 1823 to the spring of 1826. The house has been torn down.

The "Texas House," built by Thoreau and his father in 1844 on Belknap, then called Texas Street, near the Concord railroad station. Henry dug and stoned the cellar, and planted vines and trees around it. The Thoreaus lived here until August, 1850, when they moved into the "Yellow House" on Main Street. Fire and hurricane destroyed most of the Texas House in the 1930's.

Door to Thoreau's Birthplace.

chronologies, traditions, and all written revelations? The brooks sing carols and glees to the spring. The marsh hawk, sailing low over the meadow, is already seeking the first slimy life that awakes. The sinking sound of melting snow is heard in all dells, and the ice dissolves apace in the ponds. The grass flames up on the hillsides like a spring fire,— "et primitus oritur herba imbribus primoribus evocata,"—as if the earth sent forth an inward heat to greet the returning sun; not yellow but green is the color of its flame;—the symbol of perpetual youth, the grass-blade, like a long green ribbon, streams from the sod into the summer, checked indeed by the frost, but anon pushing on again, lifting its spear of last year's hay with the fresh life below. It grows as steadily as the rill oozes out of the ground. It is almost identical with that, for in the growing days of June, when the rills are dry, the grass-blades are their channels, and from year to year the herds drink at this perennial green stream, and the mower draws from it betimes their winter supply. So our human life but dies down to its root, and still puts forth its green blade to eternity.

In a pleasant spring morning all men's sins are forgiven. Such a day is a truce to vice. While such a sun holds out to burn, the vilest sinner may return. Through our own recovered innocence we discern the innocence of our neighbors. You may have known your neighbor yesterday for a thief, a drunkard, or a sensualist, and merely pitied or despised him, and despaired of the world; but the sun shines bright and warm this first spring morning, re-creating the world, and you meet him at some serene work, and see how his exhausted and debauched veins expand with still joy and bless the new day, feel the spring influence with the innocence of infancy, and all his faults are forgotten. There is not only an atmosphere of good will about him, but even a savor of holiness groping for expression, blindly and ineffectually perhaps, like a new-born instinct, and for a short hour the south hillside echoes to no vulgar jest. You see some innocent fair shoots preparing to burst from his gnarled rind and try another year's life, tender and fresh as the youngest plant. Even he has entered into the joy of his Lord. Why the jailer does not leave open his prison doors,—why the judge does not dismiss his case,—why the preacher does not dismiss his congregation! It is because they do not obey the hint which God gives them, nor accept the pardon which he freely offers to all.

SUMMER

I rest and take my lunch on Lee's Cliff, looking toward Baker Farm. What is a New England landscape this sunny August day? A weather-painted house and barn, with an orchard by its side, in midst of a sandy field surrounded by green woods, with a small blue lake on one side. A sympathy between the color of the weather-painted house and that of the lake and sky. I speak not of a country road between its fences, for this house lies off one, nor do I commonly approach them from this side. The weather-painted house. This is the New England color, homely but fit as that of a toadstool. What matter though this one has not been inhabited for thirty years? Methinks I hear the crow of a cock come up from its barn-yard.

Out of an autumn evening in 1858 came this passage in the Journal:

AUTUMN

As the afternoons grow shorter, and the early evening drives us home to complete our chores, we are reminded of the shortness of life, and become more pensive, at least in this twilight of the year. We are prompted to make haste and finish our work before the night comes. I leaned over a rail in the twilight on the Walden road, waiting for the evening mail to be distributed, when such thoughts visited me. I seemed to recognize the November evening as a familiar thing come round again, and yet I could hardly tell whether I had ever known it or only divined it. The November twilights just begun! It appeared like a part of a panorama at which I sat spectator, a part with which I was perfectly familiar just coming into view, and I foresaw how it would look and roll along, and prepared to be pleased. Just such a piece of art merely, though infinitely sweet and grand, did it appear to me, and just as little were any active duties required of me. We are independent on all that we see. The hangman whom I have seen cannot hang me. The earth which I have seen cannot bury me. Such doubleness and distance does sight prove. Only the rich and such as are troubled with ennui are implicated in the maze of phenomena. You cannot see anything until you are clear of it. The long railroad causeway through the meadows west of me, the still twilight in which hardly a cricket was heard, the dark bank of clouds in the horizon long after sunset, the villagers crowding to the post-office, and the hastening home to supper by candle-light, had I not seen all this before! What new sweet was I to extract from it? Truly they mean that we shall learn our lesson well. Nature gets thumbed like an old spelling-book. The almshouse and Frederick were still as last November. I was no nearer methinks, nor further off from my friends. Yet I sat the bench with perfect contentment, unwilling to exchange the familiar vision that was to be unrolled for any treasure or heaven that could be imagined. Sure to keep just so far apart in our orbits still, in obedience to the laws of attraction and repulsion, affording each other only steady but indispensable starlight. It was as if I was promised the greatest novelty the world has ever seen or shall see, though

The Middlesex Hotel, by the Mill-Dam in Concord, a great gathering place. At one time Sheriff Moore lived in the house at the right, and his assistant, Sam Staples, was bartender in the hotel. The jail into which Staples put Thoreau for one night was behind the stable at the left. The hotel, rebuilt in 1845 after a fire, was torn down about 1900.

the utmost possible novelty would be the difference between me and myself a year ago. This alone encouraged me, and was my fuel for the approaching winter. That we may behold the panorama with this slight improvement or change, this is what we sustain life for with so much effort from year to year.

And yet there is no more tempting novelty than this new November. No going to Europe or another world is to be named with it. Give me the old familiar walk, post-office and all, with this ever new self, with this infinite expectation and faith, which does not know when it is beaten. We'll go nutting once more. We'll pluck the nut of the world, and crack it in the winter evenings. Theatres and all other sightseeing are puppet-shows in comparison. I will take another walk to the Cliff, another row on the river, another skate on the meadow, be out in the first snow, and associate with the winter birds. Here I am at home. In the bare and bleached crust of the earth I recognize my friend.

One actual Frederick that you know is worth a million only read of. Pray, am I altogether a bachelor, or am I a widower, that I should go away and leave my bride? This Morrow that is ever knocking with irresistible force at our door, there is no such guest as that. I will stay at home and receive company.

I want nothing new, if I can have but a tithe of the old secured to me. I will spurn all wealth beside. Think of the consummate folly of attempting to go away from here! When the constant endeavor should be to get nearer and nearer here. Here are all the friends I ever had or shall have, and as friendly as ever. Why, I never had any quarrel with a friend but it was just as sweet as unanimity could be. I do not think we budge an inch forward or backward in relation to our friends. How many things can you go away from? They see the comet from the northwest coast just as plainly as we do, and the same stars through its tail. Take the shortest way round and stay at home. A man dwells in his native valley like a corolla in its calyx, like an acorn in its cup. Here, of course, is all that you love, all that you expect, all that you are. Here is your bride elect, as close to you as she can be got. Here is all the best and all the worst you can imagine. What more do you want? Bear here-away then! Foolish people imagine that what they imagine is somewhere else. That stuff is not made in any factory but their own.

And from his essay, "Autumnal Tints":

▶ But think not that the splendor of the year is over; for as one leaf does not make a summer, neither does one falling leaf make an autumn. The smallest sugar maples in our streets make a great show as early as the fifth of October, more than any other tree there. As I look up the main street, they appear like painted screens standing before the houses; yet many are green. But now, or generally by the seventeenth of October, when almost all red maples and some white maples are bare, the large sugar maples also are in their glory, glowing with yellow and red, and show unexpectedly bright and delicate tints. They are remarkable for the contrast they often afford of deep blushing red on one half and green on the other. They become at length dense masses of rich yellow with a deep scarlet blush, or more than blush, on the exposed surfaces. They are the brightest trees now in the street.

John Thoreau, Henry's father, was secretary of the Concord Fire Society. This ad appeared in the Concord *Freeman* on January 7, 1842.

Henry's father advertises his pew for sale.

[*19*]

The large ones on our Common are particularly beautiful. A delicate but warmer than golden yellow is now the prevailing color, with scarlet cheeks. Yet, standing on the east side of the Common just before sundown, when the western light is transmitted through them, I see that their yellow even, compared with the pale lemon yellow of an elm close by, amounts to a scarlet, without noticing the bright scarlet portions. Generally, they are great regular oval masses of yellow and scarlet. All the sunny warmth of the season, the Indian summer, seems to be absorbed in their leaves. The lowest and inmost leaves next the bole are, as usual, of the most delicate yellow and green, like the complexion of young men brought up in the house. There is an auction on the Common to-day, but its red flag is hard to be discerned amid this blaze of color.

Little did the fathers of the town anticipate this brilliant success, when they caused to be imported from farther in the country some straight poles with their tops cut off, which they called sugar maples; and, as I remember, after they were set out, a neighboring merchant's clerk, by way of jest, planted beans about them. Those which were then jestingly called bean-poles are to-day far the most beautiful objects noticeable in our streets. They are worth all and more than they have cost,—though one of the selectmen, while setting them out, took the cold which occasioned his death,—if only because they have filled the open eyes of children with their rich color unstintedly so many Octobers. We will not ask them to yield us sugar in the spring, while they afford us so fair a prospect in the autumn. Wealth indoors may be the inheritance of few, but it is equally distributed on the Common. All children alike can revel in this golden harvest.

Surely trees should be set in our streets with a view to their October splendor, though I doubt whether this is ever considered by the "Tree Society." Do you not think it will make some odds to these children that they were brought up under the maples? Hundreds of eyes are steadily drinking in this color, and by these teachers even the truants are caught and educated the moment they step abroad.

But of much more importance than a knowledge of the names and distinctions of color is the joy and exhilaration which these colored leaves excite. Already these brilliant trees throughout the street, without any more variety, are at least equal to an annual festival and holiday, or a week of such. These are cheap and innocent gala-days, celebrated by one and all without the aid of committees or marshals, such a show as may safely be licensed, not attracting gamblers or rum-sellers, not requiring any special police to keep the peace. And poor indeed must be that New England village's October which has not the maple in its streets. This October festival costs no powder, nor ringing of bells, but every tree is a living liberty-pole on which a thousand bright flags are waving.

2

Academy and University

"I WAS FITTED, or rather made unfit, for College, at Concord Academy & elsewhere, mainly by myself, with the countenance of Phineas Allen, Preceptor," Thoreau once wrote his class secretary at Harvard. And very little else did he write about his school days. But George F. Hoar, one of his school-day friends who later became a distinguished United States senator, gives us a vivid picture in his *Autobiography of Seventy Years* of what those school days were like:

> They had good schools in Concord, and the boys generally were good scholars and read good books. So whenever they thought fit they could use as good language as anybody; but their speech with one another was in the racy, pithy Yankee dialect, which Lowell had made immortal in the "Biglow Papers." It was not always grammatical, but as well adapted for conveying wit and humor and shrewd sense as the Scotch of Burns.
>
> The boys knew very well how to take the conceit or vanity out of their comrades. In the summer days all the boys of the village used to gather

Phineas Allen, Harvard 1825, advertises that after two years of teaching in Brookline, he has become Preceptor of Concord Academy. He boarded at Mrs. Thoreau's. Henry prepared for Harvard at the Academy, entering late in 1828, when he was going on 12.

Concord Academy.

THE subscriber respectfully informs his friends and the public, that he has engaged Miss LUCY P. F. BARRETT to assist him in teaching the English branches the next quarter which will commence on Tuesday the 3d day of September next. To those who are acquainted with Miss Barrett's qualifications for teaching, any recommendation from me would be superfluous. All the pupils will be with the Principal the greater part of each day, and he will feel himself responsible for their improvement in every branch of study pursued, in good morals, and correct manners.

TERMS—$5 per quarter. Those under 12 years of age who attend to English branches only, will be received at $3.

Aug. 10, '33.   P. ALLEN, *Preceptor.*

at a place on the river, known as Thayer's swimming-place, about half a mile from the town pump, which was the centre from which all distances were measured in those days. There was a little gravel beach where you could wade out a rod or two, and then for a rod or two the water was over the boy's head. It then became shallow again near the opposite bank. So it was a capital place to learn to swim.

After they came out, the boys would sit down on the bank and have a sort of boys' exchange, in which all matters of interest were talked over, and a great deal of good-natured chaff was exchanged. Any newcomer had to pass through an ordeal of this character, in which his temper and quality were thoroughly tried.

I suppose the outdoor winter sports have not changed much since my childhood. The sluggish Concord River used to overflow its banks and cover the broad meadows for miles, where we found excellent skating, and where the water would be only a foot or two in depth. The boys could skate for ten miles to Billerica and ten miles back, hardly going over deep water, except at the bridges, the whole way.

Sleigh-riding was not then what it is now. There were a few large sleighs owned in the town which would hold thirty or forty persons, and once or twice in the winter the boys and girls would take a ride to some neighboring town when the sleighing was good.

The indoor games were marbles, checkers, backgammon, dominoes, hunt-the-slipper, blind-man's buff, and in some houses, where they were not too strict, they played cards. High-low-jack, sometimes called all-fours or seven-up, everlasting and old maid were the chief games of cards. Most of these games have come down from a very early antiquity.

The summer outdoor games were mumble-the-peg, high-spy, snap-the-whip, a rather dangerous performance, in which a long row of boys, with the biggest boy at one end, and tapering down to the smallest at the other end, would run over a field or open space until suddenly the big boy would stop, turn half around, and stand still and hold fast with all his might. The result was that the boy next to him had to move a very little distance, but the little fellow at the end was compelled to describe a half-circle with great rapidity, and was sometimes hurled across the field, and brought up with a heavy fall. There were thread-the-needle, hunt-the-red-lion and football, played very much as it is now, except with less system and discipline, and various games of ball. These games of ball were much less scientific and difficult than the modern games. Chief were four-old-cat, three-old-cat, two-old-cat and base.

We had fewer studies at our school than now. The boys who did not go to college learned to read and write, perhaps an elementary history of the United States, and arithmetic, and occasionally made some little progress in algebra. On Saturdays we used to "speak pieces." Our favorites were

Page from the 1829 records of the Concord Academic Debating Society, presided over by schoolmaster Phineas Allen. The members met in one another's homes at 6:30 P.M. On Nov. 5, H. Thoreau won for the negative in a debate so poorly prepared by both sides that the indignant young secretary, George Moore, protested it was a waste of time and paper even to record it.

some spirited lyric, like "Scots Wha Hae" or Pierpont's "Stand, the ground's your own, my braves," "The boy stood on the burning deck," and "Bernardo del Carpio." Sometimes, though not often, some comic piece was chosen, like Jack Downing's "Tax on Old Bachelors."

Those who fitted for college added Latin and Greek to these studies. The children were sent to school earlier than is the present fashion, and had long school hours and few vacations. There were four vacations in the year, of a week each, and three days at Thanksgiving time. Little account was made of Christmas. The fashion of Christmas presents was almost wholly unknown. The boys used to be allowed to go out of school to study in the warm summer days, and would find some place in a field, and sometimes up in the belfry of the little schoolhouse. I remember studying Caesar there with George Brooks, afterward judge, and reading with him an account of some battle where Caesar barely escaped being killed, on which Brooks' comment was, "I wish to thunder he had been!"

I am afraid the boys did not respect the property of the owners of the neighboring apple orchards, as undoubtedly the better-trained boys of modern times do now. We understood the law to be that all apples that grew on the branches extending over the highway were public property, and I am afraid that when the owner was not about we were not very particular as to the boundary-line.

The discipline of the schoolmaster in those days was pretty severe. For slight offences the boys were deprived of their recess or compelled to study for an hour after the school was dismissed. The chief weapon of torture was the ferule, to the efficacy of which I can testify from much personal knowledge. The master had in his desk, however, a cowhide for gross cases. I do not remember knowing how that felt from personal experience, but I remember very well seeing it applied occasionally to the big boys.

In the infant schools, which were kept by women, of course the discipline was not expected to be so severe. The schoolmistress in those days wore what was called a busk—a flat piece of lancewood, hornbeam, or some other like tough and elastic wood, thrust into a sort of pocket or sheath in her dress, which came up almost to the chin and came down below the waist. This was intended to preserve the straightness and grace of her figure. When the small boy misbehaved, the schoolma'am would unsheath this weapon, and for some time thereafter the culprit found sitting down exceedingly uncomfortable.

Sometimes the sole of the schoolmistress's slipper answered the same purpose, and sometimes a stick from some neighboring birch-tree. It all came to pretty much the same thing in the end. The schoolmistress knew well how to accomplish her purpose. There was a diversity of gifts but the same spirit.

We were put to school much earlier than children are now, and were more advanced in our studies on the whole. I began to study Latin on my sixth birthday. When I was nine years old I was studying Greek, and had read several books of Virgil. We were not very thorough Latin scholars, even when we entered college, but could translate Virgil and Cicero and Caesar and easy Greek like Xenophon.

One of the music sheets used by Henry and his sisters in their home pleasures. A neighbor reported that for years, the family did without tea, coffee, and sugar, so that the girls could have a piano. Helen gave music lessons; Henry played the flute.

Thoreau's flute.

Years later, in 1855, Phineas Allen, the former Concord Academy master, returned to Concord for a brief visit, and chose, of all his former students, Thoreau to look up. Thoreau commented at the time in his Journal:

▶ When Allen was here the other day, I found that I could not take two steps with him. He taught school in Concord seventeen [?] years ago, and has not been here since. He wished much to see the town again, but nothing living and fair in it. He had, I should say, a very musty recollection of it. He called on no living creature among all his pupils, but insisted on going [to] the new burying-ground and reading all the epitaphs. I waited at the gate, telling him that that ground did not smell good. I remembered when the first body was placed in it. He did, however, ask after one or two juvenile scamps and one idiotic boy who came to school to him,—how they had turned out,—and also after a certain caged fool, dead since he was here, who had lived near where he boarded; also after a certain ancient tavern, now pulled down. This at odd intervals, for he improved all the rest of his time while he was here in attending a Sabbath-school convention.

Like all of us, Thoreau often looked back at those childhood school days with fond recollections. He wrote in 1851:

▶ Methinks my present experience is nothing; my past experience is all in all. I think that no experience which I have today comes up to, or is comparable with, the experiences of my boyhood. And not only this is true, but as far back as I can remember I have unconsciously referred to the experiences of a previous state of existence. "For life is a forgetting," etc. Formerly, methought, nature developed as I developed, and grew up with me. My life was ecstasy. In youth, before I lost any of my senses, I can remember that I was all alive, and inhabited my body with inexpressible satisfaction; both its weariness and its refreshment were sweet to me. This earth was the most glorious musical instrument, and

[25]

I was audience to its strains. To have such sweet impressions made on us, such ecstasies begotten of the breezes! I can remember how I was astonished. I said to myself,—I said to others,—"There comes into my mind such an indescribable, infinite, all-absorbing, divine, heavenly pleasure, a sense of elevation and expansion, and [I] have had nought to do with it. I perceive that I am dealt with by superior powers. This is a pleasure, a joy, an existence which I have not procured myself. I speak as a witness on the stand, and tell what I have perceived." The morning and the evening were sweet to me, and I led a life aloof from society of men. I wondered if a mortal had ever known what I knew. I looked in books for some recognition of a kindred experience, but, strange to say, I found none. Indeed, I was slow to discover that other men had had this experience, for it had been possible to read books and to associate with men on other grounds. The maker of me was improving me. When I detected this interference I was profoundly moved. For years I marched as to a music in comparison with which the military music of the streets is noise and discord. I was daily intoxicated, and yet no man could call me intemperate. With all your science can you tell how it is, and whence it is, that light comes into the soul?

At considerable financial sacrifice on the part of his family, Thoreau entered Harvard College in the fall of 1833. Despite the fact that he had two long periods of absence—one because of illness: apparently the first serious flare-up of the tuberculosis that was eventually to kill him—and the other to earn money by teaching school in nearby Canton under the supervision of that itinerant wanderer through all religions, Orestes Brownson—

Harvard in 1833, the year Thoreau entered. The college then had about 200 students.

Thoreau did remarkably well in his classes. So well in fact, that he was asked to read an honors paper at his commencement exercises in 1837—a paper in which quite characteristcally he asked his fellowman to reverse the Biblical instruction by working one day a week and resting six.

For many years the picture of Thoreau's life at Harvard was colored by the reminiscences of his ministerial classmate John Weiss:

> He [Thoreau] passed for nothing, it is suspected, with most of us [Thoreau's college classmates]; for he was cold and unimpressible. The touch of his hand was moist and indifferent, as if he had taken up something when he saw your hand coming, and caught your grasp upon it. How the prominent, grey-blue eyes seemed to rove down the path, just in advance of his feet, as his grave Indian stride carried him down to University Hall!
>
> He did not care for people; his classmates seemed very remote. This reverie hung always about him, and not so loosely as the odd garments which the pious household care furnished. Thought had not yet awakened his countenance; it was serene, but rather dull, rather plodding. The lips were not yet firm; there was almost a look of smug satisfaction lurking round their corners. It is plain now that he was preparing to hold his future views with great setness, and personal appreciation of their importance. The nose was prominent, but its curve fell forward without firmness over the upper lip; and we remember him as looking very much like some Egyptian sculptures of faces, large-featured, but brooding, immobile, fixed in a mystic egotism. Yet his eyes were sometimes searching, as if he had dropped, or expected to find, something. It was the look of Nature's own child learning to detect her way-side secrets; and those eyes have stocked his book with subtle traits of animate and inanimate creation which had escaped less patient observers. For he saw more upon the ground than anybody suspected to be there. His eyes slipped into every tuft of meadow or beach grass, and went winding in and out of the thickest undergrowth, like some slim, silent, cunning animal. They were amphibious besides, and slid under fishes' eggs and into their nests at the pond's bottom, to rifle all their contents. Mr. Emerson has noticed, that Thoreau could always find an Indian arrow-head in places that had been ploughed over and ransacked for years. "There is one," he would say, kicking it up with his foot. In fact, his eyes seldom left the ground, even in his most earnest conversation with you, if you can call earnest a tone and manner that was very confident, as of an opinion that had formed from granitic sediment, but also very level and unflushed with feeling. The Sphinx might have become passionate and exalted as soon.
>
> But he had no animal spirits for our sport or mischief. We cannot recollect what became of him during the scenes of the Dunkin Rebellion

[a student uprising]. He must have slipped off into some "cool retreat or mossy cell." We are half inclined to suppose that the tumult startled him into some metamorphose, that corresponded to a yearning in him of some natural kind, whereby he secured a temporary evasion till peace was restored. He may also, in this interim of qualified humanity, have established an understanding with the mute cunning of nature, which appeared afterwards in his surprising recognition of the ways of squirrels, birds, and fishes. It is certainly quite as possible that man should take off his mind, and drop into the medium of animal intelligence, as that Swedenborg, Dr. Channing, and other spirits of just men made perfect, should strip off the senses and conditions of their sphere, to come dabbling about in the atmosphere of earth among men's thoughts. However this may be, Thoreau disappeared while our young absurdity held its orgies, stripping shutters from the lower windows of the buildings, dismantling recitation rooms, greeting tutors and professors with a frenzied and groundless indignation which we symbolized by kindling the spoils of sacked premises upon the steps. It probably occurred to him that fools might rush in where angels were not in the habit of going. We recollect that he declined to accompany several fools of this description, who rushed late, all in a fine condition of contempt, with Corybantic gestures, into morning prayers,—a college exercise which we are confident was never attended by the angels.

But a letter from another classmate, A. G. Peabody, to Thoreau, written while Thoreau was home ill, gives a much livelier impression of his college days:

The Davy Club got into a little trouble the week before last, from the following momentous circumstance.

Hen. Williams gave a lecture on Pyrotechny, and illustrated it with a parcel of fire works he had prepared in the vacation. The report spread through college, that there was to be a "display of fire works," and on the night of their meeting the Davy room was crowded, and those unfortunate youths who could not get in, stood in the yard round the windows. As you may imagine, there was some slight noise on the occasion. In fact the noise was so slight, that Bowen heard it at his room in Holworthy.

This worthy, boldly determined to march forth and disperse the "rioters." Accordingly in the midst of a grand display of rockets, et cetera, he stept into the room, and having gazed round him in silent astonishment for the space of two minutes, and hearing various cries of,—Intrusion—Throw him over—Saw his leg off—Pull his wool &c &c he made two or three dignified motions with his hand to gain attention, and then kindly advised us to "retire to our respective rooms." Strange to say

The summer costume at Cambridge. The initials and date on the rock indicate this sketch was probably made by Samuel Longfellow in 1838.

The signature, "D. H. Thoreau's," is in his copy of Cicero's *Orations*. Beneath he wrote "Hollis 20," the room he shared in 1833-34 with Charles Stearns Wheeler. Thoreau entered on September 1, 1833, and apparently acquired his Cicero on September 6.

he found no one inclined to follow this good advice, and he accordingly thought fit to withdraw.

There is (as perhaps you know) a law against keeping powder in the college buildings.

The effect of "Tutor Bowen's" intrusion was evident on the next Monday night, when Williams and Bigelow were invited to call and see President Quincy, and owing to the tough reasoning of Bowen, who boldly asserted that "powder was powder," they were each presented with public admonition.

We had a miniature volcanoe at Webster's lecture the other morning, and the odours therefrom, surpassed all ever produced by Araby the blest.

Imagine to yourself all the windows and shutters of the above named lecture room closed, and then if possible stretch your fancy a little farther and conceive the delightful scent produced by the burning of nearly a bushel of Sulphur, Phospuretted Hydrogen, and other still more pleasant ingredients.

As soon as the burning commenced there was a general rush to the door, and a crowd collected there, running out every half minute to get a breath of fresh air, and then coming in to see the volcanoe.

"No noise nor nothing."

Bigelow and Dr Bacon manufactured some "laughing gas," and administered it on the Delta. It was much better than that made by Webster.

Jack Weiss took some as usual. King, Freshman, took a bag, and produced surprising effects, merely by running into all the unhappy individuals he met, who seemed by no means desirous of his company. Wheeler, Joe Allen, and Hildreth, each received a dose. Wheeler proceeded to dance for the amusement of the company, Joe signalized himself by jumping over the Delta fence, and Sam raved about Milton Shakespeare Byron &c. Sam took two doses. It produced great effect on him. He seemed to be as happy as a mortal could desire, talked with Shakespeare, Milton &c, and seemed to be quite at home with them. It was amusing to trace the connexion of his ideas, and on the whole he afforded greater entertainment than any other person there, it affected him however very strongly, and he did not get over it till he was led off the Delta and carried into Wheelers room; he was well enough however next day.

Or, again, the memoirs of his fellow-Concordian John Shepard Keyes, who entered Harvard at the time of Thoreau's graduation:

The Monday before Commencement [1837], then the last Wednesday in August, was the appointed time. To reach Cambridge in season in-

Charles Stearns Wheeler, Thoreau's first roommate at Harvard. During a college summer vacation Thoreau is said to have lived with Wheeler for six weeks in a cabin in the woods.

Jones Very, poet and tutor at Harvard in Thoreau's senior year, became a close friend through their mutual love for Greek literature. The two men met many times again at Emerson's home.

volved then going down Sunday night, and my arrangements to spend the night with David Henry Thoreau, as we all called him then, had all been comfortably agreed upon. . . . Nothing memorable can I remember happened on that momentous ride bearing a green boy to the first of his decisive trials in real life, and I was dropped at the yard gate where Thoreau met me and took me to his room in Stoughton. I was anxious of the morrow's fate, overawed by the dull old college walls, and not a little inclined to be over-thoughtful at the sudden change it all implied. But these fancies were soon dispelled, a burst of Thoreau's classmates into his room, headed by Charles Theodore Russell, Trask and others who chaffed Thoreau and his Freshman in all sorts of amusing ways, and took down some of our local pride and Concord self-conceit for which I soon found out that my host was as distinguished in college as afterwards. These roaring seniors fresh from vacation's fun and with no more college duties to worry about made a sharp contrast to a Sunday evening at home. It was seeing something of the end before even the beginning. There had been some kind of a row with the faculty and the trouble was carried into the Criminal Court and I had heard the county side of it at home and now was told the students' side by some of the actors or sympathizers and got some ideas of college discipline that varied essentially from the home notion. It was startling and novel to hear "Old Prex" and other nicknames familiarly applied to such dignitaries as Concord had almost worshipped, and I fear that the introduction wasn't of the most useful sort to just such a boy as I was.

What impression he made on the faculty can be discovered from a letter the president of the college, Josiah Quincy, wrote to Ralph Waldo Emerson on June 25, 1837, after Emerson had written suggesting that his neighbor might deserve a scholarship:

Your view concerning Thoreau is entirely in consent with that which I entertain. His general conduct has been very satisfactory and I was willing and desirous that whatever falling off there had been in his scholarship should be attributable to his sickness.

He had, however, imbibed some notions concerning emulation & College rank, which had a natural tendency to diminish his zeal, if not his exertions.

His instructors were impressed with the conviction that he was indifferent, even to a degree that was faulty and that they could not recommend him consistent with the rule, by which they are usually governed in relation to beneficiaries. I have, always, entertained a respect for, and interest in, him, and was willing to attribute any apparent neglect, or indifference to his ill-health rather than to wilfulness. I obtained from

[*31*]

Josiah Quincy, president of Harvard in Thoreau's time, as portrayed by Gilbert Stuart. Thoreau entered conditioned, with Quincy remarking, "You have barely got in."

Edward Tyrrel Channing, Boylston Professor of Rhetoric, for whom Thoreau wrote many essays. Channing, who taught many other noted writers, such as Emerson, Lowell, and Holmes, didn't think very highly of Thoreau's efforts.

In Thoreau's senior year he began a course in German taught by young Henry Wadsworth Longfellow, just back from the grand tour of Europe. Thoreau quit after the first few sessions.

Cornelius C. Felton taught Thoreau Greek. Some dozen years later, the Harvard professor of Greek literature wrote of Thoreau as "a scholar of talent, but of such pertinacious oddity in literary matters that his writings will never probably do him any justice."

The mathematician and astronomer, Benjamin Pierce, was another of Thoreau's teachers at Harvard.

the instructors the authority to state all the facts to the Corporation, and submit the result to their discretion.

This I did, and that body granted Twenty-five dollars, which was within ten, or at most fifteen dollars of any sum, he would have received had no objection been made.

There is no doubt that from some cause an unfavorable opinion has been entertained, since his return, after his sickness, of his disposition to exert himself. To what it has been owing, may be doubtful. I appreciate very fully the goodness of his heart and the strictness of his moral principle; and have done as much for him, as under the circumstances was possible.

ORDER OF EXERCISES

COMMENCEMENT,

XXX AUGUST, MDCCCXXXVII.

Exercises of Candidates for the Degree of Bachelor of Arts.

[The performers will speak in the order of their names.]

1. A Salutatory Oration in Latin.

.46   CHARLES THEODORE RUSSELL, *Princeton.*

2. A Conference. "The Influence of Young's and Cowper's Poems."

.47   DANIEL WIGHT, *Natick.*
                      WILLIAM PINKNEY WILLIAMS, *Baltimore, Md.*

3. An Essay. "The Effect upon Literature of a Belief in Immortality."

.48   JOHN FOSTER WILLIAMS LANE, *Boston.*

4. A Conference. "The Commercial Spirit of Modern Times, considered in its
Influence on the Political, Moral, and Literary Character of a Nation."

.41   CHARLES WYATT RICE, *Brookfield.*
                      DAVID HENRY THOREAU, *Concord.*
                      HENRY VOSE, *Dorchester.*

5. A Literary Disquisition. "Modern Imitation of the Ancient Greek Tragedy."

                      SAMUEL AUSTIN KENDALL, *Utica, N. Y.*

MUSIC.

6. A Dissertation. "Severity of Manners in a Republic."

                      CLIFFORD BELCHER, *Farmington, Me.*

7. A Philosophical Disquisition. "The Real or Supposed Decline of Science at
the Present Day."

                      SAMUEL TREAT, *Portsmouth, N. H.*

Thoreau was fourth on the Commencement program, August 30, 1837. He
took part in a discussion which foreshadowed a theme he was to develop at
great length. At graduation Thoreau was 19th in his class, and had accumulated
14,397 points for grades, good behavior, class and chapel attendance, etc.

But the final word should be Thoreau's. Just before his graduation he was asked to write in his Class Book, and here he said:

▶ At the age of sixteen I turned my steps towards these venerable halls, bearing in mind, as I have ever since done, that I had two ears and but one tongue. I came—I saw—I conquered—but at the hardest, another such victory and I had been undone. "One branch more," to use Mr. Quincy's own words, "and you had been turned by entirely. You barely got in." However "A man's a man for a' that," I was in, and didn't stop to ask how I got there.

Suffice it to say, that though bodily I have been a member of Harvard University, heart and soul I have been far away among the scenes of my boyhood. Those hours that should have been devoted to study have been spent in scouring the woods, and exploring the lakes and streams of my native village. Oft could I sing with the poet,

> My heart's in the Highlands, my heart is not here;
>   My heart's in the highlands a-chasing the deer;
> Chasing the wild deer, and following the roe,
> My heart's in the Highlands wherever I go.

The occasional day-dream is a bright spot in the student's history, a cloud by day, a pillar of fire by night, shedding a grateful lustre over long years of toil, and cheering him onward to the end of his pilgrimage. Immured within the dank but classic walls of a Stoughton or Hollis [Harvard dormitories in which Thoreau roomed], his wearied and care-worn spirit yearns for the sympathy of his old, and almost forgotten friend, Nature, but failing of this is fain to have recourse to Memory's perennial fount, lest her features, her teachings, and spirit-stirring revelations be forever lost.

3

I Am a Schoolmaster...

WHEN THOREAU GRADUATED from Harvard in August, 1837, he was immediately offered a teaching position in the Concord public schools. But unfortunately he held the job for only a few weeks. His friend Ellery Channing tells the story:

> Another school experience was the town school in Concord, which he took after leaving college, announcing that he should not flog, but would talk morals as a punishment instead. A fortnight sped glibly along, when a knowing deacon, one of the School Committee, walked in and told Mr. Thoreau that he must flog and use the ferule, or the school would spoil. So he did, by feruling six of his pupils after school, one of whom was the maid-servant in his own house. But it did not suit well with his conscience, and he reported to the committee that he should no longer keep their school, as they interfered with his arrangements; and they could keep it.

Unfortunately, too, the country was plunging into the worst depression of the century and Thoreau could find no other teaching positions available. Writing late in December to his old friend Orestes Brownson, under whose supervision he had taught in Canton, Massachusetts, he outlined his philosophy of education and asked Brownson for a recommendation:

▶ My apology for this letter is to ask your assistance in obtaining employment For, say what you will, this frostbitten "forked carrot" of a body must be fed and clothed after all. It is ungrateful, to say the least, to suffer this much abused case to fall into so dilapidated a condition that every northwester may luxuriate through its chinks and crevices, blasting the kindly affections it should shelter, when a few clouts would save it. Thank heaven, the toothache occurs often enough to remind me that I must be out patching the roof occasionally, and not be always keeping up a blaze upon the hearth within, with my German and metaphysical cat-sticks.

But my subject is not postponed sine die. I seek a situation as teacher of a small school, or assistant in a large one, or, what is more desirable, as private tutor in a gentleman's family.

Perhaps I should give some account of myself. I would make education a pleasant thing both to the teacher and the scholar. This discipline, which we allow to be the end of life, should not be one thing in the schoolroom, and another in the street. We should seek to be fellow students with the pupil, and we should learn of, as well as with him, if we would be most helpful to him. But I am not blind to the difficulties of the case; it supposes a degree of freedom which rarely exists. It hath not entered into the heart of man to conceive the full import of that word—Freedom—not a paltry Republican freedom, with a posse comitatus at his heels to administer it in doses as to a sick child—but a freedom proportionate to the dignity of his nature—a freedom that shall make him feel that he is a man among men, and responsible only to that Reason of which he is a particle, for his thoughts and his actions.

I have even been disposed to regard the cowhide as a nonconductor. Methinks that, unlike the electric wire, not a single spark of truth is ever transmitted through its agency to the slumbering intellect it would address. I mistake, it may teach a truth in physics, but never a truth in morals.

I shall be exceedingly grateful if you will take the trouble to inform me of any situation of the kind described that you may hear of. As referees I could mention Mr Emerson—Mr [Samuel] Hoar—and Dr [Ezra] Ripley.

When spring came and he still had no position, he asked Ezra Ripley, the family minister; Josiah Quincy, the president of Harvard; and Ralph Waldo Emerson for letters of recommendation. Ripley wrote:

The undersigned very cheerfully hereby introduces to public notice, the bearer, Mr. David Henry Thoreau, as a Teacher in the higher branches of useful literature. He is a native of this town, & a graduate of Harvard University. He is well disposed & well qualified to instruct the rising generation. His scholarship & moral character will bear the strictest scrutiny. He is modest & mild in his disposition & government, but not wanting in energy of character & fidelity in the duties of his profession. It is presumed, his character & usefulness will be appreciated more highly as an acquaintance with him shall be cultivated. Cordial wishes for his success, reputation, & usefulness attend him, as an instructor & gentleman.

Ezra Ripley

Emerson wrote:

I cordially recommend Mr. Henry D. Thoreau, a graduate of Harvard University in August, 1837, to the confidence of such parents or guardians

Henry's own school opened in July, 1838. This ad announces the second term. A quartet of the town's leaders sponsored the Academy, and John became Preceptor. In 1840, ads for the spring and summer terms announced Henry would continue to teach in the languages or classical department.

as may propose to employ him as an instructor. I have the highest confidence in Mr. Thoreau's moral character and in his intellectual ability. He is an excellent Scholar, a man of energy & kindness, & I shall esteem the town fortunate that secures his Services.

From the Harvard president, Josiah Quincy, came this letter:

I certify that Henry D. Thoreau, of Concord, in this State of Massachusetts, graduated at this seminary [Harvard College] in August, 1837; that his rank was high as a scholar in all the branches, and his morals and general conduct unexceptionable and exemplary. He is recommended as well qualified as an instructor, for employment in any public or private school or private family.

But even armed with these letters Thoreau had no success. In the fall of 1838 he was to make one more attempt, directed to the Rev. Andrew Bigelow, of Taunton, Massachusetts:

▶ Sir, I learn from my brother and sister, who were recently employed as teachers in your vicinity, that you are at present in quest of some one to fill the vacancy in your high school, occasioned by Mr. Bellows' withdrawal. As my present school, which consists of a small number of well advanced pupils, is not sufficiently lucrative, I am advised to make application for the situation now vacant. I was graduated at Cambridge in —37, and have since had my share of experience in school-keeping.

I can refer you to the President and Faculty of Harvard College—to Rev. Dr. Ripley, or Rev. R. W. Emerson—of this town, or to the parents of my present pupils, among whom I would mention—Hon. Samuel

[*38*]

Hoar—Hon. John Keyes—& Hon. Nathan Brooks. Written recommendations by these gentlemen will be procured if desired.

Again he was not successful. But as he implied in his letter to Bigelow, he had already established a private school of his own, first in his own home, and later in the deserted building of the old Concord Academy. Despite his comments to Bigelow, his school prospered and he was joined in the teaching by his brother John. Some of the students were day students; others, from out of town, boarded with the Thoreau family.

With no school board to restrain him, Thoreau adopted many new and then-radical techniques, often foreshadowing the experiments of John Dewey of half a century or more later. There was no corporal punishment and learning was achieved chiefly through doing. One of his pupils, Dr. Thomas Hosmer, reported this conversation on profanity between Thoreau and his pupils:

"Boys, if you went to talk business with a man, and he persisted in thrusting words having no connection with the subject into all parts of every sentence—Boot-jack, for instance,—wouldn't you think he was taking a liberty with you, and trifling with your time, and wasting his own?" Thoreau then thrust the "Boot-jack" violently and frequently into a sentence, to show how absurd bad street language was.

Rev. Ezra Ripley, who gave Henry a letter of recommendation "as an instructor and gentleman" when he was looking for a teaching position. Rev. Ripley married John Thoreau to Cynthia Dunbar at Concord in 1812, and baptized Henry Thoreau in 1817. He lived in the Old Manse near the Concord Bridge and had seen the famous battle of April 19. He died in 1841, at the age of 90. He was good at fires, had a strong partiality for the ladies, never let the church out of his mind, and was excellent company and counsel to all.

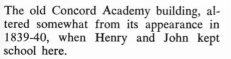

The old Concord Academy building, altered somewhat from its appearance in 1839-40, when Henry and John kept school here.

Another pupil, Henry Warren, reminiscing to F. B. Sanborn, described Thoreau's eye for detail:

An instance of Henry's close observation [was] in the matter of Indian antiquities, of which both brothers early became connoisseurs. As they were sailing through the Great Meadows, past Ball's Hill . . . Henry Thoreau called attention to a spot on the river-shore, where he fancied the Indians had made their fires, and perhaps had a fishing village. There, he said, if he had a spade, he could perchance uncover one of their rude fireplaces. "We cannot find one to-day, for we have no spade; but the next time we come I will see if that was the place of habitation." Coming to land there the next week, they drew the boat to shore, and moved up the bank a little way. "Do you see," said Henry, "anything here that would be likely to attract Indians to this spot?" One boy said, "Why, here is the river for their fishing"; another pointed to the woodland near by, which could give them game. "Well, is there anything else?" pointing out a small rivulet that must come, he said, from a spring not far off, which could furnish water cooler than the river in summer; and a hillside above it that would keep off the north and northwest wind in winter.

Then, moving inland a little farther, and looking carefully about, he struck his spade several times, without result. Presently, when the boys began to think their young teacher and guide was mistaken, his spade struck a stone. Moving forward a foot or two, he set his spade in again, struck another stone, and began to dig in a circle. He soon uncovered the red, fire-marked stones of the long-disused Indian fireplace; thus proving that he had been right in his conjecture. Having settled the point, he carefully covered up his find and replaced the turf,—not wishing to have the domestic altar of the aborigines profaned by mere curiosity.

On another walk he suddenly stopped, knelt down, and examined the ground with some care; then, plucking a minute something, he asked Henry Warren if he could see that? "Yes,—but what about it?" Drawing his microscope, Thoreau showed the boy that, thus magnified, this little thing was a perfect flower, just then in the season of its blossoming; and he went on to say that he had become so well acquainted with the flowers, large and small, of Concord and Acton and Lincoln, that without looking in the almanac, he could tell by the blooming of the flowers in what month he was. All this with no evident wish to display his own superior knowledge, but only to impress on the youthful mind how immense is the sum of Nature's activities, and to impart to others his own skill in such matters.

But perhaps the best report on the Thoreaus' school is the contemporary account of 12-year-old Edmund Sewall, brother of Ellen, the girl both schoolmasters fell in love with. Young Edmund arrived in Concord by stage on March 23, 1840; a few days later he wrote his mother:

We have a very good schoolhouse and everyone has a seat by himself. Saturday is given to writing composition. We boys who board in Mr. Thoreau's family are to write letters home once a fortnight instead of composition if we choose. I am now writing at my desk in the schoolhouse.

I have dreamed of seeing your faces twice since I have been here, and even the large pail I used to get the milk in was introduced once. I sleep with Mr. J. Thoreau in the very same room where we slept when we were here. Aunty has kindly bought me a writing book for a Journal and I made a beginning in it this morning. Wednesday afternoon before the stage got in with Joseph & Jesse, Charles and I went with Mr. Thoreau to Walden Pond. We passed through a deep little valley which had been christened by Mr. Thoreau "Laurel glen" because there is some of the large beautiful wood laurel growing there. On our return Mr. T. shot a "slate colored sparrow" which he wished to examine and while we were at the pond, for want of other game, fired a charge of buckshot through a snowball set upon a post.

Day before yesterday Mr. Thoreau took me into the printing office of the Yeoman's Gazette where I saw a compositor setting types and likewise an odd number of the Hingham Patriot. It did look so natural! He also took me to Mr. Bratt's the gunsmith's. He was just regulating the sights I think he called them of a new rifle. I saw there a number of guns, one nice little one just big enough for a boy of my size.

What did Father do with his letter to Mr. Thoreau? It was not in my trunk and I think that he must have omitted to put it in so we have been expecting to see it by mail but it has not come. How soon is Ellen's school to begin?

What the schoolday schedule was like can be learned from Edmund's letter to his father, a month after the term began:

In the morning I recite Solid Geometry. I draw the figures and write down the demonstration on the slate after Mr. Henry has taken the book and when I have done carry it to him. He examines it to see that it is right. Geography comes next, immediately after recess. Smith's geography is the one used. I borrow it of one of the boys who has done studying it. Grammar comes next. Parker and Fox's is used. It is in two parts. I have been through the first part and have begun the second. I borrow it of Mr. Thoreau.

In the afternoon I am exclusively under Mr. Henry's jurisdiction. I recite in Algebra and Latin generally before recess. In the afternoon Mr. Henry's classes go up into the hall over the schoolroom to recite. In Latin I am in company with Miss Hine. We are now on the life of Alcibiades in Nepos and in the exception in conjugation in the grammar.

A receipt Henry wrote out for the tuition of George Brooks and Samuel Burr, paid by Nathan Brooks. This was in September, 1838.

Geography is studied by a good many. We draw maps of the states. Saturday morning is devoted to writing composition. The two that I have written have been on birds and berries. We boys who live away from home can write home instead of writing compositions if we wish every other Saturday. I have hitherto availed myself of this permission. We write every other day, that is to say half write one day and half the next.

The school hours are from half past eight to half past twelve in the morning and from two to four in the afternoon. Mr. Thoreau reads loud those compositions which he thinks will please the scholars, which sometimes occasions a great deal of laughter. The boys sometimes write their lives or those of some venerable Aunt Hannah or Uncle Ichabod.

In his diary Edmund recorded how he handled a difficult writing assignment:

NOTICE.

A Lecture on Slavery, will be delivered by J. N. BROWNE, Esq. of Lynn, at the Rev. Mr Wilders Meeting House, on Wednesday evening next, at 7 o'clock.

LYCEUM.

The Members of Concord Lyceum, will meet at Lyceum Hall, on Wednesday evening next at 7 o'clock, P. M. for the choice of officers. A full attendance is requested, as business of importance will be laid before the meeting, in relation to the admission of members. Per order of the Curators.

INSTRUCTION IN VOCAL MUSIC.

THE subscriber respectfully gives notice, that he will commence a course of Lessons of instruction in the elementary principles of Vocal Music, at the Lyceum Hall on Monday Oct. 15th at six o'clock, P. M.

TERMS—$1,00 for twenty four lessons. Those who wish to attend are requested to leave their names previous to the 15th.

THOMAS HUNT.

Concord, Oct. 2, 1838.

Dancing School.

J. DELANO, Respectfully informs the young and Gentlemen of Concord, that he will mence an Evening School for the instruction of who may wish to attend to the acquisition of this ionable accomplishment, on WEDNESDAY E October 31, at Shepards' Hall. In which will be the latest and most fashionable Dances.

TUITION—$3 per couple.

☞ Mr D. trusts by his long experience in the fession, he will be able to give satisfaction to thos may honor him with their patronage.

Concord, Oct. 13, 1838.

Culture in Concord.

Mr. Thoreau said that he should give me something to write about of which I did not know much about so I wrote on the Ostrich the Eagle and Falcon which everybody knows something about. I suppose he thought I should write about Bobolinks and Chickadees of which I am wholly ignorant. I cunningly took half a sheet of paper to write on so on the whole I managed to fill out my pages.

The school program sometimes extended into the evenings. The pupils were taken to the Lyceum on occasion, as Edmund reported in his diary:

We went to the Lyceum expecting that a phrenologist would lecture. His apparatus was there but the lecturer had not arrived. A man there set out his casts and several real skulls on the desk but immediately put them back again. One of the skulls was that of a British soldier who fell in the Battle of Concord. It was dug up in Lincoln. It was only the upper half of the head. There was the bullet hole through which the ball that killed him had passed. A Mr. Haskins lectured on Roger Williams the founder of Rhode Island—a description of his life. Bought 2 cents worth of burnt almonds going home.

But field trips with the Thoreau brothers on a Saturday afternoon provided, Edmund thought, the best part of his education:

In the afternoon we went off into the woods with a parcel of the boys of the school where we played awhile and drank out [sic] a jug of lemonade we had carried with us. We then left the jug till we came back and started for Walden pond. As we were coming back we saw Aunt and Mr. Thoreau, and I went and joined her while the rest of the boys kept on. We went to Goose pond where we heard a tremendous chirping of frogs. It has been disputed whether the noise was caused by frogs so we were very curious to know what it was. Mr. Thoreau however caught three very small frogs, two of them in the act of chirping. While bringing them home one of them chirped in his hat. He carried them to Mr. Emerson in a tumbler of water. They chirped there also. On Sunday morning I believe he put them into a barrel with some rain water in it. He threw in some sticks for them to rest on. They sometimes crawled up the side of the barrel. I saw one of them chirping. He had swelled out the loose skin of his throat like a little bladder.

The school continued to prosper. Most of the time there was a waiting list of students who wished to enroll. But in 1841 John's health deteriorated and he was forced to give up teaching. Henry, not wishing to carry the burden alone, abandoned the school.

The Thoreau family moved into the Parkman House in 1837. The brothers kept school there in 1838. They soon moved the school to the old unused Concord Academy buildings, but Mrs. Thoreau continued to board pupils from outside the village. Henry wrote his first lecture and his first journal in his room in the attic of the Parkman House. The house was then where the Concord Library now stands.

In later years, recalling his teaching experience, he meditated:

▶ How vain to try to teach youth. or anybody, truths! They can only learn them after their own fashion, and when they get ready. I do not mean by this to condemn our system of education, but to show what it amounts to. A hundred boys at college are drilled in physics and metaphysics, languages, etc. There may be one or two in each hundred, prematurely old perchance, who approaches the subject from a similar point of view to his teachers, but as for the rest, and the most promising, it is like agricultural chemistry to so many Indians. They get a valuable drilling, it may be, but they do not learn what you profess to teach. They at most only learn where the arsenal is, in case they should ever want to use any of its weapons. The young men, being young, necessarily listen to the lecturer in history, just as they do to the singing of a bird. They expect to be affected by something he may say. It is a kind of poetic pabulum and imagery that they get. Nothing comes quite amiss to their mill.

I AM A SCHOOLMASTER . . .

In his 1852 Journal, he examined the culture of Concord:

▶   We boast that we belong to the Nineteenth Century, and are making the most rapid strides of any nation. But consider how little this village does for its own culture. We have a comparatively decent system of common schools, schools for infants only, as it were, but, excepting the half starved Lyceum in the winter, no school for ourselves. It is time that we had uncommon schools, that we did not leave off our education when we begin to be men. Comparatively few of my townsmen evince any interest in their own culture, however much they may boast of the school tax they pay. It is time that villages were universities, and their elder inhabitants the fellows, with leisure—if they are indeed so well off—to pursue liberal studies as long as they live. In this country the village should in many respects take the place of the nobleman who has gone by the board. It should be the patron of the fine arts. It is rich enough; it only wants the refinement. It can spend money enough on such things as farmers value, but it is thought utopian to propose spending money for things which more intelligent men know to be of far more worth. If we live in the Nineteenth Century, why should our life be in any respect provincial? As the nobleman of cultivated taste surrounds himself with whatever conduces to his culture,—books, paintings, statuary, etc.,—so let the village do. This town,—how much has it ever spent directly on its own culture? To act collectively is according to the spirit of our institutions, and I am confident that, as our circumstances are more flourishing, our means are greater. New England can hire all the wise men in the world to come and teach her, and board them round the while, and not be provincial at all. That is the uncommon school we want. The one hundred and twenty-five dollars which is subscribed in this town every winter for a Lyceum is better spent than any other equal sum. Instead of noblemen, let us have noble towns or villages of men. This town has just spent sixteen thousand dollars for a town-house. Suppose it had been proposed to spend an equal

Helen Thoreau announced she would open a school for girls in May, 1842, a year after her brother John's death led to the closing of his and Henry's Academy.

sum for something which will tend far more to refine and cultivate its inhabitants, a library, for instance. We have sadly neglected our education. We leave it to Harper & Brothers and Redding & Co.

What had education or books to say about the subject of getting an honest living? Little or nothing, as Thoreau saw it:

▶ Neither the New Testament nor Poor Richard speaks to our condition. I cannot think of a single page which entertains, much less answers, the questions which I put to myself on this subject. How to make the getting our living poetic! for if it is not poetic, it is not life but death that we get. Is it that men are too disgusted with their experience to speak of it? or that commonly they do not question the common modes? The most practically important of all questions, it seems to me, is how shall I get my living, and yet I find little or nothing said to the purpose in any book. Those who are living on the interest of money inherited, or dishonestly, i.e. by false methods, acquired, are of course incompetent to answer it. I consider that society with all its arts, has done nothing for us in this respect. One would think, from looking at literature, that this question had never disturbed a solitary individual's musings. Cold and hunger seem more friendly to my nature than those methods which men have adopted and advise to ward them off. If it were not that I desire to do something here,—accomplish some work,—I should certainly prefer to suffer and die rather than be at the pains to get a living by the modes men propose.

4

We Two, Brothers,
Weighed Anchor

IN THE LATE SUMMER of 1839, the two brothers, John and Henry Thoreau, decided to take a vacation from the school teaching duties and go on an excursion to the White Mountains of New Hampshire. Earlier they had built themselves a rowboat, and now having outfitted it with a sail and various provisions, they set off down the Concord River and up the Merrimack to the foothills of the White Mountains.

As Thoreau later described in his journal:

▶   We had appointed Saturday, August 31st, 1839, for the commencement of our White Mountain expedition. We awake to a warm, drizzling

The boat-landing Thoreau used in Concord.

A summer scene on the Concord River, drawn by May Alcott. The river, Thoreau said, "is remarkable for the gentleness of its current, which is scarcely perceptible, and some have referred to its influence the proverbial moderation of the inhabitants of Concord, as exhibited in the Revolution, and on later occasions. It has been proposed that the town should adopt for its coat of arms a field verdant, with the Concord circling nine times around."

rain which threatens delay to our plans, but at length the leaves and grass are dried, and it comes out a mild afternoon, of such a sober serenity and freshness that Nature herself seems maturing some greater scheme of her own. All things wear the aspect of a fertile idleness. It is the eventide of the soul. After this long dripping and oozing from every pore Nature begins to respire again more healthily than ever. So with a vigorous shove we launch our boat from the bank, while the flags and bulrushes curtsy a Godspeed, and drop silently down the stream. As if we had launched our bark in the sluggish current of our thoughts, and were bound no-whither.

Gradually the village murmur subsides, as when one falls into a placid dream and on its Lethe tide is floated from the past into the future, or as silently as fresh thoughts awaken us to new morning or evening light.

Our boat was built like a fisherman's dory, with thole-pins for four oars. Below it was green with a border of blue, as if out of courtesy [to] the green sea and the blue heavens. It was well calculated for service, but of consequence difficult to be dragged over shoal places or carried round falls.

A boat should have a sort of life and independence of its own. It is a sort of amphibious animal, a creature of two elements, a fish to swim and a bird to fly, related by one half of its structure to some swift and shapely fish and by the other to some strong-winged and graceful bird. The fins of the fish will tell where to set the oars, and the tail give some hint for the form and position of the rudder. And so may we learn where there should be the greatest breadth of beam and depth in the hold. The bird will show how to rig and trim the sails, and what form to give to the prow, that it may balance the boat and divide the air and water best.

John Thoreau, Jr., as painted by his sister Sophia. After John's sudden death of lockjaw on January 12, 1842 (below is the Concord *Freeman*'s obituary notice), Henry decided to make his record of their rowboat excursion a memorial tribute. The book did not appear, however, until nine years after the excursion. Although Henry worshiped his older brother (even suffering a severe sympathetic case of lockjaw), there is little in *A Week* that reflects that feeling.

DIED:

In this town, on Tuesday last, suddenly of the lock jaw, Mr JOHN THOREAU, Jr., aged 27.

In Acton, on the 6th inst., Mr JONAS WOOD, aged

The boat took to the water; from of old there had been a tacit league struck between these two, and now it gladly availed itself of the law that the heavier shall float the lighter.

Two masts we had provided, one to serve for a tentpole at night, and likewise other slender poles, that we might exchange the tedium of rowing for poling in shallow reaches. At night we lay on a buffalo-skin under a tent of drilled cotton eight feet high and as many in diameter, which effectually defended from dampness, so short a step is it from tiled roofs to drilled cotton, from carpeted floors to a buffalo-skin.

There were a few berries left still on the hills, hanging with brave content by the slenderest threads.

As the night stole over, such a freshness stole across the meadow that every blade of cut-grass seemed to teem with life.

We stole noiselessly down the stream, occasionally driving a pickerel from the covert of the pads, or a bream from her nest, and the small green bittern would now and then sail away on sluggish wings from some recess of the shore. With its patient study by rocks and sandy capes, has it wrested the whole of her secret from Nature yet? It has looked out from its dull eye for so long, standing on one leg, on moon and stars sparkling through silence and dark, and now what a rich experience is its! What says it of stagnant pools, and reeds, and damp night fogs? It would be worth while to look in the eye which has been open and seeing at such hours and in such solitudes. When I behold that dull yellowish green, I wonder if my own soul is not a bright, invisible green. I would fain lay my eye side by side with its and learn of it.

And so they continued along their way. On Thursday, September 5, they reached Hooksett, New Hampshire. They stored their boat and gear with a friendly farmer and made their way by stage-coach and foot to the mountains, via Concord and Plymouth. They visited the Flume and the Old Man, Crawford Notch, and the top of Mount Washington, finally returning to Hooksett on Thursday, the 12th, and picking up their boat, made their return hastily down the river, arriving back in Concord on Friday evening.

What at first glance might seem an insignificant two-week vacation later assumed great importance in Thoreau's life, for the account of that excursion became the basis of his first book, *A Week on the Concord and Merrimack Rivers*. Greatly expanding his original journal entries and padding them with miscellaneous essays and poems on subjects as varied as Chaucer, the Hindus, friendship, and religion, he enlarged the tale of a rowboat journey into a personal epic.

5

A Friend of Emerson

WHEN THOREAU and his Concord neighbor Ralph Waldo Emerson became acquainted is a question that cannot be answered specifically. Emerson became a resident of Concord in 1835, while Thoreau was away at college. Emerson wrote a letter of recommendation for Thoreau as early as June, 1837, several months before he officially returned to Concord from Harvard. One legend has it that they became acquainted when Emerson heard that Thoreau had walked twenty miles to hear him lecture. Another states that Mrs. Lucy Brown, Emerson's sister-in-law who was boarding with the Thoreaus at the time, called Emerson's attention to a passage in one of Thoreau's journals that was similar to an idea Emerson had expressed in a public lecture (on the other hand, Thoreau himself has implied that he didn't start a journal until Emerson had personally suggested the idea to him). At any rate, by February 11, 1838, Emerson was recording in his journal, "I delight much in my young friend, who seems to have as free and erect a mind as any I have ever met."

Their friendship rapidly ripened and deepened. Thoreau's down-to-earth practicality complemented Emerson's philosophical abstractness; Emerson's wider fame served to introduce Thoreau to new men and new horizons. In 1841, after the Thoreau brothers had abandoned their school, Henry was invited to live with the Emersons, exchanging his handiwork around the Emerson household for board and room. When Thoreau's brother John and Emerson's son Waldo died within a few weeks of each other, their mutual grief tightened the bonds of friendship between the two men. Then, after the Walden experiment, Thoreau again lived in the Emerson house, looking out for the family while Emerson was on a lecture tour abroad.

In the early days of their friendship Thoreau quite naturally idolized Emerson:

▶ Emerson . . . is a critic, poet, philosopher, with talent not so conspicuous, not so adequate to his task; but his field is still higher, his task more arduous. Lives a far more intense life; seeks to realize a divine life;

[*51*]

his affections and intellect equally developed. Has advanced farther, and a new heaven opens to him. Love and Friendship, Religion, Poetry, the Holy are familiar to him. The life of an Artist; more variegated, more observing, finer perception; not so robust, elastic; practical enough in his own field; faithful, a judge of men. There is no such general critic of men and things, no such trustworthy and faithful man. More of the divine realized in him than in any. A poetic critic, reserving the unqualified nouns for the gods.

The young Ralph Waldo Emerson in an engraving which appeared in one of the early illustrated weeklies. Born in 1803, he was 14 years older than Thoreau.

A note from Emerson to Thoreau, asking him to come up to the southern side of Concord's Fair Haven Hill, which was called the Cliff, and to bring his flute. It was written probably in November, 1838, when the two had become friendly, but not to a degree that permitted dropping the "dear Sir" salutation. In fact, it took Thoreau ten years to reach that point with Emerson.

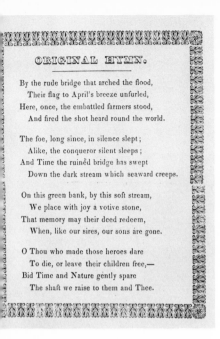

On July 4, 1837, Concord dedicated its monument to the battle of April 19, 1775. The land was given the town by Rev. Ezra Ripley, Emerson's stepgrandfather, who made the benediction that day. The "original Hymn by a citizen of Concord" had been written by Emerson, and was sung by the assembled townspeople (including Thoreau) to the tune of "Old Hundred." They read the stanzas from leaflets printed for the occasion. One of the two known surviving copies is reproduced here.

Emerson's first child, Waldo, whose death in January, 1842, came only two weeks after the death of Thoreau's brother John. This engraving is probably from the daguerreotype that John arranged to have made of the five-year-old just before his death. Of little Waldo, who was his favorite in these years he was living with the Emersons, Thoreau wrote "he died as the mist rises from the brook. . . . He had not even taken root here."

Emerson has special talents unequalled. The divine in man has had no more easy, methodically distinct expression. His personal influence upon young persons greater than any man's. In his world every man would be a poet. Love would reign, Beauty would take place, Man and Nature would harmonize.

Emerson does not consider things in respect to their essential utility, but an important partial and relative one, as works of art perhaps. His probes pass one side of their centre of gravity. His exaggeration is of a part, not of the whole.

[53]

An 1852 drawing of the Emerson home.

But then as Thoreau matured, he slowly became more critical, more objective, more independent.

▶ I bethought myself, while my fire was kindling, to open one of Emerson's books, which it happens that I rarely look at, to try what a chance sentence out of that could do for me; thinking, at the same time, of a conversation I had with him the other night, I finding fault with him for the stress he had laid on some of Margaret Fuller's whims and superstitions, but he declaring gravely that she was one of those persons whose experiences warranted her attaching importance to such things,—as the Sortes Virgilianae, for instance, of which her numerous friends could tell remarkable instances. At any rate, I saw that he was disposed [to] regard such things more seriously than I. The first sentence which I opened upon in his book was this: "If, with a high trust, he can thus submit himself, he will find that ample returns are poured into his bosom out of what seemed hours of obstruction and loss. Let him not grieve too much on account of unfit associates. . . . In a society of perfect sympathy, no word, no act, no record, would be. He will learn that it is not much matter what he reads, what he does. Be a scholar, and he shall have the scholar's part of everything."

Most of this responded well enough to my mood, and this would be as good an instance of the Sortes Virgilianae as most to quote. But what makes this coincidence very little if at all remarkable to me is the fact of the obviousness of the moral, so that I had, perhaps, thought the same thing myself twenty times during the day, and yet had not been contented with that account of it, leaving me thus to be amused by the coincidence, rather than impressed as by an intimation out of the deeps.

Then, by the mid-1850's there was a definite cooling of their friendship. Perhaps Thoreau was irritated by the frequent charges, such as those by James Russell Lowell in his "Fable For Critics," that he was too imitative of Emerson:

> Fie, for shame, brother bard; with good fruit of your own,
> Can't you let Neighbor Emerson's orchards alone?

In the summer of 1847 blueberrying parties for the Emerson family were scouted by Henry Thoreau, who selected the best spots for the pickers to work and drove the hayrack which carried the family off to the woods for the excursions. That summer, too, Thoreau served as assistant carpenter to Bronson Alcott who at Emerson's request began building a summerhouse in the garden. Alcott fancied a "sylvan" style, curving the rafters in a "mystic serpentine," much to the distaste of both Thoreau and the town. Henry fell off the roof at one point, but luckily landed in a nearby haystack. This is May Alcott's drawing of the "Bower" in which the "Bard" would "entertain the Muses," in Alcott's words.

Or perhaps as Emerson grew older and more conservative, Thoreau felt he was compromising his ideals. At any rate, there are more and more entries in his journals expressing a disappointment, a disillusionment with Emerson:

> I had two friends. The one offered me friendship on such terms that I could not accept it, without a sense of degradation. He would not meet me on equal terms, but only be to some extent my patron. He would not come to see, but was hurt if I did not visit him. He would not readily accept a favor, but would gladly confer one. He treated me with ceremony occasionally, though he could be simple and downright sometimes; and from time to time acted a part, treating me as if I were a distinguished stranger; was on stilts, using made words. Our relation was one long tragedy, yet I did not directly speak of it. I do not believe in complaint, nor in explanation. The whole is but too plain, alas, already. We grieve that we do not love each other, that we cannot confide in each other. I could not bring myself to speak, and so recognize an obstacle to our affection.

Nor was the break one-sided. Emerson too was confiding in his own journal such comments as this on Thoreau, written only a few days before Thoreau's comment above:

> If I knew only Thoreau, I should think cooperation of good men impossible. Must we always talk for victory, and never once for truth, for

Mr. Emerson gives a Virgil lesson to his children Edith and Edward. An ambrotype made in 1858. Thoreau had the run of their house on the two occasions when Emerson was away for long periods, and "was to us children the best kind of an older brother," Edward recalled. "He soon became the guide and companion of our early expeditions afield, and, later, the advisor of our first camping trips." By the fireside he told them stories of his childhood, or more often of squirrels, muskrats, hawks, of the duel of mud turtles in the river, or the great Homeric battle of the red and black ants. He would make their pencils and knives disappear, and find them in their ears and noses, and finally would get down the heavy copper warming-pan from the garret and pop corn for them.

comfort, and joy? Centrality he has, and penetration, strong understanding, and the higher gifts,—the insight of the real, or from the real, and the moral rectitude that belongs to it; but all this and all his resources of wit and invention are lost to me, in every experiment, year after year, that I make, to hold intercourse with his mind. Always some weary captious paradox to fight you with, and the time and temper wasted.

A few years later when Thoreau was asked to join Emerson and some of his friends on a camping trip in the Adirondacks, he laughingly rejected the invitation in his journal:

▶ Emerson is gone to the Adirondack country with a hunting party. Eddy [Emerson's son] says he has carried a double-barrelled gun, one side for shot, the other for ball, for Lowell killed a bear there last year. But the story on the Mill-Dam is that he has taken a gun which throws shot from one end and ball from the other!

After Emerson's return, Thoreau reported what had happened:

▶ Emerson says that he and Agassiz and Company broke some dozens of ale-bottles, one after another, with their bullets, in the Adirondack country, using them for marks! It sounds rather Cockneyish. He says that he shot a peetweet for Agassiz, and this, I think he said, was the first game he ever bagged. He carried a double-barrelled gun,—rifle and shotgun,—which he bought for the purpose, which he says received much commendation,—all parties thought it a very pretty piece. Think of Emerson shooting a peetweet (with shot) for Agassiz, and cracking an ale-bottle (after emptying it) with his rifle at six rods! They cut several pounds of lead out of the tree. It is just what Mike Saunders, the merchant's clerk, did when he was there.

But the break between the two men was never absolute. They could each find much to admire in the other. And when Thoreau died in 1862, Emerson was able to say honestly:

The country knows not yet, or in the least part, how great a son it has lost. It seems an injury that he should leave in the midst his broken task which none else can finish, a kind of indignity to so noble a soul that he should depart out of Nature before yet he had been really shown to his peers for what he is. But he, at least is content. His soul was made for the noblest society; he had in a short life exhausted the capabilities of this world; wherever there is knowledge, wherever there is virtue, wherever there is beauty, he will find a home.

6

No Remedy for Love

THOREAU LOST HIS HEART just once—to Ellen Devereux Sewall of Scituate, Massachusetts. Ellen was the older sister of Edmund Sewall, Thoreau's favorite pupil in his school. In July, 1839, when Ellen was seventeen and Thoreau twenty-two, she visited the Thoreau family for two weeks at the invitation of Mrs. Thoreau. Both of the Thoreau brothers felt her charm and continued the acquaintance the following winter. In July, 1840, John visited the Sewalls in Scituate and asked Ellen to marry him. She was surprised, and in her surprise she accepted him. But on further thought she decided she was more in love with Henry than John and so withdrew her acceptance. Apparently Henry did not know until years later of that acceptance and rejection. Meanwhile he continued to see Ellen on occasion, as is indicated by his journal entry of June 19, 1840:

▶   The other day I rowed in my boat a free, even lovely young lady, and, as I plied the oars, she sat in the stern, and there was nothing but she between me and the sky. So might all our lives be picturesque if they were free enough, but mean relations and prejudices intervene to shut out the sky, and we never see a man as simple and distinct as the man-weather-cock on a steeple.

In the fall of 1840, Ellen journeyed to Watertown, New York, to visit relatives, and while she was there she received a letter from Henry proposing marriage. Knowing that her father, a rather conservative Unitarian minister, would object to her marrying one of "those radical followers of Ralph Waldo Emerson, those transcendentalists," she communicated with her father. She later told her aunt:

He wished me to write immediately in a short, explicit, and cold manner to Mr. Thoreau. . . . I wrote to H. T. that evening. I never felt so badly at sending a letter in my life. I could not bear to think that both those friends [John and Henry] whom I had enjoyed so much with, would no

Emerson's wife, Lidian, who became Thoreau's friend when he lived in the Emerson home in 1841-43. Lidian was Emerson's second wife, married to him in 1835, four years after the death of his first wife. This is a crayon drawing of her by Samuel Worcester Rowse.

A silhouette of Mary Moody Emerson, aunt of Ralph Waldo, who was born on the eve of the Revolution and lived into the middle of the Civil War. A mystic and a thinker, she charmed and challenged Thoreau. For some years, longing for death, she had her bed made in the form of a coffin and prepared her shroud. But since the end was long postponed, she wore out several shrouds as night and day dress, rather than to see them lie idle.

Mrs. Lucy Jackson Brown, a boarder with the Thoreau family, was an older sister of Emerson's wife Lidian, and Henry's first literary confidante. She was the means of bringing Thoreau and Emerson together.

Mrs. Mary Russell Watson, of Plymouth, Mass. As a young girl, when she tutored the Emersons' boy, Waldo, she seems to have drawn Thoreau's affections, although only briefly.

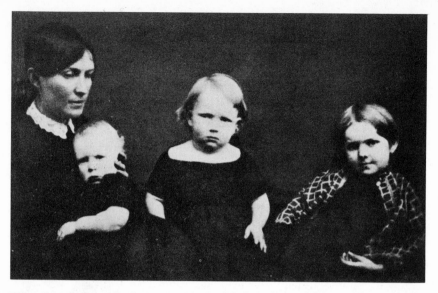

Ellen Sewall Osgood, daguerreotyped with her three children. The only girl Thoreau fell in love with, Ellen Sewall, met Henry when he was 22 and she 17. But she married a Unitarian minister instead of Henry—or his brother John, who also proposed to her.

longer be able to have free pleasant intercourse with us as formerly. My letter was very short indeed. But I hope it was the thing.

Several years later she became acquainted with Joseph Osgood, a young Unitarian minister in nearby Cohasset. The two were soon married and spent half a century together in wedded happiness. But throughout her life she continued her interest in Henry Thoreau and kept in close contact with the Thoreau family. Thoreau, in his turn, unquestionably continued an interest in her until the end of his life.

There are indications that for a brief period in the early 1840's he was romantically inclined towards another girl—Mary Russell of Plymouth, Massachusetts. Miss Russell was a friend of the Emerson family and spent the summer of 1841 in the Emerson household tutoring young Waldo Emerson. Tradition has it that Thoreau wrote his poem "To a Maiden in the East" about her:

▶ TO THE MAIDEN IN THE EAST

Low in the eastern sky
Is set thy glancing eye;
And though its gracious light

Ne'er riseth to my sight,
Yet every star that climbs
Above the gnarled limbs
   Of yonder hill,
Conveys thy gentle will.

Believe I knew thy thought,
And that the zephyrs brought
Thy kindest wishes through,
As mine they bear to you;
That some attentive cloud
Did pause amid the crowd
   Over my head,
While gentle things were said.

Believe the thrushes sung,
And that the flower-bells rung,
That herbs exhaled their scent,
And beasts knew what was meant,
The trees a welcome waved,
And lakes their margins laved,
   When thy free mind
To my retreat did wind.

It was a summer eve,
The air did gently heave
While yet a low-hung cloud
Thy eastern skies did shroud;
The lightning's silent gleam,
Startling my drowsy dream,
   Seemed like the flash
Under thy dark eyelash.

From yonder comes the sun,
But soon his course is run,
Rising to trivial day
Along his dusty way;
But thy noontide completes
Only auroral heats,
   Nor ever sets,
To hasten vain regrets.

Direct thy pensive eye
Into the western sky;
And when the evening star

Does glimmer from afar
Upon the mountain line,
Accept it for a sign
    That I am near,
And thinking of thee here.

I'll be thy Mercury,
Thou Cytherea to me,
Distinguished by thy face
The earth shall learn my place;
As near beneath thy light
Will I outwear the night,
    With mingled ray
Leading the westward way.

Still will I strive to be
As if thou wert with me;
Whatever path I take,
It shall be for thy sake,
Of gentle slope and wide,
As thou wert by my side,
    Without a root
To trip thy gentle foot.

I'll walk with gentle pace,
And choose the smoothest place,
And careful dip the oar,
And shun the winding shore,
And gently steer my boat
Where water-lilies float,
    And cardinal-flowers
Stand in their sylvan bowers.

But the romance, if such it was, was a short-lived one and Miss Russell later married Thoreau's Harvard friend and classmate Marston Watson, settling down to live in her native Plymouth.

Like many idealistic and intellectual youths, Thoreau several times formed Platonic attachments for older women. One of the first was for Lucy Jackson Brown, Emerson's sister-in-law, who for a time boarded with the Thoreaus so that she might be near the Emersons after her husband became involved in financial difficulties and fled the country. Thoreau found Mrs. Brown intellectually stimulating and in a romantic moment tossed a bouquet of violets in through her window, accompanying it with what has become one of his best known poems, "Sic Vita":

SIC VITA

I am a parcel of vain strivings tied
  By a chance bond together,
Dangling this way and that, their links
  Were made so loose and wide,
      Methinks,
    For milder weather.

A bunch of violets without their roots,
  And sorrel intermixed,
Encircled by a wisp of straw
  Once coiled about their shoots,
      The law
    By which I'm fixed.

A nosegay which Time clutched from out
  Those fair Elysian fields,
With weeds and broken stems, in haste,
  Doth make the rabble rout
      That waste
    The day he yields.

And here I bloom for a short hour unseen,
  Drinking my juices up,
With no root in the land
  To keep my branches green,
      But stand
    In a bare cup.

Some tender buds were left upon my stem
  In mimicry of life,
But ah! the children will not know,
  Till time has withered them,
      The woe
    With which they're rife.

But now I see I was not plucked for naught,
  And after in life's vase
Of glass set while I might survive,
  But by a kind hand brought
      Alive
    To a strange place.

That stock thus thinned will soon redeem its hours,
And by another year,
Such as God knows, with freer air,
More fruits and fairer flowers
Will bear,
While I droop here.

Later he was attracted to Mrs. Emerson, Lucy Brown's sister. Their friendship developed in the years 1841, 1842, and 1843 when Thoreau lived in the Emerson home. And shortly after Thoreau went to Staten Island in 1843 to act as tutor for Emerson's nephews, he wrote Mrs. Emerson a memorably affectionate letter:

▶ *My very dear Friend,*
    I have only read a page of your letter and have come out to the top of the hill at sunset where I can see the ocean to prepare to read the rest. It is fitter that it should hear it than the walls of my chamber. The very crickets here seem to chirp around me as they did not before. I feel as if it were a great daring to go on and read the rest, and then to live accordingly. There are more than thirty vessels in sight going to sea. I am almost afraid to look at your letter. I see that it will make my life very steep, but it may lead to fairer prospects than this.
    You seem to me to speak out of a very clear and high heaven, where any one may be who stands so high. Your voice seems not a voice, but comes as much from the blue heavens, as from the paper.
    My dear friend it was very noble in you to write me so trustful an answer. It will do as well for another world as for this. Such a voice is for no particular time nor person, and it makes him who may hear it stand for all that is lofty and true in humanity. The thought of you will constantly elevate my life; it will be something always above the horizon to behold, as when I look up at the evening star. I think I know your thoughts without seeing you, and as well here as in Concord. You are not at all strange to me.
    I could hardly believe after the lapse of one night that I had such a noble letter still at hand to read—that it was not some fine dream. I looked at midnight to be sure that it was real. I feel that I am unworthy to know you, and yet they will not permit it wrongfully.
    I, perhaps, am more willing to deceive by appearances than you say you are; it would not be worth the while to tell how willing—but I have the power perhaps too much to forget my meanness as soon as seen, and not be incited by permanent sorrow. My actual life is unspeakably mean, compared with what I know and see that it might be—Yet the ground from which I see and say this is some part of it. It ranges from heaven

to earth and is all things in an hour. The experience of every past moment but belies the faith of each present. We never conceive the greatness of our fates. Are not these faint flashes of light which sometimes obscure the sun, their certain dawn?

My friend, I have read your letter as if I was not reading it. After each pause I could defer the rest forever. The thought of you will be a new motive for every right action. You are another human being whom I know, and might not our topic be as broad as the universe. What have we to do with petty rumbling news? We have our own great affairs. Sometimes in Concord I found my actions dictated, as it were, by your influence, and though it lead almost to trivial Hindoo observances, yet it was good and elevating.

To hear that you have sad hours is not sad to me. I rather rejoice at the richness of your experience. Only think of some sadness away in Pekin—unseen and unknown there. What a mine it is. Would it not weigh down the Celestial empire, with all its gay Chinese? Our sadness is not sad, but our cheap joys. Let us be sad about all we see and are, for so we demand and pray for better. It is the constant prayer and whole Christian religion. I could hope that you would get well soon, and have a healthy body for this world, but I know this cannot be—and the Fates after all, are the accomplishers of our hopes. Yet I do hope that you may find it a worthy struggle, and life seems grand still through the clouds.

What wealth is it to have such friends that we cannot think of them without elevation. And we can think of them any time, and any where, and it costs nothing but the lofty disposition. I cannot tell you the joy your letter gives me—which will not quite cease till the latest time. Let me accompany your finest thought.

I send my love to my other friend and brother, whose nobleness I slowly recognize.

Henry

Henry Seidel Canby, in his biography of Thoreau (1939), came to the conclusion that "Thoreau was what the common man would call in love with Emerson's wife." But in so stating, he ignored Thoreau's own words in another letter to Mrs. Emerson from Staten Island: "I think of you as some elder sister of mine. . . . You must know that you represent to me woman." Brooks Atkinson has better evaluated their relationship when he said, "Thoreau had—I suppose unconsciously—a tender, romantic attachment to her. I think he was longing for affection. Since she was older than he and also married, I think he found her a safe and no doubt worthy object of adoration."

But there was another woman from whom Thoreau was not so safe. In

1847, Thoreau wrote a letter to Emerson, who was at the time in Europe, stating in part:

▶ I have had a tragic correspondence, for the most part all on one side, with Miss [Ford]. She did really wish to—I hesitate to write—marry me. That is the way they spell it. Of course I did not write a deliberate answer. How could I deliberate upon it? I sent back as distinct a no as I have learned to pronounce after considerable practice, and I trust that this no has succeeded. Indeed, I wished that it might burst, like hollow shot, after it had struck and buried itself and made itself felt there. There was no other way. I really had anticipated no such foe as this in my career.

Sophia Ford (or Foord, as she sometimes spelled her name) was a friend of the Alcotts and was for a while a tutor of Emerson's children. She once confided to a friend that she thought herself Thoreau's "soul's twin" and that she expected to be united with him in heaven if not on this earth. The rumor spread after Thoreau's rejection of her suit that she committed suicide in despair, but in actuality she outlived Thoreau by twenty years, remaining devoted to him to the end.

One of Thoreau's favorites was Mary Moody Emerson, the maiden aunt of Ralph Waldo, who spent a good deal of her time in Concord. Although she was far more orthodox in her religious beliefs than either her nephew or Thoreau, she provided both of them with a great deal of intellectual stimulation, as Thoreau's Journal shows.

In 1845-46 Sophia Foord of Milton, Massachusetts, tutored the Emerson and Alcott children in Concord and, although 15 years older than Thoreau, seems to have fallen in love with him. She returned home in 1847. Her signature appears on this inscription on the flyleaf of a first edition of Ellery Channing's biography of *Thoreau: the Poet-Naturalist*. She was always remembered by the Chace children whom she tutored in the 1850's as "a dark skinned, pudgy-featured woman." Unfortunately, no known pictures of her survive.

▶ Just spent a couple of hours (eight to ten) with Miss Mary Emerson at Holbrook's. The wittiest and most vivacious woman that I know, certainly that woman among my acquaintance whom it is most profitable to meet, the least frivolous, who will most surely provoke to good conversation and the expression of what is in you. She is singular, among women at least, in being really and perseveringly interested to know what thinkers think. She relates herself surely to the intellectual where she goes. It is perhaps her greatest praise and peculiarity that she, more surely than any other woman, gives her companion occasion to utter his best thought. In spite of her own biases, she can entertain a large thought with hospitality, and is not prevented by any intellectuality in it, as women commonly are. In short, she is a genius, as woman seldom is, reminding you less often of her sex than any woman whom I know. In that sense she is capable of a masculine appreciation of poetry and philosophy. I never talked with any other woman who I thought accompanied me so far in describing a poetic experience. Miss Fuller is the only woman I think of in this connection, and of her rather from her fame than from any knowledge of her. Miss Emerson expressed to-night a singular want of respect for her own sex, saying that they were frivolous almost without exception, that woman was the weaker vessel, etc.; that into whatever family she might go, she depended more upon the "clown" for society than upon the lady of the house. Men are more likely to have opinions of their own.

On another occasion, wrote Thoreau, as he was "reading from my manuscript to Miss Emerson this evening and using the word 'god,' in one instance, in perchance a merely heathenish sense, she inquired hastily in a tone of dignified anxiety, 'Is that god spelt with a little g?' Fortunately it was. (I had brought in the word 'god' without any solemnity of voice or connection.) So I went on as if nothing had happened."

7

Says I to Myself

ALMOST EVERY DAY for twenty-four years Thoreau jotted down the true history of himself in a series of blank notebooks. " 'Says I to myself' should be the motto of my journal," he wrote in it on November 11, 1851. When the journal trailed to its end, just a few months before Thoreau's death, about two million words had gone into it.

It began on October 22, 1837, three months after Thoreau had graduated from Harvard College. On the journal's first page are the lines, " 'What are you doing now?' he asked. 'Do you keep a journal?' So I make my first entry today." Probably it was at Emerson's prompting that this huge storehouse of a man's time, feelings, and thoughts was begun. Printed long after Thoreau's death, it runs to 14 volumes, with 6,000 pages of text.

How personal it would be Thoreau knew:

"Is not the poet bound to write his own biography? Is there any other work for him but a good journal? We do not wish to know how his imaginary hero, but how he, the actual hero, lived from day to day."

Yet it was not the orthodox record of time and event and place he wanted to make:

▶ In a true history or biography, of how little consequence those events of which so much is commonly made! For example, how difficult for a man to remember in what towns or houses he has lived, or when! Yet one of the first steps of his biographer will be to establish these facts, and he will thus give an undue importance to many of them. I find in my Journal that the most important events in my life, if recorded at all, are not dated.

▶ A journal [he believed] is a record of experiences and growth, not a preserve of things well done or said. I am occasionally reminded of a statement which I have made in conversation and immediately forgotten, which would read much better than what I put in my journal. It is a ripe, dry fruit of long-past experience which falls from me easily, without

Thoreau's first writing to see print was this brief obituary notice for Anna Jones, in the *Yeoman's Gazette* for November 25, 1837.

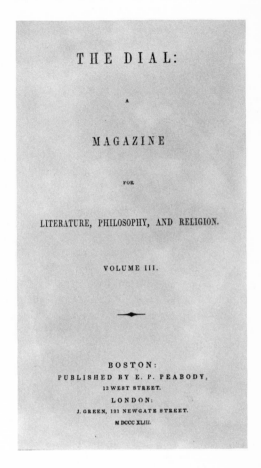

itle page of a volume of *The Dial*, founded 1840 with Margaret Fuller as editor. radually Emerson took over her duties, nd Thoreau became his assistant. In 1843 e April issue was entirely under Thoreau's irection. The magazine's circulation ran om 500 to 1,000 readers at best. In its short ut important life, which ended with the pril, 1844, issue, it published 31 contribuons from Thoreau.

giving pain or pleasure. The charm of the journal must consist in a certain greenness, though freshness, and not in maturity. Here I cannot afford to be remembering what I said or did, my scurf cast off, but what I am and aspire to become.

But it was also important "in a few words to describe the weather, or character of the day, as it affects our feelings. That which was so important at the time cannot be unimportant to remember."

He believed, too, in rewriting. His first impressions were usually jotted down rapidly, notes made on the spot, as when he was out in the fields and woods. Later, at home, he expanded these, and got a fuller version down in the notebook. In 1857, he explained why two tries at the same thing were often better than one:

▶   If you are describing any occurrence, or a man, make two or more distinct reports at different times. Though you may think you have said all, you will tomorrow remember a whole new class of facts which perhaps interested most of all at the time, but did not present themselves to be reported. If we have recently met and talked with a man, and would report our experience, we commonly make a very partial report at first, failing to seize the most significant, picturesque, and dramatic points; we describe only what we have had time to digest and dispose of in our minds, without being conscious that there were other things really more novel and interesting to us, which will not fail to recur to us and impress us suitably at last.

A few days later, he discussed it again:

▶   I would fain make two reports in my Journal, first the incidents and observations of today; and by tomorrow I review the same and record what was omitted before, which will often be the most significant and poetic part. I do not know at first what it is that charms me. The men and things of today are wont to lie fairer and truer in tomorrow's memory.

"Often," he said, "I can give the truest and most interesting account of any adventure I have had after years have elapsed, for then I am not confused, only the most significant facts surviving in my memory. Indeed, all that continues to interest me after such a lapse of time is sure to be pertinent, and I may safely record all that I remember."

His interest in the particular and the minute is what makes many of his best pages, but there was something more than facts which he wished to set down:

▶   Facts should only be as the frame to my pictures; they should be material to the mythology which I am writing; not facts to assist men to make money, farmers to farm profitably, in any common sense; facts to tell who I am, and where I have been or what I have thought: as now the bell rings for evening meeting, and its volumes of sound, like smoke which rises from where a cannon is fired, make the tent in which I dwell. My facts shall be falsehoods to the common sense. I would so state facts that they shall be significant, shall be myths or mythologic. Facts which the mind perceived, thoughts which the body thought,—with these I

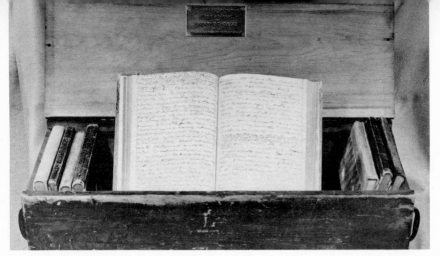

Some of the notebooks in which Thoreau kept his Journal, and the chest he made to hold them.

deal. I, too, cherish vague and misty forms, vaguest when the cloud at which I gaze is dissipated quite and naught but the skyey depths are seen.

All the while the Journal was building Thoreau was doing many other things, of course—lecturing, pencil-making, surveying, odd jobs. Yet, he said:

▶ I find that whatever hindrances may occur I write just about the same amount of truth in my Journal; for the record is more concentrated, and usually it is some very real and earnest life, after all, that interrupts. All flourishes are omitted. If I saw wood from morning to night, though I grieve that I could not observe the train of my thoughts during that time, yet, in the evening, the few scrannel lines which describe my day's occupations will make the creaking of the saw more musical than my freest fancies could have been. I find incessant labor with the hands, which engrosses the attention also, the best method to remove palaver out of one's style. One will not dance at his work who has wood to cut and cord before the night falls in the short days of winter; but every stroke will be husbanded, and ring soberly through the wood; and so will his lines ring and tell on the ear, when at evening he settles the accounts of the day. I have often been astonished at the force and precision of style to which busy laboring men, unpracticed in writing, easily attain when they are required to make the effort. It seems as if their sincerity and plainness were the main thing to be taught in schools,—and yet not in the schools, but in the fields, in actual service, I should say. The scholar not unfrequently envies the propriety and emphasis with which the

[*71*]

A WALK TO WACHUSETT.

The needles of the pine,
All to the west incline.

Concord, July, 19, 1842.

Summer and winter our eyes had rested on the dim outline of the mountains, to which distance and indistinctness lent a grandeur not their own, so that they served equally to interpret all the allusions of poets and travellers; whether with Homer, on a spring morning, we sat down on the...

Through your defiles windeth the way to heaven;
And yonder still, in spite of history's page,
Linger the golden and the silver age;
Upon the laboring gale
The news of future centuries is brought,
And of new dynasties of thought,
From your remotest vale.

This essay, Thoreau's report on a hike taken with Richard Fuller, Margaret's younger brother, in July, 1842, appeared in the January, 1843, issue of *The Boston Miscellany*. A poem Margaret had rejected for *The Dial* Thoreau got before the public by embedding it in this essay. The editor never got around to paying for the piece.

farmer calls to his team, and confesses that if that lingo were written it would surpass his labored sentences.

Who is not tired of the weak and flowing periods of the politician and scholar, and resorts not even to the Farmer's Almanac, to read the simple account of the month's labor, to restore his tone again? I want to see a sentence run clear through to the end, as deep and fertile as a well-drawn furrow which shows that the plow was pressed down to the beam. If our scholars would lead more earnest lives, we should not witness those lame conclusions to their ill-sown discourses, but their sentences would pass over the ground like loaded rollers, and not mere hollow and wooden ones, to press in the seed and make it germinate.

A well-built sentence, in the rapidity and force with which it works, may be compared to a modern cornplanter, which furrows out, drops the seed, and covers it up at one movement.

Thoreau's use of his Journal as a source for his lectures and then their conversion into essays he explained while at Walden:

Thoreau's excursion to Maine appeared serially in Sartain's *Union Magazine* from July through November, 1848. After his death, the articles became part of *The Maine Woods* volume.

KTAADN, AND THE MAINE WOODS.

BY HENRY D. THOREAU.

No. IV.

THE ASCENT OF KTAADN.

We had been told by McCauslin that we should here find trout enough: so while some prepared the camp, the rest fell to fishing. Seizing the birch poles which some party of Indians or white hunters had left on the shore, and baiting our

remedy this evil: for one, who had lost his hook, stood on shore to catch them as they fell in a perfect shower around him—sometimes, wet and slippery, full in his face and bosom and his hands were outside...

GRAHAM'S MAGAZINE.

Vol. XXX.   PHILADELPHIA, MARCH, 1847.   No. 3.

THOMAS CARLYLE AND HIS WORKS.

BY HENRY D. THOREAU.

THOMAS CARLYLE is a Scotchman, born about fifty years ago, "at Ecclefechan, Annandale," according to one authority. "His parents 'good farmer people,' his father an elder in the Secession church there, and a man of strong native sense, whose words were said ... puttock, a wild and solitary farm-house in the upper part of Dumfriesshire," at which last place, amid barren heather hills, he was visited by our countryman Emerson. With Emerson he still corresponds. He was early intimate with Edward Irving, and ...

Written while Thoreau was at Walden, this piece was first used as a lecture before the Concord Lyceum in 1846. When Horace Greeley became Thoreau's literary agent, he got it into the March and April numbers of *Graham's,* but more than a year passed before the magazine paid the $75 due Thoreau.

▶ From all points of the compass, from the earth beneath and the heavens above, have come these inspirations and been entered duly in the order of their arrival in the journal. Thereafter, when the time arrived, they were winnowed into lectures, and again, in due time, from lectures into essays. And at last they stand, like the cubes of Pythagoras, firmly on either basis; like statues on their pedestals, but the statues rarely take hold of hands. There is only such connection and series as is attainable in the galleries. And this affects their immediate practical and popular influence.

To speak the truth, Thoreau said, is the one great rule of composition:

▶ Literary gentlemen, editors, and critics think that they know how to write because they have studied grammar and rhetoric; but the art of composition is as simple as the discharge of a bullet from a rifle, and its masterpieces imply an infinitely greater force behind it. This unlettered man's speaking and writing is standard English. Some words

This brief piece was published in January, 1849. It was apparently pirated from Sartain's *Union Magazine* articles without Thoreau's knowledge or consent. The sentence structure and vocabulary are both watered down from the original version, probably to make it "more suitable" for a juvenile audience.

68   THE STUDENT.

THE BACKWOODS OF MAINE.

BY HENRY D. THOREAU.

WHAT is most striking in the Maine wilderness is the continuousness of the forest, with fewer open intervals or glades than you had imagined. Except the few burnt lands, the narrow intervals on the rivers, the bare tops of the high mountains, and the lakes and streams, the forest is uninterrupted ...

While the Republic has already acquired a history world-wide, America is still unsettled and unexplored. Like the English in New Holland, we live only on the shores of a continent even yet, and hardly know where the rivers come from which float our navy. The very timber and boards, and shingles which our houses are made ... day in a ...

and phrases deemed vulgarisms and Americanisms before, he has made standard American. "It will pay." It suggests that the one great rule of composition—and if I were a professor of rhetoric I should insist on this—is to speak the truth. This first, this second, this third. This demands earnestness and manhood chiefly.

The kind of man the writer is, is what counts:

▶ You can't read any genuine history—as that of Herodotus or the Venerable Bede—without perceiving that our interest depends not on the subject but on the man,—on the manner in which he treats the subject and the importance he gives it. A feeble writer and without genius must have what he thinks a great theme, which we are already interested in through the accounts of others, but a genius—a Shakespeare, for instance—would make the history of his parish more interesting than another's history of the world.

Wherever men have lived there is a story to be told, and it depends chiefly on the story-teller or historian whether that is interesting or not. You are simply a witness on the stand to tell what you know about your neighbors and neighborhood. Your account of foreign parts which you have never seen should by good rights be less interesting.

What about the writer's audience?

▶ Those authors are successful who do not write down to others, but make their own taste and judgment their audience. By some strange infatuation we forget that we do not approve what yet we recommend to others. It is enough if I please myself with writing; I am then sure of an audience.

He had something to say too about the acrobatic writer, a word of warning:

▶ Write often, write upon a thousand themes, rather than long at a time, not trying to turn too many feeble somersets in the air,—and so come

"Chesuncook" is the story of Thoreau's second trip to the Maine woods, taken in 1853 with his Bangor cousin George Thatcher. He sent the piece to *Atlantic* editor James Russell Lowell, in response to the new editor's request for material. Lowell, whom Thoreau had known at Harvard, deleted one sentence about a pine tree ("It is as immortal as I am, and perchance will go to as high a heaven, there to tower above me still"). When Thoreau saw the censorship in the July issue, he exploded, called it "mean and cowardly, . . . bigoted and timid," and a liberty he would not permit any editor to take. The sentence was put back when *The Maine Woods* was published.

down upon your head at last. Antaeus-like, be not long absent from the
ground. Those sentences are good and well discharged which are like
so many little resiliencies from the spring floor of our life,—a distinct
fruit and kernel itself, springing from terra firma.

But he did not mean to dig deeper than you have lived. He wrote:

▶   It is of no use to plow deeper than the soil is, unless you mean to
follow up that mode of cultivation persistently, manuring highly and
carting on muck at each plowing,—making a soil, in short. Yet many a
man likes to tackle mighty themes, like immortality, but in his discourse
he turns up nothing but yellow sand, under which what little fertile and
available surface soil he may have is quite buried and lost. He should
teach frugality rather,—how to postpone the fatal hour,—should plant
a crop of beans. He might have raised enough of these to make a deacon
of him, though never a preacher. Many a man runs his plow so deep in
heavy or stony soil that it sticks fast in the furrow. It is a great art in the
writer to improve from day to day just that soil and fertility which he has,
to harvest that crop which his life yields, whatever it may be, not be
straining as if to reach apples or oranges when he yields only groundnuts.
He should be digging, not soaring. Just as earnest as your life is, so deep
is your soil. If strong and deep, you will sow wheat and raise bread of
life in it.

Thoreau had contempt for easy books, but not for simple words:

▶   There are many words, which are genuine and indigenous and have
their root in our natures, not made by scholars, and as well understood
by the illiterate as others. There are also a great many words which are
spurious and artificial, and can only be used in a bad sense, since the
thing they signify is not fair and substantial,—such as the church, the
judiciary, to impeach, etc., etc. They who use them do not stand on solid
ground. It is in vain to try to preserve them by attaching other words to
them as the true church, etc. It is like towing a sinking ship with a canoe.

And again, a little later in the Journal:

▶   Some men have a peculiar taste for bad words, mouthing and licking
them into lumpish shapes like the bear her cubs,—words like "tribal"
and "ornamentation," which drag a dead tail after them. They will pick
you out of a thousand the still-born words, the falsettos, the wing-clipped
and lame words, as if only the false notes caught their ears. They cry
encore to all the discords.

8

Sea Beach and City

TOWARD THE END of Thoreau's two-year stay at Emerson's house, he wrote Emerson that he was "meditating some other method of paying debts than by lectures and writing,—which will only do to talk about. If anything of that 'other' sort should come to your ears in New York, will you remember it for me?"

Ten weeks later, on May 6, 1843, Thoreau left Concord for Staten Island, to take up a job as tutor to a son of Emerson's brother William. In return for board, a room for himself to study in, and $100 a year, Thoreau had agreed to be the "friend and educator" of William Jr., a boy "not yet subdued by schoolmaster," as Emerson put it.

The salary would only cover his expenses, Thoreau knew, and he hoped the boy's father—a county judge—would help him find clerical work to supplement it, at least until he could gain a footing in New York's publishing world.

"No truer no purer person lives in wide New York," Emerson assured his brother. "He is bold and a profound thinker," he continued, "though he may easily chance to pester you with some accidental crochets and perhaps a village exaggeration of the value of facts."

Thoreau arrived at William Emerson's home, "The Snuggery," feeling the effects of the illness which had seized him in February. A bad cough took hold at once, but did not dampen the spirit of the letter he got off to his family on May 11:

▶ We arrived here safely at ten o'clock on Sunday morning, having had as good a passage as usual, though we ran aground and were detained a couple of hours in the Thames River, till the tide came to our relief. At length we curtseyed up to a wharf just the other side of their Castle Garden,—very incurious about them and their city. I believe my vacant look, absolutely inaccessible to questions, did at length satisfy an army of starving cabmen that I did not want a hack, cab, or anything of that sort as yet. It was the only demand the city made on us; as if a wheeled

Judge William Emerson, elder brother of Ralph Waldo, who hired Thoreau to tutor his son Willie in their house on Staten Island, called "The Snuggery."

vehicle of some sort were the sum and summit of a reasonable man's wants. "Having tried the water," they seemed to say, "will you not return to the pleasant securities of land carriage? Else why your boat's prow turned toward the shore at last?" They are a sad-looking set of fellows, not permitted to come on board, and I pitied them. They had been expecting me, it would seem, and did really wish that I should take a cab; though they did not seem rich enough to supply me with one.

It was a confused jumble of heads and soiled coats, dangling from flesh-colored faces,—all swaying to and fro, as by a sort of undertow, while each whip-stock, true as the needle to the pole, still preserved that level and direction in which its proprietor had dismissed his forlorn interrogatory. They took sight from them,—the lash being wound up thereon, to prevent your attention from wandering, or to make it concentre upon its object by the spiral line. They began at first, perhaps, with

A view of the Narrows as it probably looked to Thoreau from the hill behind Judge Emerson's house.

the modest, but rather confident inquiry, "Want a cab, sir?" but as their despair increased, it took the affirmative tone, as the disheartened and irresolute are apt to do: "You want a cab, sir," or even, "You want a nice cab, sir, to take you to Fourth Street." The question which one had bravely and hopefully begun to put, another had the tact to take up and conclude with fresh emphasis,—twirling it from his particular whipstick as if it had emanated from his lips—as the sentiment did from his heart. Each one could truly say, "Them's my sentiments." But it was a sad sight.

I am seven and a half miles from New York, and, as it would take half a day at least, have not been there yet. I have already run over no small part of the island, to the highest hill, and some way along the shore. From the hill directly behind the house I can see New York, Brooklyn, Long Island, the Narrows, through which vessels bound to and from all parts of the world chiefly pass,—Sandy Hook and the Highlands of Neversink (part of the coast of New Jersey)—and, by going still farther up the hill, the Kill van Kull, and Newark Bay. From the pinnacle of one Madame Grimes' house the other night at sunset, I could see almost round the island. Far in the horizon there was a fleet of sloops bound up the Hudson, which seemed to be going over the edge of the earth; and in view of these trading ships, commerce seems quite imposing.

But it is rather derogatory that your dwelling-place should be only a neighborhood to a great city,—to live on an inclined plane. I do not like their cities and forts, with their morning and evening guns, and sails flapping in one's eye. I want a whole continent to breathe in, and a good deal of solitude and silence, such as all Wall Street cannot buy,—nor Broadway with its wooden pavement. I must live along the beach, on the southern shore, which looks directly out to sea,—and see what that great parade of water means, that dashes and roars, and has not yet wet me, as long as I have lived.

I must not know anything about my condition and relations here till what is not permanent is worn off. I have not yet subsided. Give me time enough, and I may like it. All my inner man heretofore has been a Concord impression; and here come these Sandy Hook and Coney Island breakers to meet and modify the former; but it will be long before I can make nature look as innocently grand and inspiring as in Concord.

As soon as his bronchitis let up, Thoreau began to botanize. He wrote sister Sophia on May 22:

▶   The cedar seems to be one of the most common trees here, and the fields are very fragrant with it. There are also the gum and tulip trees. The latter is not very common, but is very large and beautiful, having flowers as large as tulips and as handsome. It is not time for it yet. The woods are now full of a large honeysuckle in full bloom, which differs from ours in being red instead of white, so that at first I did not know its genus. The painted cup is very common in the meadows here. Peaches, and especially cherries, seem to grow by all the fences.

Things are very forward here compared with Concord. The apricots growing out of doors are already as large as plums. The apple, pear, peach, cherry and plum trees, have shed their blossoms. The whole island is like a garden, and affords very fine scenery. In front of the house is a very extensive wood, beyond which is the sea, whose roar I can hear all night long, when there is no wind, if easterly winds have prevailed on the Atlantic. There are always some vessels in sight—ten, twenty, or thirty miles off and Sunday before last there were hundreds in long procession, stretching from New York to Sanday [sic] Hook, and far beyond, for Sunday is a lucky day.

His illness did not long delay a trip to New York; a week after arriving Thoreau set out to explore the city he had not seen since the visit with his father in 1836.

▶ In New York [he told Sophia] I saw Geo. Ward, and also Giles Waldo and William Tappan, whom I can describe better when I have seen them more—They are young friends of Mr. Emerson. Waldo came down to the Island to see me the next day. I also saw the Great Western, the Croton Waterworks, and the picture gallery of the National Academy of Design. But I have not had time to see or do much in N.Y. yet.

Tell Miss [Prudence] Ward I shall try to put my microscope to a good use, and if I find any new and pressible flower, will throw it into my common place book. Garlic, the original of the common onion, grows like grass here all over the fields, and during its season spoils the cream and butter for the market, as the cows like it very much. Tell Helen there are two schools just established in this neighborhood, with large prospects, or rather designs, one for boys, and another for girls. The latter by a Miss Errington—and though it is very small as yet—will keep my ears open for her in such directions—The encouragement is very slight.

I hope you will not be washed away by the Irish sea. Tell mother I think my cold was not wholly owing to imprudence. Perhaps I was being acclimated.

Tell father that Mr. Tappan whose son I know—and whose clerks young Tappan and Waldo are—has invented and established a new and very important business—which Waldo thinks could allow them to burn 99 out of 100 of the stores in N.Y. which now only offset and cancel one another. It is a kind of intelligence office for the whole country—

THE LANDLORD.

BY HENRY D. THOREAU.

UNDER the one word, house, are included the school house, the alms house, the jail, the tavern, the dwelling house ; and the meanest shed or cave in which men live, contains the elements of all these. But no where on the earth ·s·ands the entire and perfect· house. The Parthenon ~~~~~ genial a human nature, that he would fain sacrifice the tender but narrow ties of private friendship, to a broad, sunshiny, fair-weather-and foul friendship for his race ; who loves men, not as a philosopher, with philanthropy, nor as an overseer of the poor, with charity, ~~~~~

"Literature comes to a poor market here," Thoreau wrote Emerson in mid-September, "and even the little I write is more than will sell. I have tried the *Democratic Review,* the *New Mirror,* and *Brother Jonathan.* The last two, as well as the *New World,* are overwhelmed with contributions which cost nothing, and are worth no more. The *Knickerbocker* is too poor, and only the *Ladies' Companion* pays." In the next two months, however, the *Democratic Review* printed Thoreau's familiar essay, "The Landlord," and his review of a pamphlet on social reform.

with branches in the principal cities, giving information with regard to the credit and affairs of every man of business in the country. Of course it is not popular at the South and West. It is an extensive business, and will employ a great many clerks.

To Emerson, Thoreau had more to say about his first reactions to New York:

▶ You must not count much upon what I can do or learn in New York. I feel a good way off here—and it is not to be visited, but seen and dwelt in. I have been there but once, and have been confined to the house since. Everything there disappoints me but the crowd—rather I was disappointed with the rest before I came. I have no eyes for their churches and what else they find to brag of. Though I know but little about Boston, yet what attracts me in a quiet way seems much meaner and more pretending than these—Libraries—Pictures—and faces in the street—You don't know where any respectability inhabits.—It is in the crowd in Chatham street. The crowd is something new and to be attended to. It is worth a thousand Trinity Churches and Exchanges while it is looking at them—and will run over them and trample them under foot one day. There are two things I hear, and am aware that I live in the neighborhood of—The roar of the sea—and the hum of the city. I have just come from the beach (to find your letter) and I like it much. Everything there is on a grand and generous scale—sea-weed, water, and sand; and even the dead fishes, horses and hogs have a rank luxuriant odor. Great shad nets spread to dry, crabs and horse-shoes crawling over the sand— Clumsy boats, only for service, dancing like sea-fowl on the surf, and ships afar off going about their business.

In answer to what must have been a request for more details about his everyday life, and the new people he was meeting, Thoreau wrote his family:

▶ I have been to N.Y. four or five times, and have run about the island a good deal. Geo. Ward when I last saw him, which was at his house in Brooklyn, was studying the daguerreotype process, preparing to set up in that line. The boats run now almost every hour, from 8 A.M. to 7 P.M. back and forth, so that I can get to the city much more easily than before. I have seen there one Henry James, a lame man, of whom I had heard before, whom I like very much, and he asks me to make free use of his house, which is situated in a pleasant part of the city, adjoining the University. I have met several people whom I knew before, and among the rest Mr. Wright, who was on his way to Niagara.

I feel already about as well acquainted with New York as with Boston, that is about as little, perhaps. It is large enough now and they intend it shall be larger still. 15th Street, where some of my new acquaintances live, is two or three miles from the battery where the boat touches, clear brick and stone and no give to the foot; and they have layed out though not built, up to the 149th Street above. I had rather see a brick for a

Horace Greeley as he looked when Thoreau met him. The two became friends in 1843 when Thoreau was tutoring on Staten Island. Greeley had founded the *New York Tribune* two years earlier. (Although there were 11 dailies in a town of 250,000, the competition didn't worry him.) The influential editor took on the additional chore of literary agent —often without fee—for his new friend. He placed Thoreau's work in magazines, promoted his books in the *Tribune,* and heckled editors for cash. To his sister Helen, Thoreau sent his first impression of Greeley as "cheerfully in earnest—his office of all work —a hearty New Hampshire boy as one would wish to meet. And says 'now be neighborly'—and believes only or mainly, first, in the Sylvania Association somewhere in Pennsylvania—and secondly and most of all, in a new association to go into operation soon in New Jersey, with which he is connected." Greeley told Thoreau he wanted "to let the public know something of your way of thinking and seeing." Greeley must have meant something special to Thoreau, who once borrowed $75 from him.

specimen for my part such as they exhibited in old times. You see it is quite a day's training to make a few calls in different parts of the city. (to say nothing of 12 miles by water and three by land, i.e. not brick and stone) especially if it does not rain shillings which might interest omnibuses in your behalf. Some Omnibuses are marked "Broadway—Fourth Street"—and they go no further—others "8th Street" and so on, and so of the other principal streets. This letter will be circumstantial enough for Helen.

This is in all respects a very pleasant residence—much more rural than you would expect of the vicinity of New York. There are woods all around.

We breakfast at half past six—lunch if we will at twelve—and dine or sup at five. Thus is the day partitioned off. From 9 to 2 or thereabouts I am the schoolmaster—and at other times as much the pupil as I can be. Mr. and Mrs. Emerson & family are not indeed of my kith or kin in any sense—but they are irreproachable and kind.

I have met no one yet on the Island whose acquaintance I shall actually cultivate—or hoe around—unless it be our neighbor Capt. Smith—an old fisherman who catches the fish called moss-bonkers—(so it sounds) and invites me to come to the beach where he spends the week and see him and his fish.

Farms are for sale all around here—and so I suppose men are for purchase.

North of us live Peter Wandell—Mr. Mell—and Mr. Disusway (dont mind the spelling) as far as the Clove road; and south John Britton—Van Pelt and Capt Smith as far as the Fingerboard road. Behind is the hill, some 250 feet high—on the side of which we live, and in front the forest and the sea—the latter at the distance of a mile and a half.

Tell Helen that Miss Errington is provided with assistance. This were as good a place as any to establish a school if one could wait a little. Families come down here to board in the summer—and three or four have been already established this season.

As for money matters I have not set my traps yet, but I am getting the bait ready. Pray how does the garden thrive and what improvement in the pencil line? I miss you all very much. Write soon and send a Concord paper.

To Emerson, who had provided a letter of introduction to the elder Henry James, Thoreau reported:

▶ I have been to see Henry James, and like him very much. It was a great pleasure to meet him. It makes humanity seem more erect and respectable. I never was more kindly and faithfully catechised. It made me respect myself more to be thought worthy of such wise questions. He is a man, and takes his own way, or stands still in his own place. I know of no one so patient and determined to have the good of you. It is almost friendship, such plain and human dealing. I think that he will not write or speak inspiringly; but he is a refreshing forward-looking and forward-moving man, and he has naturalized and humanized New York for me. He actually reproaches you by his respect for your poor words. I had three hours' solid talk with him, and he asks me to make free use of his house. He wants an expression of your faith, or to be sure that it is faith, and confesses that his own treads fast upon the neck of his understanding. He exclaimed, at some careless answer of mine, "Well, you Transcendentalists are wonderfully consistent. I must get hold of this somehow!" He likes Carlyle's book, but says that it leaves him in an excited and unprofitable state, and that Carlyle is so ready to obey his humor that he makes the least vestige of truth the foundation of any superstructure, not keeping faith with his better genius nor truest readers.

Arthur Brisbane, the American propagandist for Fourier's socialist theories, Thoreau saw by chance on the street.

▶   Brisbane, with whom I did not converse, did not impress me favorably. He looks like a man who has lived in a cellar, far gone in consumption. I barely saw him, but he did not look as if he could let Fourier go, in any case, and throw up his hat.

New York did not grow on Thoreau, he wrote Emerson:

▶   I don't like the city better, the more I see it, but worse. I am ashamed of my eyes that behold it. It is a thousand times meaner than I could have imagined. It will be something to hate,—that's the advantage it will be to me; and even the best people in it are a part of it and talk coolly about it. The pigs in the street are the most respectable part of the population. When will the world learn that a million men are of no importance compared with one man? But I must wait for a shower of shillings, or at least a slight dew or mizzling of sixpences, before I explore New York very far.
    The sea-beach is the best thing I have seen. It is very solitary and remote, and you only remember New York occasionally. The distances, too, along the shore, and inland in sight of it, are unaccountably great and startling. The sea seems very near from the hills but it proves a long way over the plain, and yet you may be wet with the spray before you can believe that you are there. The far seems near, and the near far. Many rods from the beach, I step aside for the Atlantic, and I see men drag up their boats on to the sand, with oxen, stepping about amid the surf, as if it were possible they might draw up Sandy Hook.

[*83*]

I do not feel myself especially serviceable to the good people with whom I live, except as inflictions are sanctified to the righteous. And so, too, must I serve the boy. I can look to the Latin and mathematics sharply, and for the rest behave myself. But I cannot be in his neighborhood hereafter as his Educator, of course, but as the hawks fly over my own head. I am not attracted toward him but as to youth generally. He shall frequent me, however, as much as he can, and I'll be I.

Reporting the local news, Emerson said the town was full of Irish and the woods of engineers with theodolite and red flag singing out their feet and inches as they advanced the new Fitchburg-railroad from station to station. The Alcotts were experimenting with paradise at Fruitlands. Ellery Channing was saying that Thoreau ought not to see Concord again for ten years, that he ought to "grind up fifty Concords" in his mill.

News from friends and family intensified a homesickness Thoreau hastened to deny. In August, he wrote his mother:

▶ I am chiefly indebted to your letters for what I have learned of Concord and family news, and am very glad when I get one. I should have liked to be in Walden woods with you, but not with the railroad. I think of you all very often, and wonder if you are still separated from me only by so many miles of earth, or so many miles of memory. This life we live is a strange dream, and I don't believe at all any account men give of it. Methinks I should be content to sit at the back-door in Concord, under the poplar-tree, henceforth forever. Not that I am homesick at all, —for places are strangely indifferent to me,—but Concord is still a cynosure to my eyes, and I find it hard to attach it, even in imagination, to the rest of the globe, and tell where the seam is.

I fancy that this Sunday evening you are poring over some select book almost transcendental perchance, or else "Burgh's Dignity," or Massillon,

So slim was the New York literary market that Thoreau turned from trying to write for the magazines to trying to sell them. "I carried the *Agriculturist* about the city," he reported to Emerson, "and up as far as Manhattanville, and called at the Croton Reservoir, where indeed they did not want any *Agriculturist*."

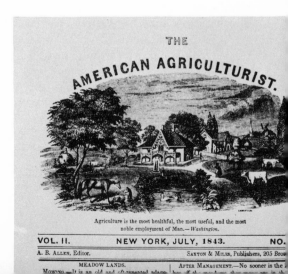

THE
AMERICAN AGRICULTURIST

Agriculture is the most healthful, the most useful, and the most noble employment of Man.—*Washington.*

VOL. II.   NEW YORK, JULY, 1843.   NO.

A. B. ALLEN, Editor.   SAXTON & MILES, Publishers, 205 Broa

The elder Henry James, with Henry, Jr., the son who was to become the novelist. The father of William and Henry James met Thoreau in New York in 1843, at Emerson's prompting. Thoreau visited him at his home. He liked to argue with James as "a hearty man" of "good temper," but he thought his Swedenborgian doctrines and notions of reform "would leave us about where we are now."

or the "Christian Examiner." Father has just taken one more look at the garden, and is now absorbed in Chaptelle, or reading the newspaper quite abstractedly, only looking up occasionally over his spectacles to see how the rest are engaged, and not to miss any newer news that may not be in the paper. Helen has slipped in for the fourth time to learn the very latest item. Sophia, I suppose, is at Bangor; but Aunt Louisa, without doubt, is just flitting away to some good meeting to save the credit of you all.

I have been translating some Greek, and reading English poetry, and it seems, am thought to be a surveyor,—an Eastern man inquiring narrowly into the condition and value of land, etc., here, preparatory to an extensive speculation. One neighbor observed to me, in a mysterious and half inquisitive way, that he supposed I must be pretty well acquainted with the state of things; that I kept pretty close; he didn't see any surveying instruments, but perhaps I had them in my pocket.

The New York literary market had opened only a crack to Thoreau. O'Sullivan's *Democratic Review* put a book review and an essay into print, and the *Boston Miscellany* had taken "A Walk to Wachusett." Thoreau sounded only faintly hopeful in a letter to his mother:

▶ I may yet accomplish something in the literary way—indeed I should have done so before now but for the slowness and poverty of the Reviews themselves. I have tried sundry methods of earning money in the

[*85*]

city of late but without success. have rambled into every bookseller's or publisher's house and discussed their affairs with them. Some propose to me to do what an honest man cannot—Among others I conversed with the Harpers—to see if they might not find me useful to them—but they say that they are making fifty thousand dollars annually, and their motto is to let well alone. I find that I talk with these poor men as if I were over head and ears in business and a few thousands were no consideration with me—I almost reproach myself for bothering them thus to no purpose—but it is very valuable experience—and the best introduction I could have.

The news that the great Daniel Webster, who had recently retired from Tyler's Cabinet, was now handling a case in Concord, stirred Thoreau.

▶ I should have liked to see Dan. Webster walking about Concord, I suppose the town shook every step he took—But I trust there were some sturdy Concordians who were not tumbled down by the jar, but represented still the upright town. Where was Geo. Minott? he would not have gone far to see him. Uncle Charles should have been there—he might as well have been catching cat naps in Concord as anywhere. And then what a whetter up of his memory this event would have been! You'd have had all the classmates again in alphabetical order reversed—and Seth Hunt & Bob Smith—and he was a student of my fathers—and where's Put now? and I wonder, you, if Henry's been to see Geo. Jones yet—A little account with Stow—Balcolm—Bigelow—poor miserable to-a-d (sound asleep) I vow you—what noise was that?—saving grace—and few there be—That's clear as preaching—Easter Brooks—mora[lly] depraved—How charming is divine p[hi]losophy—Some wise and some otherwise—Heighho! (Sound asleep again)
Webster's a smart fellow—bears his age well—how old should you think he was—you does he look as if he were ten years younger than I?

Making a domestic report, Thoreau wrote "I hold together remarkably well as yet, speaking of my outward linen and woolen man, no holes more than I brought away, and no stitches needed yet. It is marvellous."
There was some modest shopping: "I have bought some pantaloons—and stockings show no holes yet. Thin pantaloons cost $2.25 ready made."
He was reading a good deal, and had worked his way in with the librarian of the New York Society Library—"Who has lately been to Cambridge to learn liberality, and has come back to let me take out some untake-out-able books, which I was threatening to read on the spot."
From his vantage point on the heights of Staten Island, overlooking the Bay, Thoreau was able

▶ . . . to observe one aspect of the modern world at least—I mean the migratory—the western movement. Sixteen hundred immigrants arrived at quarantine ground on the fourth of July, and more or less every day since I have been here. I see them occasionally washing their persons and clothes, or men women and children gathered on an isolated quay near the shore, stretching their limbs and taking the air, the children running races and swinging—on their artificial piece of the land of liberty—while the vessels are undergoing purification. They are detained but a day or two, and then go up to the city, for the most part without having landed here.

I have crossed the bay 20 or 30 times and have seen a great many immigrants going up to the city for the first time—Norwegians who carry their old fashioned farming tools to the west with them, and will buy nothing here for fear of being cheated.—English operatives, known by their pale faces and stained hands, who will recover their birth-rights in a little cheap sun and wind,—English travellers on their way to the Astor House, to whom I have done the honors of the city.—Whole families of immigrants cooking their dinner upon the pavements, all sunburnt—so that you are in doubt where the foreigner's face of flesh begins—their tidy clothes laid on, and then tied to their swathed bodies which move about like a bandaged finger—caps set on the head, as if woven of the hair, which is still growing at the roots—each and all busily cooking, stooping from time to time over the pot, and having something to drop into it, that so they may be entitled to take something out, forsooth. They look like respectable but straightened [sic] people, who may turn out to be counts when they get to Wisconsin—and will have their experience to relate to their children.

A copy of the October *Dial* arrived, and Thoreau set about telling Emerson what he thought of the issue, including, especially, Emerson's own verse contribution:

▶ I feel as if I were ready to be appointed a committee on poetry, I have got my eyes so whetted and proved of late, like the knife-sharpener I saw at the Fair certified to have been in constant use in a gentleman's family for more than two years. Yes, I ride along the ranks of the English poets casting terrible glances, and some I blot out, and some I spare. . . . I have a good deal of fault to find with your ode to Beauty. The tune is altogether unworthy of the thoughts. You slope too quickly to the rhyme, as if that trick had better be performed as soon as possible or as if you stood over the line with a hatchet and chopped off the verses as they came out—some short and some long. But give us a long reel and we'll cut it up to suit ourselves. It sounds like a parody. "Thee knew I of old"

"Remediless thirst" are some of those stereotyped lines. I am frequently reminded, I believe of Jane Taylors Philosopher's Scales and how the world
"Flew out with a bounce"
which—"jerked the philosopher out of his cell." or else of "From the climes of the sun all war-worn and weary." I had rather have the thoughts come ushered with a flourish of oaths and curses. Yet I love your poetry as I do little else that is near and recent—especially when you get fairly around the end of the line, and are not thrown back upon the rocks.

Criticism out of the way, Thoreau was again on his favorite topic: "Methinks I could look with equanimity upon a long street of Irish cabins and pigs and children revelling in the genial Concord dirt, and I should still find my Walden wood and Fair Haven in their tanned and happy faces."

A month later, he was home for Thanksgiving. He had learned that his Eldorado was far off yet. On November 29 he lectured on the ancient poets before the Concord Lyceum. Early the next month he returned briefly to Staten Island to pack his things. He was never again to live away from Concord.

9

Friends and Neighbors

IT IS ONE of the most remarkable phenomena of American literary history that so many of our great writers should have lived in one tiny town—Concord, of course—with a population then of only two thousand people. Thoreau was born there. Emerson came to the town because it was the home of his ancestors. Hawthorne came chiefly because he was offered the use of the Old Manse as a residence. Bronson Alcott and many others came to be near Emerson. But whatever the reason for their residence there, it is still nonetheless remarkable that so many famous writers gathered together in so small a town.

Because the town was small, it was inevitable that Thoreau would get to know all the others and get to know them well. With Alcott, for example, he developed a particularly strong friendship. Although Thoreau was annoyed that Alcott would rather sit and talk than walk, he was one of the earliest to recognize Alcott's genius, writing in his journal for May 8, 1853:

▶ I have devoted most of my day to Mr. Alcott. He is broad and genial, but indefinite; some would say feeble; forever feeling about vainly in his speech and touching nothing. But this is a very negative account of him, for he thus suggests far more than the sharp and definite practical mind. The feelers of his thought diverge,—such is the breadth of their grasp, —not converge; and in his society almost alone I can express at my leisure, with more or less success, my vaguest but most cherished fancy or thought. There are never any obstacles in the way of our meeting. He has no creed. He is not pledged to any institution. The sanest man I ever knew; the fewest crotchets after all, has he.

It has occurred to me, while I am thinking with pleasure of our day's intercourse, "Why should I not think aloud to you?" Having each some shingles of thought well dried, we walk and whittle them, trying our knives, and admiring the clear yellowish grain of the pumpkin pine. We wade so gently and reverently, or we pull together so smoothly, that the

"Hillside," the Concord house on the Lexington Road into which the Alcotts moved in the spring of 1845. Alcott made the house over himself, and developed the gardens into the best in town. This is from Alcott's 1845 drawing.

fishes of thought are not scared from the stream, but come and go grandly, like yonder clouds that float peacefully through the western sky. When we walk it seems as if the heavens—whose mother-o'-pearl and rainbow tints come and go, form and dissolve—and the earth had met together, and righteousness and peace had kissed each other. I have an ally against the arch-enemy. A blue-robed man dwells under the blue concave. The blue sky is a distant reflection of the azure serenity that looks out from under a human brow. We walk together like the most innocent children, going after wild pinks with case-knives.

Alcott, in his turn, was equally early in recognizing Thoreau's abilities and we find some perceptive comments on Thoreau scattered through Alcott's journals:

September 11, 1856.
Thoreau is persistently manly and independent as of old. His criticisms on men and the times as characteristic, individual, and urged with all the

Bronson Alcott, photographed at Orchard House, into which his family moved in 1857. The house is next door to "Hillside."

[*90*]

honest pertinacity befitting a descent of the Scandinavian Thor. A man of a genealogy like his—Franko-Norman-Scotish-American—may well be forgiven for a little foolhardiness, if not pugnacity, amidst his great common sense and faithfulness to the core of natural things.

July 3, 1859.

Thoreau comes and stays an hour or two. Students of Nature alike, our methods differ. He is an observer of Nature pure, and I discern her as exalted and mingled in Man. Her brute aspects and qualities interest him, and these he discriminates with a sagacity unsurpassed. He is less thinker than observer; a naturalist in tendency but of a mystic habit, and a genius for detecting the essence in the form and giving forth the soul of things seen. He knows more of Nature's secrets than any man I have known, and of Man as related to Nature. He thinks and sees for himself in way eminently original, and is formidably individual and persistent.

When Hawthorne settled in Concord in 1842, he soon met Thoreau— or "Mr. Thorow" as he misspelled his name. Although Emerson and Hawthorne were never to find much in common, Thoreau and Hawthorne quickly became friends and Thoreau dropped in frequently to see Hawthorne and his bride at the Old Manse. Hawthorne kept a record of those visits in his "American Notebooks":

Sept. 1st [1842] Thursday.

Mr. Thorow [sic] dined with us yesterday. He is a singular character— a young man with much of wild original nature still remaining in him; and so far as he is sophisticated, it is in a way and method of his own. He is as ugly as sin, long-nosed, queer-mouthed, and with uncouth and somewhat rustic, although courteous manners, corresponding very well with such an exterior. But his ugliness is of an honest and agreeable fashion, and becomes him much better than beauty. He was educated, at Cambridge, and formerly kept school in this town; but for two or three years back, he has repudiated all regular modes of getting a living, and seems inclined to lead a sort of Indian life among civilized men— an Indian life, I mean, as respects the absence of any systematic effort for a livelihood. He has been for some time an inmate of Mr. Emerson's family; and, in requital, he labors in the garden, and performs such other offices as may suit him—being entertained by Mr. Emerson for the sake of what true manhood there is in him. Mr. Thorow is a keen and delicate observer of nature—a genuine observer, which, I suspect, is almost as rare a character as even an original poet; and Nature, in return for his love, seems to adopt him as her especial child, and shows him secrets which few others are allowed to witness. He is familiar with beast, fish, fowl, and reptile, and has strange stories to tell of adventures, and friendly passages with these lower brethren of mortality. Herb and flower, likewise, wherever they grow, whether in garden, or wild wood, are his familiar friends. He is also on intimate terms with the clouds, and can tell the portents of storms. It is a characteristic trait, that he has a great regard for the memory of the Indian tribes, whose wild life would have suited him so well; and strange to say, he seldom walks over a ploughed field without picking up an arrow-point, a spear-head, or other relic of the red men—as if their spirits willed him to be the inheritor of their simple wealth.

With all this he has more than a tincture of literature—a deep and true taste for poetry, especially the elder poets, although more exclusive than is desirable, like all other Transcendentalists, so far as I am acquainted with them. He is a good writer—at least, he has written one good article, a rambling disquisition on Natural History in the last Dial, —which, he says, was chiefly made up from journals of his own observa-

Nathaniel Hawthorne: a crayon drawing by Eastman Johnson, done in 1846. The Hawthornes moved into the Old Manse in Concord immediately after their marriage in July, 1842. Nathaniel, owed $700 by George Ripley after the failure of Brook Farm, was told to take it out in rent at the Old Manse, which was now owned by Ripley.

Louisa May Alcott, whose *Little Women* made her family the best-known in America. Henry Thoreau was teacher and elder brother alike to Louisa and her sisters Anna and Beth. In her first novel, *Moods,* published two years after Thoreau's death, Louisa used Thoreau as the basis for one of her major characters.

In May, 1852—after living in Salem and the Berkshires for several years—the Hawthornes returned to Concord, purchasing Alcott's "Hillside" home and rebaptizing it "The Wayside." Here they stayed for a year, until Hawthorne's consulship drew him to England. In 1860 the family was back at "The Wayside," for the four years remaining before Hawthorne's death. This engraving of "The Wayside" shows it in 1852, with the many improvements Alcott had made in the house and nine acres.

tions. Methinks this article gives a very fair image of his mind and character—so true, minute, and literal in observation, yet giving the spirit as well as letter of what he sees, even as a lake reflects its wooded banks, showing every leaf, yet giving the wild beauty of the whole scene;— then there are passages in the article of cloudy and dreamy metaphysics, partly affected, and partly the natural exhalations of his intellect;—and also passages where his thoughts seem to measure and attune themselves into spontaneous verse, as they rightfully may, since there is real poetry in him. There is a basis of good sense and moral truth, too, throughout the article, which also is a reflection of his character; for he is not unwise to think and feel, however imperfect in his own mode of action. On the whole, I find him a healthy and wholesome man to know.

After dinner (at which we cut the first watermelon and musk melon that our garden has ripened) Mr. Thorow and I walked up the bank of the river; and, at a certain point, he shouted for his boat. Forthwith, a young man paddled it across the river, and Mr. Thorow and I voyaged further up the stream, which soon became more beautiful than any picture, with its dark and quiet sheet of water, half shaded, half sunny, between high and wooded banks. The late rains have swollen the stream so much, that many trees are standing up to their knees, as it were, in the water; and boughs, which lately swung high in air, now dip and drink deep of the passing wave. As to the poor cardinals, which glowed upon the bank, a few days since, I could see only a few of their scarlet caps, peeping above the water. Mr. Thorow managed the boat so perfectly, either with two paddles or with one, that it seemed instinct with his own will, and to require no physical effort to guide it. He said that, when some

Indians visited Concord a few years since, he found that he had acquired, without a teacher, their precise method of propelling and steering a canoe. Nevertheless, being in want of money the poor fellow was desirous of selling the boat, of which he is so fit a pilot, and which was built by his own hands; so I agreed to give him his price (only seven dollars) and accordingly became possessor of the Musketaquid. I wish I could acquire the aquatic skill of its original owner at as a reasonable a rate.

Sept. 2d. Friday.

Yesterday afternoon, while my wife, and Louisa, and I, were gathering the windfallen apples in our orchard, Mr. Thorow arrived with the boat. The adjacent meadow being overflowed by the rise of the stream, he had rowed directly to the foot of the orchard, and landed at the boards, after floating over forty or fifty yards of water, where people were making hay, a week or two since. I entered the boat with him, in order to have the benefit of a lesson in rowing and paddling. My little wife, who was looking on, cannot feel very proud of her husband's proficiency. I managed, indeed, to propel the boat by rowing with two oars; but the use of the single paddle is quite beyond my present skill. Mr. Thorow had assured me that it was only necessary to will the boat to go in any particular direction, and she would immediately take that course, as if imbued with the spirit of the steersman. It may be so with him, but certainly not with me; the boat seemed to be bewitched, and turned its head to every point of the compass except the right one. He then took the paddle himself, and though I could observe nothing peculiar in his management of it, the Musketaquid immediately became as docile as a trained steed. I suspect that she has not yet transferred her affections from her old master to her new one. By and by, when we are better acquainted, she will grow more tractable; especially after she shall have had the honor of bearing my little wife, who is loved by all things, living or inanimate. We propose to change her name from Musketaquid (the Indian name of Concord river, meaning the river of meadows) to the Pond Lily—which will be very beautiful and appropriate, as, during the summer season, she will bring home many a cargo of pond lilies from along the river's weedy shore. It is not very likely that I shall make such long voyages in her as Mr. Thorow has. He once followed our river down to the Merrimack, and thence, I believe, to Newburyport—a voyage of about eighty miles, in this little vessel.

Lesser known was Ellery Channing, nephew of the famed Unitarian divine, William Ellery Channing. Ellery moved to Concord in the early 1840's after dropping out of Harvard and spending some time living alone in a hut on the Illinois prairies. Later he married Margaret Fuller's sister

Ellen. (Edward Channing, the famed historian, was a child of that marriage.) Ellery was a born eccentric, one of the most undependable persons who ever lived. His family life was in a constant turmoil and he quarreled with almost anyone at the least—or with no provocation. Thoreau once found his mother and Ellery standing back to back on his front porch. Ellery had come to see Henry, but Mrs. Thoreau by chance had answered his knock at the door. Ellery, in a huff, turned his back. And Mrs. Thoreau, not to be outdone, turned hers.

But despite his eccentricities, Ellery, to Thoreau at least, was a worthy companion. Thoreau usually refused to permit anyone to accompany him on his long walks through the Concord fields and woods. But Ellery was always welcome, though Thoreau was often amused at his actions.

▶   In our walks C. takes out his note-book sometimes and tries to write as I do, but all in vain. He soon puts it up again, or contents himself with scrawling some sketch of the landscape. Observing me still scribbling, he will say that he confines himself to the ideal, purely ideal remarks; he leaves the facts to me. Sometimes, too, he will say a little petulantly, "I am universal; I have nothing to do with the particular and definite." He is the moodiest person, perhaps, that I ever saw. As naturally whimsical as a cow is brindled, both in his tenderness and his roughness he belies himself. He can be incredibly selfish and unexpectedly generous. He is conceited, and yet there is in him far more than usual to ground conceit upon.

Channing, in turn, had his comments to make about Thoreau—in fact, a book full of them, for in 1873 he published the first book-length biography of Thoreau. But one of his best comments was made to their mutual friend, Franklin Benjamin Sanborn, who reported it in his 1917 biography of Thoreau:

Henry was fond of making an ado, a wonder, a surprise, of all facts that took place out of doors; but a picture, a piece of music, a novel, did not affect him in that fashion. This trait of exaggeration was as pleasing as possible to his companions. Nothing was more delightful than the enormous curiosity, the effervescing wonder, of this child of Nature —glad of everything its mother said or did. This joy in Nature is something we can get over, like love. And yet love,—that is a hard toy to smash and fling under the grate, for good. But Henry made no account at all of love, apparently; he had notions about friendship.

The townspeople readily recognized the affinity of the Transcendentalists for one another. In 1857, Thoreau told how he knew this:

▶ About a month ago, at the post office, Abel Brooks, who is pretty deaf, sidling up to me, observed in a loud voice which all could hear, "Let me see, your society is pretty large, ain't it?" "Oh, yes, large enough," said I, not knowing what he meant. "There's Stewart belongs to it, and Collier, he's one of them, and Emerson, and my boarder" (Pulsifer), "and Channing, I believe, I think he goes there." "You mean the walkers; don't you?" "Ye-es, I call you the Society. All go to the woods, don't you?" "Do you miss any of your wood?" I asked. "No, I hain't worried any yet. I believe you're a pretty clever set, as good as the average." etc., etc.

Telling Sanborn of this, he said that, when he first came to town and boarded at Holbrook's, he asked H. how many religious societies there were in town. H. said that there were three,—the Unitarian, the Orthodox, and the Walden Pond Society. I asked Sanborn with which Holbrook classed himself. He said he believes that he put himself with the last.

Thoreau found warm friends too among some of the farmers and even the ne'er-do-wells of the town. Some of the more prosperous farmers and particularly the businessmen of the town he did not always look on with favor. To him they were "coarse and boisterous money-making fellows." They in turn looked upon Thoreau as a hopeless eccentric, who, despite a good education, had inexplicably gone to seed.

But the "poetic" farmers—such men as Edmund Hosmer, George Minott, and Reuben Rice—men who could see beyond the noses of their horses and appreciate the beauty of the world about them, men who were willing to take time out for thought and contemplation—these men found in Thoreau a worthy companion. And he in turn found much to admire in them. Even some of the hunters and trappers—such men as Melvin and Goodwin, who lived only a hand-to-mouth existence—won Thoreau's admiration, for at least they had the courage to do what they wanted.

▶ How I love the simple, reserved countrymen, my neighbors, who mind their own business and let me alone, who never waylaid nor shot at me, to my knowledge, when I crossed their fields, though each one has a gun in his house! For nearly twoscore years I have known, at a distance, these long-suffering men, whom I never spoke to, who never spoke to me, and now feel a certain tenderness for them, as if this long probation were but the prelude to an eternal friend-ship. What a long trail we have withstood, and how much more admirable we are to each other, perchance, than if we had been bedfellows! I am not only grateful because Veias, and Homer, and Christ, and Shakespeare have lived, but I am grateful for Minott, and Rice, and Melvin, and Goodwin, and Puffer even. I see Melvin all alone filling his sphere, in russet suit, which no other could fill or suggest. He takes up as much room in nature as the most famous.

That was 1856. In the same period:

▶ It is interesting to me to talk with Rice, he lives so thoroughly and satisfactorily to himself. He has learned that rare art of living, the very elements of which most professors do not know. His life has been not a failure but a success. Seeing me going to sharpen some plane-irons, and hearing me complain of the want of tools, he said that I ought to have a chest of tools. But I said it was not worth the while. I should not use them enough to pay for them. "You would use them more, if you had them," said he. "When I came to do a piece of work I used to find commonly that I wanted a certain tool, and I made it a rule first always to make that tool. I have spent as much as $3000 thus on my tools." Comparatively speaking, his life is a success; not such a failure as most men's. He gets more out of any enterprise than his neighbors, for he helps himself more and hires less. Whatever pleasure there is in it he enjoys. By good sense and calculation he has become rich and has invested his property well, yet practices a fair and neat economy, dwells not in untidy luxury. It costs him less to live, and he gets more out of life, than others. To get his living, or keep it, is not a hasty or disagreeable toil. He works slowly but surely, enjoying the sweet of it. He buys a piece of meadow at a profitable rate, works at it in pleasant weather, he and his son, when they are inclined, goes a-fishing or a-bee-hunting or a-rifle-shooting quite as often, and thus the meadow gets redeemed, and potatoes get planted, perchance, and he is very sure to have a good crop stored in his cellar in the fall, and some to sell. He always has the best of potatoes there. In the same spirit in which he and his son tackle up their Dobbin (he never keeps a fast horse) and go a-spearing or a-fishing through the ice, they also tackle up and go to their Sudbury farm to hoe or harvest a little, and when they return they bring home a load of stumps in their hay-rigging, which impeded their labors, but, perchance, supply them with their winter wood. All the woodchucks they shoot or trap in the bean-field are brought home also. And thus their life is a long sport and they know not what hard times are.

He had a lot to say about George Minott:

▶ I am surprised to see how bare Minott's hillside is already. It is already spring there, and Minott is puttering outside in the sun. How wise in his grandfather to select such a site for a house, the summers he has lived have been so much longer! How pleasant the calm season and the

George Minott's "small, square, one-storied and un-painted house" on the hillside, described by Thoreau on these pages. Minott's tall clock (right), which ticked in the corner on Thoreau's visits, was said to be 200 years old then. "The most poetical farmer" was Thoreau's term for Minott, and there is more about him in the Journal than perhaps anyone else.

warmth—the sun is even like a burning-glass on my back—and the sight and sound of melting snow running down the hill! I look in among the withered grass blades for some starting greenness. I listen to hear the first bluebird in the soft air. I hear the dry clucking of hens which have come abroad.

Minott's is a small, square, one-storied and unpainted house, with a hipped roof and at least one dormer-window, a third the way up the south side of a long hill which is some fifty feet high and extends east and west. A traveller of taste may go straight through the village without being detained a moment by any dwelling, either the form or surround-ings being objectionable, but very few go by this house without being agreeably impressed, and many are therefore led to inquire who lives in it. Not that its form is so incomparable, nor even its weather-stained color, but chiefly, I think, because of its snug and picturesque position on the hillside, fairly lodged there, where all children like to be, and its perfect harmony with its surroundings and position. For if, preserving this form and color, it should be transplanted to the meadow below, nobody would notice it more than a schoolhouse which was lately of the same form. It is there because somebody was independent or bold enough to carry out the happy thought of placing it high on the hillside. It is the locality, not the architecture, that takes us captive. There is exactly such a site, only of course less room on either side, between this house and the next westward, but few if any, even of the admiring travellers, have thought of this as a house-lot, or would be bold enough to place a cottage there.

Without side fences or gravelled walks or flower-plats, that simple sloping bank before it is pleasanter than any front yard, though many a visitor—and many times the master—has slipped and fallen on the steep path. From its position and exposure, it has shelter and warmth and dryness and prospect. He overlooks the road, the meadow and brook, and houses beyond, to the distant woods. The spring comes earlier to that dooryard than to any, and summer lingers longest there.

Minott is, perhaps, the most poetical farmer—who most realizes to me the poetry of the farmer's life—that I know. He does nothing with haste and drudgery, but as if he loved it. He makes the most of his labor, and takes infinite satisfaction in every part of it. He is not looking forward to the sale of his crops or any pecuniary profit, but he is paid by the constant satisfaction which his labor yields him. He has not too much land to trouble him,—too much work to do,—no hired man nor boy,—but simply to amuse himself and live. He cares not so much to raise a large crop as to do his work well. He knows every pin and nail in his barn. If another linter is to be floored, he lets no hired man rob him of that amusement, but he goes slowly to the woods and, at his leisure, selects a pitch pine tree, cuts it, and hauls it or gets it hauled to the mill; and so he knows the history of his barn floor.

Farming is an amusement which has lasted him longer than gunning or fishing. He is never in a hurry to get his garden planted and yet [it] is always planted soon enough, and none in the town is kept so beautifully clean.

He always prophesies a failure of the crops, and yet is satisfied with what he gets. His barn floor is fastened down with oak pins, and he pre-

Edmund Hosmer was one of Thoreau's friends who helped him at the raising of his cabin by Walden Pond. Thoreau spent many evenings in discussion with "the philosophic farmer" at his house. Thoreau's Uncle Charlie Dunbar threw Hosmer twice in a wrestling match. "Better men never lecture than they hire to come here," Thoreau confided to his Journal in 1851. "Why don't they ask Edmund Hosmer or George Minott? I would rather hear them decline than most of these hirelings lecture."

fers them to iron spikes, which he says will rust and give away. He handles and amuses himself with every ear of his corn crop as much as a child with its playthings, and so his small crop goes a great way. He might well cry if it were carried to market. The seed of weeds is no longer in his soil.

He loves to walk in a swamp in windy weather and hear the wind groan through the pines. He keeps a cat in his barn to catch the mice. He indulges in no luxury of food or dress or furniture, yet he is not penurious but merely simple. If his sister dies before him, he may have to go to the almshouse in his old age; yet he is not poor, for he does not want riches. He gets out of each manipulation in the farmers' operations a fund of entertainment which the speculating drudge hardly knows. With neverfailing rheumatism and trembling hands, he seems yet to enjoy perennial health. Though he never reads a book,—since he has finished the "Naval Monument,"—he speaks the best of English.

One evening in December, 1856, Thoreau

▶ . . . saw Melvin's lank bluish-white black-spotted hound, and Melvin with his gun near, going home at eve. He follows hunting, praise be to him, as regularly in our tame fields as the farmers follow farming. Persistent Genius! How I respect him and thank him for him [sic] I trust the Lord will provide us with another Melvin when he is gone. How good in him to follow his own bent, and not continue at the Sabbath-school all his days! What a wealth he thus becomes in the neighborhood! Few know how to take the census. I thank my stars for Melvin. I think of him with gratitude when I am going to sleep, grateful that he exists,— that Melvin who is such a trial to his mother. Yet he is agreeable to me as a tinge of russet on the hillside. I would fain give thanks morning and evening for my blessings. Awkward, gawky, loose-hung, dragging his legs after him. He is my contemporary and neighbor. He is one tribe, I am another, and we are not at war.

Of course there were parties in Concord. Thoreau got to one—at least once.

▶ In the evening went to a party. It is a bad place to go to,—thirty or forty persons, mostly young women, in a small room, warm and noisy. Was introduced to two young women. The first one was as lively and loquacious as a chickadee; had been accustomed to the society of watering-places, and therefore could get no refreshment out of such a dry fellow as I. The other was said to be pretty-looking, but I rarely look people in their faces, and moreover, I could not hear what she said, there

The young Franklin B. Sanborn. Fresh from Harvard in 1855, he moved to Concord to open a private school, and boarded with the Thoreaus for some years. He introduced John Brown to Thoreau. After Thoreau's death, he considered himself an official biographer and editor of his material, publishing many works on the writer.

In 1843, just before Thoreau left Concord for his half-year stay on Staten Island, Ellery Channing moved to Concord. They had met earlier; soon Channing became Henry's most intimate friend. Channing, the same age as Thoreau, lived much longer, until 1901. He published the first biography of Thoreau in 1873.

Samuel Hoar, Concord's leading citizen. When Thoreau was a little boy the Squire, observing his gravity, nicknamed him "the Judge." The Squire sent his son George to Thoreau's school. Another son, Edward, was often Henry's companion on excursions.

Three of Squire Samuel Hoar's children, friends of Thoreau's. Elizabeth Hoar (left), one of the town's intellectuals, called "Elizabeth the Wise" by Emerson, whose brother Charles died just before Elizabeth was to have married him. She said of Thoreau, "I love Henry, but do not like him." Ebenezer Rockwood (center) and George Frisbie (right) were lawyers, like their father. Rockwood became a Massachusetts Supreme Court Justice and then Attorney General in Grant's cabinet. George was a pupil at Thoreau's school. He was elected Congressman and then Senator.

was such a clacking,—could only see the motion of her lips when I looked that way. I could imagine better places for conversation, where there should be a certain degree of silence surrounding you, and less than forty talking at once. Why, this afternoon, even, I did better. There was old Mr. Joseph Hosmer and I ate our luncheon of cracker and cheese together in the woods. I heard all he said, though it was not much, to be sure, and he could hear me. And then he talked out of such a glorious repose, taking a leisurely bite at the cracker and cheese between his words; and so some of him was communicated to me, and some of me to him, I trust.

But even the best of his fellow-townsmen, men like Edmund Hosmer, the "long-headed farmer" mentioned so appreciatively in *Walden,* could at times be disappointing to a man of such high ideals as Thoreau was.

▶ I am disappointed that Hosmer, the most intelligent farmer in Concord, and perchance in Middlesex, who admits that he has property enough for his use without accumulating more, and talks of leaving off hard work, letting his farm, and spending the rest of his days easier and better, cannot yet think of any method of employing himself but in work with his hands; only he would have a little less of it. Much as he is inclined to speculation in conversation—giving up any work to it for the time— and long-headed as he is, he talks of working for a neighbor for a day now and then and taking his dollar. He "would not like to spend his time sitting on the mill-dam." He has not even planned an essentially better life.

And then were those—many of them—who could see little good in Thoreau. Even today in Concord there are those who are astounded at his twentieth-century fame. They remember him chiefly as the man who burned the woods, not as the author of *Walden* or "Civil Disobedience."

In April of 1844, Thoreau and his friend Edward Hoar went out fishing on Fairhaven Bay—but let Thoreau tell the story himself:

▶ I once set fire to the woods. Having set out, one April day, to go to the sources of Concord River in a boat with a single companion, meaning to camp on the bank at night or seek a lodging in some neighboring country inn or farmhouse, we took fishing tackle with us that we might fitly procure our food from the stream, Indian-like. At the shoemaker's near the river, we obtained a match, which we had forgotten. Though it was thus early in the spring, the river was low, for there had not been much rain, and we succeeded in catching a mess of fish sufficient for our dinner before we had left the town, and by the shores of Fair Haven Pond we proceeded to cook them. The earth was uncommonly dry, and our fire, kindled far from the woods in a sunny recess in the hillside on the east of the pond, suddenly caught the dry grass of the previous year which grew about the stump on which it was kindled. We sprang to extinguish it at first with our hands and feet, and then we fought it with a board obtained from the boat, but in a few minutes it was beyond our reach; being on the side of a hill, it spread rapidly upward, through the long, dry, wiry grass interspersed with bushes.

"Well, where will this end?" asked my companion. I saw that it might be bounded by Well Meadow Brook on one side, but would, perchance, go to the village side of the brook. "It will go to town," I answered. While my companion took the boat back down the river, I set out through the woods to inform the owners and to raise the town. The fire had already spread a dozen rods on every side and went leaping and crackling wildly and irreclaimably toward the wood. That way went the flames with wild delight, and we felt that we had no control over the demonic creature to which we had given birth. We had kindled many fires in the woods before, burning a clear space in the grass, without ever kindling such a fire as this.

As I ran toward the town through the woods, I could see the smoke over the woods behind me marking the spot and the progress of the flames. The first farmer whom I met driving a team, after leaving the woods, inquired the cause of the smoke. I told him. "Well," said he, "it is none of my stuff," and drove along. The next I met was the owner in his field, with whom I returned at once to the woods, running all the way. I had already run two miles. When at length we got into the neighborhood of the flames, we met a carpenter who had been hewing timber, an infirm man who had been driven off by the fire, fleeing with his axe. The farmer returned to hasten more assistance. I, who was spent with running, remained. What could I do alone against a front of flame half a mile wide?

I walked slowly through the wood to Fair Haven Cliff, climbed to the highest rock, and sat down upon it to observe the progress of the flames, which were rapidly approaching me, now about a mile distant from the spot where the fire was kindled. Presently I heard the sound of the distant bell giving the alarm, and I knew that the town was on its way to the scene. Hitherto I had felt like a guilty person,—nothing but shame and regret. But now I settled the matter with myself shortly. I said to myself: "Who are these men who are said to be the owners of these woods, and how am I related to them? I have set fire to the forest, but I have done no wrong therein, and now it is as if the lightning had done it. These flames are but consuming their natural food." (It has never troubled me from that day to this more than if the lightning had done it. The trivial fishing was all that disturbed me and disturbs me still.) So shortly I settled it with myself and stood to watch the approaching flames. It was a glorious spectacle, and I was the only one there to enjoy it. The fire now reached the base of the cliff and then rushed up its sides. The squirrels ran before it in blind haste, and three pigeons dashed into the midst of the smoke. The flames flashed up the pines to their tops, as if they were powder.

When I found I was about to be surrounded by the fire, I retreated and joined the forces now arriving from the town. It took us several hours to surround the flames with our hoes and shovels and by back fires subdue them. In the midst of all I saw the farmer whom I first met, who had turned indifferently away saying it was none of his stuff, striving earnestly to save his corded wood which the fire had already seized and which it after all consumed.

It burned over a hundred acres or more and destroyed much young wood. When I returned home late in the day, with others of my townsmen, I could not help noticing that the crowd who were so ready to condemn the individual who had kindled the fire did not sympathize with the owners of the wood, but were in fact highly elate and as it were thankful for the opportunity which had afforded them so much sport; and it was only half a dozen owners, so called, though not all of them who looked sour or grieved, and I felt that I had a deeper interest in the

Fire in the Woods.—A fire broke out in the woods near Fairhaven Pond, in this town, about ten o'clock, last Tuesday forenoon. It extended with great rapidity, and was not subdued until late in the afternoon. The extent of ground over which the fire prevailed, is variously estimated, the lowest estimate placing it at not less than 300 acres. The damage is estimated at about $2000, and falls principally upon Mr A. H. Wheeler, Mr Cyrus Hubbard, and Mr Darius Hubbard. Several other persons have lost something by the disaster, but not so largely as the gentlemen named. Mr Wheeler had some sixty cords of wood which had been cut and piled, destroyed. Our citizens turned out very generally, and labored with great zeal and efficiency to stay the progress of the fire. Their labors were crowned with all the success that could have been expected, when we consider the exceeding dryness of the woods, —there having been no rain of consequence for weeks, —and the difficulties against which they had to contend. By trenching, beating the fire with pine branches, and lighting 'back fires,' all of which was coolly and systematically, a large quantity of property was saved, and the fire prevented from spreading. fire at times made a very magnificent appearance as it was mainly confined to the young wood, underbrush, and leaves, it could not have been seen a very great distance. Dense clouds of smoke rose at times, and gave the impression that the fire was more destructive than it really was. We were forcibly reminded of the scene in Cooper's ' Pioneers,' in which a burning forest is so graphically described.

The fire, we understand, was communicated to the woods through the thoughtlessness of two of our citizens, who kindled it in a *pine stump*, near the Pond for the purpose of making a chowder. As every thing around them was as combustible almost as a firebrand, the flames spread with rapidity, and hours elapsed before it could be subdued. It is to be hoped that this unfortunate result of sheer carelessness, will be borne in mind by those who may visit the woods in future recreation.

The Concord paper reports Thoreau's fire in the woods.

woods, knew them better and should feel their loss more, than any or all of them. The farmer whom I had first conducted to the woods was obliged to ask me the shortest way back, through his own lot. Why, then, should the half-dozen owners [and] the individuals who set the fire alone feel sorrow for the loss of the wood, while the rest of the town have their spirits raised? Some of the owners, however, bore their loss like men, but other some declared behind my back that I was a "damned rascal;" and a flibbertigibbet or two, who crowed like the old cock, shouted some reminiscences of "burnt woods" from safe recesses for some years after. I have had nothing to say to any of them. The locomotive engine has since burned over nearly all the same ground and more, and in some measure blotted out the memory of the previous fire. For a long time after I had learned this lesson I marvelled that while matches and tinder were contemporaries the world was not consumed; why the houses that have hearths were not burned before another day; if the flames were not as hungry now as when I waked them. I at once ceased to regard the owners and my own fault,—if fault there was any in the matter— and attended to the phenomenon before me, determined to make the most of it. To be sure, I felt a little ashamed when I reflected on what a trivial occasion this had happened, that at the time I was no better employed than my townsmen.

That night I watched fire, where some stumps still flamed at midnight in the midst of the blackened waste, wandering through the woods by myself; and far in the night I threaded my way to the spot where the fire had taken, and discovered the now broiled fish,—which had been dressed,—scattered over the burnt grass.

Add to the repercussions of that fire the fact that Thoreau refused to conform to what we now would call the "status-seeking" practices of most of his contemporaries and it is a wonder that he was not ostracized even more than he was. Although usually he was enough of an individualist to ignore the cynical comments of many of his fellow-townsmen, unquestionably at times he must have felt his was a lonely path through life. There seemed to be no one to satisfy the real hunger for true companionship deep down in his heart.

▶   I do not know if I am singular when I say that I believe there is no man with whom I can associate who will not, comparatively speaking, spoil my afternoon. That society or encounter may at last yield a fruit which I am not aware of, but I cannot help suspecting that I should have spent those hours more profitably alone.   •

Even the best of his friends—men such as Emerson and Channing—

[*105*]

failed to come up to the highly idealistic standards by which he wished to measure them:

> ▶ Men are very generally spoiled by being so civil and well-disposed. You can have no profitable conversation with them, they are so conciliatory, determined to agree with you. They exhibit such long-suffering and kindness in a short interview. I would meet with some provoking strangeness, so that we may be guest and host and refresh one another. It is possible for a man wholly to disappear and be merged in his manners. The thousand and one gentlemen whom I meet, I meet despairingly and but to part from them, for I am not cheered by the hope of any rudeness from them. A cross man, a coarse man, an eccentric man, a silent, a man who does not drill well,—of him there is some hope. Your gentlemen, they are all alike. They utter their opinions as if it was not a man that uttered them. It is "just as you please;" they are indifferent to everything. They will talk with you for nothing. The interesting man will rather avoid [you], and it is a rare chance if you get so far as talk with him. The laborers whom I know, the loafers, fishers, and hunters, I can spin yarns with profitably, for it is hands off; they are they and I am I still; they do not come to me and quarter themselves on me for a day or an hour to be treated politely, they do not approach me with a flag of truce. They do not go out of themselves to meet me. I am never electrified by my gentleman; he is not an electric eel, but one of the common kind that slip through your hands, however hard you clutch them, and leave them covered with slime. He is a man, every inch of him; is worth a groom.

Seven years later, in 1858, on the same theme:

> ▶ How long we will follow an illusion! On meeting that one whom I call my friend, I find that I had imagined something that was not there. I am sure to depart sadder than I came. Nothing makes me so dejected as to have met my friends, for they make me doubt if it is possible to have any friends. I feel what a fool I am. I cannot conceive of persons more strange to me than they actually are; not thinking, not believing, not doing as I do; interrupted by me. My only distinction must be that I am the greatest bore they ever had. Not in a single thought agreed; regularly balking one another. But when I get far away, my thoughts return to them. That is the way I can visit them. Perhaps it is unaccountable to me why I care for them. Thus I am taught that my friend is not an actual person. When I have withdrawn and am alone, I forget the actual person and remember only my ideal. Then I have a friend again. I am not so ready to perceive the illusion that is in Nature. I certainly come nearer, to say the least, to an actual and joyful intercourse with

her. Every day I have more or less communion with her, as I think. At least, I do not feel as if I must withdraw out of nature. I feel like a welcome guest. Yet, strictly speaking, the same must be true of nature and of man; our ideal is the only real. It is not the finite and temporal that satisfies or concerns us in either case.

I associate the idea of friendship, methinks, with the person the most foreign to me. This illusion is perpetuated, like superstition in a country long after civilization has been attained to. We are attracted toward a particular person, but no one has discovered the laws of this attraction. When I come nearest to that other actually, I am wont to be surprised at my selection. It may be enough that we have met some time, and now can never forget it. Some time or other we paid each other this wonderful compliment, looked largely, humanly, divinely on one another, and now are fated to be acquaintances forever. In the case of nature I am not so conscious of this unsatisfied yearning.

And from another aspect:

▶   What if we feel a yearning to which no breast answers? I walk alone. My heart is full. Feelings impede the current of my thoughts. I knock on the earth for my friend. I expect to meet him at every turn; but no friend appears, and perhaps none is dreaming of me. I am tired of frivolous society, in which silence is forever the most natural and the best manners. I would fain walk on the deep waters, but my companions will only walk on shallows and puddles. I am naturally silent in the midst of twenty from day to day, from year to year. I am rarely reminded of their presence. Two yards of politeness do not make society for me. One complains that I do not take his jokes. I took them before he had done uttering them, and went my way. One talks to me of his apples and pears, and I depart with my secret untold. His are not the apples that tempt me.

But Thoreau was no misanthrope. Unquestionably he was sometimes disappointed in his fellow man. But when there were people who needed help, Thoreau was there to help them. Consider, for example, Thoreau and the Irish laborers of Concord.

The potato famine struck Ireland in the late 1830's and early 1840's. By the thousands those who could scrape together the few dollars necessary for transportation across the Atlantic by steerage fled to this country. But instead of finding themselves welcomed into the "land of the free," they found themselves almost completely ostracized by the old-time Yankees who considered the new immigrants hardly members of the human race. The only jobs open to them were the most menial labor. They were condemned to live in shanties and slums. They were denied aid from the numerous charitable societies. Their churches were desecrated and their convent in nearby Chelsea burned. Businessmen were interested in them only as a source of cheap labor on the rapidly developing railroads. And large numbers of them swarmed into Concord with the coming of the Fitchburg railroad in 1844.

At first Thoreau was somewhat aloof. One can sense that aloofness in parts of *Walden*. But very quickly his resistance broke down and he became one of their staunchest friends and defenders in Concord.

In 1853 he described his experience in trying to borrow money for a poor Irishman who wished to get his family to this country.

▶   One will never know his neighbors till he has carried a subscription paper among them. Ah! it reveals many and sad facts to stand in this relation to them. To hear the selfish and cowardly excuses some make,— that if they help any they must help the Irishman who lives with them, —and him they are sure never to help! Others, with whom public opinion weighs, will think of it, trusting you never will raise the sum and so they will not be called on again; who give stingily after all. What a satire in the fact that you are much more inclined to call on a certain slighted and so-called crazy woman in moderate circumstances rather than on the president of the bank! But some are generous and save the town from the distinction which threatened it, and some even who do not lend, plainly would if they could.

Not long after, Thoreau's indignation was roused when he heard:

▶   One of my townsmen, notorious for meanness, was endeavoring to get and keep a premium of four dollars which a poor Irish laborer whom he hired had gained by fifteen minutes' spading at our Agricultural Fair. To-night a free colored woman is lodging at our house, whose errand to the North is to get money to buy her husband, who is a slave to one Moore in Norfolk, Virginia. She persuaded Moore, though not a kind master, to buy him that he might not be sold further South. Moore paid six hundred dollars for him, but asks her eight hundred. My most natural reflection was that he was even meaner than my townsman. As mean as a slaveholder!

A particular object of his concern and interest was the little Irish lad Johnny Riordan. Some of the most delightful pages of Thoreau's *Journal* are devoted to Johnny:

▶   They showed me little Johnny Riordan the other day, as bright a boy of five years as ever trod our paths, whom you could not see for five minutes without loving and honoring him. He lives in what they call the shanty in the woods. He had on, in the middle of January of the coldest winter we have had for twenty years, one thickness only of ragged cloth sewed on to his pantaloons over his little shirt, and shoes with large holes in the toes, into which the snow got, as he was obliged to confess, he who had trodden five winters under his feet! Thus clad he walked a mile to school every day, over the bleakest of railroad causeways, where I know by experience the grown man would frequently freeze his ears or nose if they were not well protected,—for his parents have no thermometer,—all to get learning and warmth and there sit at the head of his bench. These clothes with countless patches, which had for vehicle— O shame! shame!—pantaloons that had been mine, they whispered to me, set as if his mother had fitted them to a tea-kettle first.

I glimpsed him the other morning taking his last step from his last snow-drift on to the schoolhouse door-step, floundering still; saw not his face nor his profile, only his mien, but saw clearly in imagination his "old-worthy" face behind the sober visor of his cap, and he revived to my mind the grave nobility and magnanimity of ancient heroes. He never was drawn in a willow wagon, but progresses by his own brave steps. Has not the world waited for such a generation? Here he condescends to his a-b-c without one smile, who has the lore of worlds uncounted in his brain. He speaks not of the adventures of the causeway. What was the bravery of Leonidas and his three hundred boys at the pass of Thermopylae to this infant's? They dared but to die; he dares to live, and takes his reward of merit, perchance, without relaxing his face into a smile, that does not reward a thousandth part of his merits, that overlooks his unseen and unrewardable merits,—Little Johnny Riordan, who faces cold and routs it like a Persian army, who, yet innocent, carries in his knees the strength of a thousand Indras. Not to be so tenderly nurtured as you and I forsooth? All day he plays with his coevals and equals, and then they go to their several homes.

> I am the little Irish boy,
>   That lives in the shanty.
> I am five years old to-day,
>   And shall soon be one and twenty . . .

> At recess I play
> With little Billy Gray
> And when school is done,
> Then away I run

> And if I meet the cars,
>   I get on the other track,

And then I know, whatever comes,
I needn't look back.

Having carried off the palm in the intellectual contest with the children of luxury, how bravely he contemplates his destiny:—

I shall grow up
And be a great man,
And shovel all day
As hard as I can.

This tender gobbet for the fates, cast into a cold world, with a torn lichen leaf wrapped about him! I would rather hear that America's first-born were all slain than that his little fingers and toes should feel cold while I am warm. Is man so cheap that he cannot be clothed but with a mat or a rag? that we should abandon to him our wornout clothes or our cold victuals? Infancy pleads with equal eloquence from all platforms. Rather let the mature rich wear the rags and insufficient clothing, the infant poor and rich, if any, wear the costly furs, the purple and fine linen. Our charitable institutions are an insult to humanity,—a charity which dispenses the crumbs that fall from its overloaded tables! whose waste and whose example helped to produce that poverty!

While the charitable waddle about cased in furs and finery, this boy, lively as a cricket, passes them on his way to school. I see that, for the present, the child is happy, is not puny, and has all the wonders of nature for his toys. Have I not faith that his tenderness will in some way be cherished and protected, as the buds of spring in the remotest wintry dell no less than in the garden and summer-house?

"Carried a new cloak to Johnny Riordan," he noted in February, 1852:

▶   I found that the shanty was warmed by the simple social relations of the Irish. On Sunday they come from the town and stand in the doorway and so keep out the cold. One is not cold among his brothers and sisters. What if there is less fire on the hearth, if there is more in the heart!

These Irish are not succeeding so ill after all. The little boy goes to the primary school and proves a forward boy there, and the mother's brother, who has let himself in the village, tells me that he takes the "Flag of our Union" (if that is the paper edited by an Irishman). It is musical news to hear that Johnny does not love to be kept at home from school in deep snows.

10

Three Ultra-Reformers

"IT WAS A TIME when the air was full of reform," Emerson wrote years later when he looked back on the 1840's. "Madmen, madwomen, men with beards, Dunkers, Muggletonians, Come-outers, Groaners, Agrarians, Seventh-day Baptists, Quakers, Abolitionists, Calvinists, Unitarians and Philosophers,—all came successively to the top, and seized their moment, if not their hour, wherein to chide, or pray, or preach, or protest."

So far as Thoreau was concerned, these reformers were all beginning the wrong end to. They wanted to reform society, thinking that thereby the reformation of man would automatically follow. Thoreau, true to his Transcendentalist principles, believed that all reform must begin with the individual. Reform the individual and society would not need reformation. As he wrote in *Cape Cod:*

▶ Alas! this is the crying sin of the age, this want of faith in the prevalence of a man. Nothing can be effected but by one man. He who wants help wants everything. True, this is the condition of our weakness, but it can never be the means of our recovery. We must first succeed alone, that we may enjoy our success together. We trust that the social movements which we witness indicate an aspiration not to be thus cheaply satisfied. In this matter of reforming the world, we have little faith in corporations; not thus was it first formed.

Later, in the same book, he said:

▶ Love is the wind, the tide, the waves, the sunshine. Its power is incalculable; it is many horse-power. It never ceases, it never slacks; it can move the globe without a resting-place; it can warm without fire; it can feed without meat; it can clothe without garments; it can shelter without roof; it can make a paradise within which will dispense with a paradise without. But though the wisest men in all ages have labored to publish this force, and every human heart is, sooner or later, more or less, made to feel it, yet how little is actually applied to social ends! True, it is the motive-power of all successful social machinery; but as in physics we have made the elements do only a little drudgery for us,—steam to take the place of a few horses, wind of a few oars, water of a few cranks and handmills,—as the mechanical forces have not yet been generously and largely applied to make the physical world answer to the ideal, so the power of love has been but meanly and sparingly applied, as yet. It has patented only such machines as the almshouse, the hospital, and the Bible Society, while its infinite wind is still blowing, and blowing down these very structures too, from time to time. Still less are we accumulating its power, and preparing to act with greater energy at a future time. Shall we not contribute our shares to this enterprise, then?

Concord, quite naturally, with all its intellectual ferment, was a center for these reform movements. Reformers and reform movements bubbled and seethed through the town. Mrs. Thoreau's boarding house was often the temporary residence for transient reformers, in Concord to conduct a meeting, proselytize for followers, or interview Emerson and his friends. Thoreau himself was not amused at their antics. He lashed out in his Journal:

▶   Here have been three ultra-reformers, lecturers on Slavery, Temperance, the Church, etc., in and about our house and Mrs. Brooks's the last three or four days,—A. D. Foss, once a Baptist minister in Hopkinton, N.H.; Loring Moody, a sort of traveling pattern-working chaplain; and H. C. Wright, who shocks all the old women with his infidel writings. Though Foss was a stranger to the others, you would have thought them old and familiar cronies. (They happened here together by accident.)

"The great Dr. Channing"—uncle of William Ellery and William Henry—Transcendentalist and one of the chief wedges that cracked the grim front of New England Calvinism. For forty years in Boston the Unitarian clergyman was a pioneer in social reform, opposing slavery and war, and the exploitation of labor.

They addressed each other constantly by their Christian names, and rubbed you continually with the greasy cheeks of their kindness. They would not keep their distance, but cuddle up and lie spoon-fashion with you, no matter how hot the weather nor how narrow the bed,—chiefly ————. I was awfully pestered with his benignity; feared I should get greased all over with it past restoration; tried to keep some starch in my clothes. He wrote a book called "A Kiss for a Blow," and he behaved as if there were no alternative between these, or as if I had given him a blow. I would have preferred the blow, but he was bent on giving me the kiss, when there was neither quarrel nor agreement between us. I wanted that he should straighten his back, smooth out those ogling wrinkles of benignity about his eyes, and, with a healthy reserve, pronounce something in a downright manner. It was difficult to keep clear in his slimy benignity, with which he sought to cover you before he swallowed you and took you fairly into his bowels. It would have been far worse than the fate of Jonah. I do not wish to get any nearer to a man's bowels than usual. They lick you as a cow her calf. They would fain wrap you about with their bowels. ———— addressed me as "Henry" within one minute from the time I first laid eyes on him, and when I spoke, he said with drawling, sultry sympathy, "Henry, I know all you would say; I understand you perfectly; you need not explain anything to me;" and to another, "I am going to dive into Henry's inmost depths." I said, "I trust you will not strike your head against the bottom." He could tell in a dark room, with his eyes blinded and in perfect stillness, if there was one there whom he loved. One of the most attractive things about the flowers is their beautiful reserve. The truly beautiful and noble puts its lover, as it were, at an infinite distance, while it attracts him more strongly than ever. I do not like the men who come so near with their bowels. It is

George Ripley, a Unitarian minister for 14 years, found it impossible to reconcile Christian doctrine with the social conditions he knew. A financial crisis had seized the country in 1837; it lasted until 1844. The widespread suffering destroyed the confidence of many in the economic system and led them to explore the advantages of a planned, cooperative system. All the utopian communities had their birth in this period. Ripley resigned his pulpit to establish Brook Farm as a self-sufficient cooperative community, a kind of practical demonstration of Transcendentalism, in which thought would be free and work without drudgery.

[*113*]

the most disagreeable kind of snare to be caught in. Men's bowels are far more slimy than their brains. They must be ascetics indeed who approach you by this side. What a relief to have heard the ring of one healthy reserved tone! With such a forgiving disposition, as if he were all the while forgiving you for existing. Considering our condition or habit of soul,—maybe corpulent and asthmatic,—maybe dying of atrophy, with all our bones sticking out,—is it kindness to embrace a man? They lay their sweaty hand on your shoulder, or your knee, to magnetize you.

Most memorable of the many reform movements of the time were the various experimental communities. As Emerson wrote Thomas Carlyle in 1840, "We are all a little wild here with numberless projects of social reform. Not a reading man but has a draft of a new Community in his waistcoat pocket."

Best known of these communities and, comparatively speaking, one of the most successful, was Brook Farm, which the Rev. George Ripley, a Unitarian minister and distant relative of Emerson by marriage, established in West Roxbury, a suburb of Boston, in 1841. The major purpose of Brook Farm was to free the individual at least partially from the toils of society. Theoretically its members would earn their living by spending their mornings working for the community in the gardens, the barns, the dormitories, or participating in its various money-earning projects. The afternoons then

Charles King Newcomb, a member of Brook Farm, friend of Emerson and occasional walking companion of Thoreau.

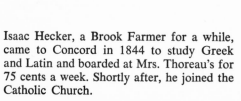

Isaac Hecker, a Brook Farmer for a while, came to Concord in 1844 to study Greek and Latin and boarded at Mrs. Thoreau's for 75 cents a week. Shortly after, he joined the Catholic Church.

they could devote to creative work—such as writing or painting. And their evenings could be social occasions. The artist—whether in words or paints or music—could thus devote nearly 50 per cent of his time to his craft and still be assured of his living.

But unfortunately Brook Farm never succeeded in fulfilling its hopes. From the very beginning there was a shortage of both converts and cash. And too few of the converts it did have took their work seriously. As Emerson wryly commented, "It was a perpetual picnic, a French Revolution in small, an Age of Reason in a patty-pan."

Nathaniel Hawthorne was one of its earliest members, but, disillusioned, he dropped out before the end of the first year. Ripley begged Emerson to join, but he replied:

It is quite time I made an answer to your proposition that I should join you in your new enterprise. The design appears to me so noble & humane, proceeding, as I plainly see, from a manly & expanding heart & mind that it makes me & all men its friends & debtors. It becomes a matter of conscience to entertain it friendly & to examine what it has for us.

I have decided not to join it & yet very slowly & I may almost say penitentially. I am greatly relieved by learning that your coadjutors are now so many that you will no longer ascribe that importance to the defection of individuals which you hinted in your letter to me it might attach to mine.

The ground of my decision is almost purely personal to myself. I have some remains of skepticism in regard to the general practicability of the plan, but these have not much weighed with me. That which determines me is the conviction that the Community is not good for me. Whilst I

Charles A. Dana (left) and George W. Curtis were among the first Brook Farmers. Dana became editor of the New York *Sun,* and Curtis editor of *Putnam's* and *Harper's Weekly*. Dana, his friends of the community days said, was the man who later departed furthest from Brook Farm's aspirations. Curtis and Thoreau, old friends, fell out in 1853 when the former, as *Putnam's* editor, tried to censor "heretical" passages in Thoreau's report of his trip to Canada.

see it may hold out many inducements for others it has little to offer me which with resolution I cannot procure for myself.

There is no record that Thoreau was asked to join the community. Unquestionably he would have been welcomed because many of his friends were among its members. But apparently—and quite rightfully—they realized that he was too much of the individualist to even consider such a move.

In 1843 when Charles Lane and Bronson Alcott started their own community in nearby Harvard, Massachusetts, they were very anxious to have Thoreau join. Lane wrote Thoreau in June of 1843:

You have no doubt seen the neighborhood; but from these very fields, where you may at once be at home and out, there is enough to love and revel in for sympathetic souls like yours. On the estate are about fourteen acres of wood, part of it extremely pleasant as a retreat, a very sylvan realization, which only wants a Thoreau's mind to elevate it to classic beauty.

I have some imagination that you are not so happy and so well housed in your present position as you would be here amongst us; although at present there is much hard manual labor,—so much that, as you perceive, my usual handwriting is very greatly suspended. We have only two associates in addition to our own families; our house accommodations are poor and scanty; but the greatest want is of good female aid. Far too much labor devolves on Mrs. Alcott. If you should light on any such assistance, it would be charitable to give it a direction this way. We may, perhaps, be rather particular about the quality; but the conditions will pretty well determine the acceptability of the parties without a direct adjudication on our part. For though to me our mode of life is luxurious in the highest degree, yet generally it seems to be thought that the setting aside of all impure diet, dirty habits, idle thoughts, and selfish feelings, is a course of self-denial, scarcely to be encountered or even thought of in such an alluring world as this in which we dwell.

Besides the busy occupations of each succeeding day, we form, in this ample theatre of hope, many forthcoming scenes. The nearer little copse is designed as the site of the cottages. Fountains can be made to descend from their granite sources on the hill-slope to every apartment if required. Gardens are to displace the warm grazing glades on the south, and numerous human beings, instead of cattle, shall here enjoy existence. The farther wood offers to the naturalist and the poet an exhaustless haunt; and a short cleaning of the brook would connect our boat with the Nashua. Such are the designs which Mr. Alcott and I have just sketched, as, resting from planting, we walked around this reserve.

But Thoreau, like Emerson, felt there were other solutions to the problems of the day. Two years earlier he had confided to his Journal his personal opinion of the new utopias:

▶ As for these communities, I think I had rather keep bachelor's hall in hell than go to board in heaven. Do you think your virtue will be boarded with you? It will never live on the interest of your money, depend upon it. The boarder has no home. In heaven I hope to bake my own bread and clean my own linen. The tomb is the only boarding-house in which a hundred are served at once. In the catacomb we may dwell together and prop one another without loss.

Some years later, meeting the New York artist Bellew, he summed up his objections to cooperative projects:

▶ Talking with Bellew this evening about Fourierism and communities, I said that I suspected any enterprise in which two were engaged together. "But," said he, "it is difficult to make a stick stand unless you slant two or more against it." "Oh, no," answered I, "you may split its lower end into three, or drive it single into the ground, which is the best way; but most men, when they start on a new enterprise, not only figuratively, but really, pull up stakes. When the sticks prop one another, none, or only one, stands erect."

Although Thoreau traveled little in professional Transcendentalist circles, preferring instead to "travel much in Concord," he became acquainted with most of the leaders of the movement chiefly through the fact that they hovered around Emerson's home in Concord like bees around honey.

Well in advance of their time there were many "blue-stocking" women among the Transcendentalists. Most outstanding of them all was Margaret Fuller. Daughter of a Congressman from Cambridge, Massachusetts, she was a child prodigy. Upon achieving chronological—if not emotional—maturity (modern psychiatrists would have had a field day with some of her problems), Margaret quickly associated herself with the leaders of the Transcendentalist movement. She was the first editor of their magazine, *The Dial*. Emerson, anxious as always to forward Thoreau's literary career, frequently suggested that she include Thoreau's essays and poems in the pages of *The Dial*. Although she did accept some of his writings, she was not as appreciative of their worth as was Emerson. Typical of her reactions is a letter she wrote Thoreau on December 1, 1840, rejecting an essay entitled "The Service" that he had submitted:

I am to blame for so long detaining your manuscript. But my thoughts have been so engaged that I have not found a suitable hour to reread it as I wished till last night. This second reading only confirms my impression from the first. The essay is rich in thoughts, and I should be pained not to meet it again. But then the thoughts seem to me so out of their natural order, that I cannot read it through without pain. I never once feel myself in a stream of thought, but seem to hear the grating of tools on the mosaic. It is true, as Mr. E[merson] says, that essays not to be compared with this have found their way into the Dial. But then these are more unassuming in their tone, and have an air of quiet good-breeding which induces us to permit their presence. Yours is so rugged that it ought to be commanding. Yet I hope you will give it me again, and if you see no force in my objections disregard them.

One anecdote about Thoreau and Margaret Fuller holds that a double wedding was arranged with Henry and Margaret as one pair of principals. But when asked about it, Henry had merely shaken his head and said, "In the first place, Margaret Fuller is not fool enough to marry me; and second, I am not fool enough to marry her." Amusing as the story is, it is undoubtedly apocryphal.

In 1844 Margaret joined the staff of Horace Greeley's New York *Tribune* as its first woman reporter. She wrote book reviews, travel sketches, and articles on various reforms of the day. Abroad in 1848, she found herself in the midst of the great European revolutions of that year, and became America's first woman war correspondent. Before the revolution was over, she had become the Marchioness Ossoli and the mother of a son. Returning to this country with her family and the manuscript of her book on the Italian Revolution she lost her life in a shipwreck on the coast of Long Island. At Emerson's request, Thoreau was sent to search for the bodies of the Ossoli family and the manuscript of the book. On July 25th, 1850, Thoreau sent Emerson his findings:

▶ I am writing this at the house of Smith Oakes, within one mile of the wreck. He is the one who rendered the most assistance. Wm H Channing [a New York clergyman and cousin of Ellery] came down with me, but I have not seen Arthur Fuller—nor [Horace] Greeley, nor [Marcus] Spring [a close friend of Margaret Fuller]. Spring & [Senator Charles] Sumner [whose brother was lost in the wreck] were here yesterday, but left soon. Mr. Oakes & wife tell me (all the survivors came or were brought dir[ec]tly to their house) that the ship struck at 10 minutes after 4 A.M. and all hands, being mostly in their night clothes made haste to the forecastle—the water coming in [at o]nce. There they remained, the passengers in the forecastle, the crew above it doing what they could. Every wave lifted the forecastle roof & washed over those within. The

Margaret Fuller, writer, critic, *The Dial* editor, was often seen in Concord and at Brook Farm, where she had conversations on Goethe and Greek mythology. Greeley, whose *Tribune* staff she joined, said of her, "I never met a woman who conversed more freely and lucidly." She is reported to have said of herself: "I know now all the people worth knowing in America, and I find no intellect comparable to my own." At Emerson's request Thoreau hurried to Fire Island in July, 1850, to try to salvage her manuscripts and other belongings from the wreck of her ship.

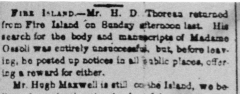

Fire Island.—Mr. H. D Thoreau returned from Fire Island on Sunday afternoon last. His search for the body and manuscripts of Madame Ossoli was entirely unsuccessful, but, before leaving, he posted up notices in all public places, offering a reward for either.

Mr. Hugh Maxwell is still on the Island, we believe, investigating the plunder of the wreck. We hope he will succeed in bringing to justice the ringleaders.

The press notes Thoreau's failure to find the body of Margaret Fuller after her boat was shipwrecked off Fire Island on her voyage back from Italy.

first man got ashore at 9, many from 9 to noon—. At floodtide about 3½ o'clock when the ship broke up entirely—they came out of the forecastle & Margaret sat with her back to the foremast with her hands over her knees—her husband & child already drowned—a great wave came & washed her off. The Steward? had just before taken her child & started for shore; both were drowned.

The broken desk in a bag—containing no very valuable papers—a large black leather trunk—with an upper and under apartment—the upper holding books & papers—A carpet bag probably Ossolis and one of his? shoes—are all the Ossolis' effects known to have been found.

Four bodies remain to be found—the two Ossoli's—Horace Sumner —& a sailor.

I have visited the child's grave—Nobody will probably be taken away today.

The wreck is to be sold at auction—excepting the hull—today. The mortar would not go off. Mrs. Hartz the Captain's wife, told Mrs. Oakes that she & Margaret divided their money—& tied up the halves in handkerchiefs around their persons that Margaret took 60 or 70 dol[lars.]

Mrs. Hartz who can tell all about Margaret up to 11 'oclock on Friday is said to be going to Portland Me. today—She & Mrs. Fuller must & probably will come together. The cook, the last to leave, & the Steward? will know the rest. I shall try to see them. In the meanwhile I shall do what I can to recover property & obtain particulars here abouts. Wm H. Channing—did I write it? has come with me. Arthur Fuller has this moment reached this house. He reached the beach last night—we got here yesterday noon. A good part of the wreck still holds together where she struck, & something may come ashore with her fragments. The last body was found on Tuesday 3 miles west. Mrs. Oakes dried the papers which were in the trunk—and she says they appeared to be of various kinds. "Would they cover that table"?, a small round one—"They would spread out"—Some were tied up. There were 20 or 30 books in the same half of the trunk. Another, smaller trunk empty, came ashore, but there is no mark on it—She speaks of [Celesta] Pardena as if she might have been a sort of nurse to the child"—I expect to go to Patchogue whence the pilferers must have chiefly come—& advertise &c &c.

Some months later, as he strolled along the sandy beaches of Cape Cod, Thoreau was reminded of that Fire Island search:

▶   I once went in search of the relics of a human body—a week after a wreck—which had been cast up the day before on to the beach, though the sharks had stripped off the flesh. I got the direction from a lighthouse. I should find it a mile or two distant over the sand, a dozen rods from the water, by a stick which was stuck up covered with a red cloth. Pursuing the direction pointed out, I expected that I should have to look very narrowly at the sand to find so small an object, but so completely smooth and bare was the beach—half a mile wide of sand—and so magnifying the mirage toward the sea that when I was half a mile distant the insignificant stick or sliver which marked the spot looked like a broken mast in the sand. As if there was no other object, this trifling sliver had puffed itself up to the vision to fill the void; and there lay the relics in a certain state, rendered perfectly inoffensive to both bodily and spiritual eye by the surrounding scenery,—a slight inequality in the sweep of the shore. Alone with the sea and the beach, attending to the sea, whose hollow roar seemed addressed to the ears of the departed,—articulate speech to them. It was as conspicuous on that sandy plain as if a generation had labored to pile up a cairn there. Where there were so few objects, the least was obvious as a mausoleum. It reigned over the shore. That dead body possessed the shore as no living one could. It showed a title to the sands which no living ruler could.

This speculation was promoted by Margaret Fuller's death:

▶   I find the actual to be far less real to me than the imagined. Why this singular prominence and importance is given to the former, I do not know. In proportion as that which possesses my thoughts is removed from the actual, it impresses me. I have never met with anything so truly visionary and accidental as some actual events. They have affected me less than my dreams. Whatever actually happens to a man is wonderfully trivial and insignificant,—even to death itself, I imagine. He complains of the fates who drown him, that they do not touch him. They do not deal directly with him. I have in my pocket a button which I ripped off the coat of the Marquis of Ossoli on the seashore the other day. Held up, it intercepts the light and casts a shadow,—an actual button so called,—and yet all the life it is connected with is less substantial to me than my faintest dreams. This stream of events which we consent to call actual, and that other mightier stream which alone carries us with it,—what makes the difference? On the one our bodies float, and we have sympathy with it through them; on the other, our spirits. We are ever dying to one world and being born into another, and possibly no man knows whether he is at any time dead in the sense in which he affirms that phenomenon of another, or not. Our thoughts are the epochs of our life: all else is but as a journal of the winds that blew while we were here.

Isaac Hecker was another of the Transcendentalists with whom Thoreau became well acquainted. Hecker, a New York City baker, joined the Brook Farm community briefly, and later Fruitlands. In 1844 he settled for a time in Concord, boarding with the Thoreaus while he pursued his studies. A few months later he was baptized into the Roman Catholic Church in New York City and made plans to go on a walking tour of Europe. He wrote Thoreau asking him to join him on this trip:

I have been stimulated to write to you at this present moment on account of a certain project which I have formed in which your influence has no slight share I imagine in forming. It is to work out passage to Europe, and to walk, work, and beg, if needs be, as far when there as we are inclined to do. We wish to see how it looks. And to court difficulties, for we feel an unknown depth of untried virgin strength which we know of no better way at the present time to call into activity and so dispose of. We desire to go without purse or staff, depending upon the all embracing love of God, Humanity, and the spark of courage imprisoned in us.

How does the idea strike you? I prefer at least to go this way before going farther in the woods. The past let us take with us. We reverence, we love it, but forget not that our eyes are in our face set to the beautiful unimagined future. Let us be Janus faced with a beard and beardless face. Will you accept this invitation? Let me know what your impressions are.

Thoreau, although tempted, replied in the negative:

▶ I am strongly tempted by your proposal and experience a decided schism between my outward and inward tendencies. Your method of travelling especially—to live along the road—citizens of the world, without haste or petty plans—I have often proposed this to my dreams, and still do—But the fact is, I cannot so decidedly postpone exploring the Farther Indies, which are to be reached you know by other routs and other methods of travel. I mean that I constantly return from every external enterprise with disgust to fresh faith in a kind of Brahminical Artesian, Inner Temple, life. All my experience, as yours probably, proves only this reality.

Channing wonders how I can resist your invitation, I, a single man—unfettered—and so do I. Why—there are Roncesvalles, the cape de Finisterre, and the three kings of Cologne; Rome, Athens, & the rest—to be visited in serene untemporal hours—and all history to revive in one's memory as he went by the way with splendors too bright for this world—I know how it is. But is not here too Roncesvalle with greater lustre? Unfortunately it may prove dull and desultory weather enough here, but better trivial days with faith than the fairest ones lighted by sunshine alone. Perchance my wanderjahre has not arrived. But you cannot wait for that. I hope you will find a companion who will enter as heartily into your schemes as I should have done.

Hecker, not discouraged, went off to Europe by himself. He joined the order of the Redemptorist Fathers at St. Trond in Belgium. Thus their brief acquaintance came to an end. Some years later Hecker returned to this country and established the Paulist order in New York City, but he was never to meet Thoreau again.

Margaret Fuller and Isaac Hecker were only two of the many Transcendentalists Thoreau knew well. Among the others were Henry G. Wright, an English reformer who joined Charles Lane and Bronson Alcott at Fruitlands; Henry C. Wright, a Unitarian minister who shocked his Newburyport parish by swimming the Merrimack River in the nude; Edward Palmer, the "no-money" man, who felt money to be tainted and refused ever to carry it with him; Joseph Palmer, who achieved nationwide fame for being jailed for wearing a beard when beards were out of fashion; George William Curtis, who later became editor of *Harper's Monthly;*

Theodore Parker, the leading theologian of the group; Jones Very, Emerson's "brave saint," who wrote some of America's best sonnets;—the list could be extended almost indefinitely, a strange combination of eccentricity and genius. Thoreau knew them all. Although he thought many of them to be "men of one idea like a hen with one chicken and that a duckling," nonetheless he was sympathetic to the extent that they were unselfishly trying to create a better world for their fellow man.

11

I Go Abroad Lecturing

A THOREAU LECTURE could be "tom-foolery and nonsense" to one part of the audience, and "wise and valuable" to the other. Reviewing his appearance before the Salem Lyceum, the local newspaper noted this diversity of opinion and attributed it to a style that was "rather too allegorical for a popular audience." Nevertheless, Thoreau sometimes was very entertaining on the platform, for the *Salem Observer* reported on another occasion that Thoreau's story of his life in the woods was "done in an admirable manner, in a strain of exquisite humor, with a strong undercurrent of delicate satire against the follies of the times." Keeping the audience "in almost constant mirth," the performance "created 'quite a sensation' amongst the Lyceum goers."

Other performers were in constant demand by Lyceum managers, but not Thoreau. He said in 1857:

▶ For some years past I have partially offered myself as a lecturer; have been advertised as such several years. Yet I have had but two or three invitations to lecture in a year, and some years none at all. I congratulate myself on having been permitted to stay at home thus, I am so much richer for it. I do not see what I should have got of much value, but money, by going about, but I do see what I should have lost. It seems to me that I have a longer and more liberal lease of life thus. I cannot afford to be telling my experience, especially to those who perhaps will take no interest in it. I wish to be getting experience. You might as well recommend to a bear to leave his hollow tree and run about all winter scratching at all the hollow trees in the woods. He would be leaner in the spring than if he had stayed at home and sucked his claws. As for the lecturegoers, it is none of their business what I think.

When not in this mood, Thoreau ventured to tell audiences what he thought of a great variety of subjects, from his first lecture, on "Society," heard by the Concord Lyceum in 1838, to Raleigh, Carlyle, Maine, Cape

A newspaper notice of the lecturers offered
by the Concord Lyceum for the 1842-43
season. H. D. Thoreau is announced for
February 8. He lectured on Sir Walter
Raleigh. "It was as bright a night as you
could wish," he wrote to Emerson in England. "I hope there were no stars thrown
away on the occasion." The Lyceum was introduced locally in 1829, when Thoreau was
12, the minimum age for joining. He attended the Lyceum, lectured there himself at
least 19 times, and as Curator for the 1843-
44 season managed to spend only $100 for
a full complement of talent. Neither Thoreau
nor any of the townspeople received fees
from the Concord Lyceum. Speakers from
outside, however, were paid from $5 to $25.

The Salem *Observer* for November 25, 1848,
reviewed Thoreau's first lecture outside Concord. Invited to speak by his friend Nathaniel
Hawthorne, he read part of the first chapter
of *Walden,* and was paid $20.

SALEM LYCEUM.

Mr Thoreau, of Concord, gave his au-
ditors a lecture on Wednesday evening,
sufficiently *Emersonian* to have come from
the great philosopher himself. We were
reminded of Emerson continually. In
thought, style & delivery, the similarity was
equally obvious. There was the same keen
philosophy running through him, the same
jutting forth of " brilliant edges of meaning " as Gilfillan has it. Even in tone of
voice, Emerson was brought strikingly to
the ear ; and in personal appearance also,
we fancied some little resemblance. The
close likeness between the two would almost justify a charge of plagiarism, were it
not that Mr Thoreau's lecture furnished
ample proof of being a native product, by affording all the charm of an original. Rather
than an imitation of Emerson, it was the
unfolding of a like mind with his ; as if the
two men had grown in the same soil and
under the same culture.

The reader may remember having recently see an article from the N. Y. Tribune, describing the recluse life led by a
scholar, who supported himself by manual
labor, and on a regime which cost only *twenty seven cents a week,* making it necessary to
labor but six weeks to provide sufficient of
the necessaries of life to serve the balance of
the year. Mr Thoreau is the hero of that
story —although he claims no heroism, considering himself simply as an economist.

The subject of this lecture was Economy,
illustrated by the experiment mentioned.—
This was done in an admirable manner, in
a strain of exquisite humor, with a strong
under current of delicate satire against the
follies of the times. Then there were interspersed observations, speculations, and suggestions upon dress, fashions, food, dwellings,
furniture, &c. &c., sufficiently queer to keep
the audience in almost constant mirth, and
sufficiently wise and new to afford many
good practical hints and precepts.

The performance has created " quite a
sensation " amongst the Lyceum goers.

[*125*]

Cod, Canada, Walden, walking, wild apples, autumnal tints, John Brown, and "the history of myself."

After lecturing twice one winter, he wrote:

▶ I feel that I am in danger of cheapening myself by trying to become a successful lecturer, i.e. to interest my audiences. I am disappointed to find that most that I am and value myself for is lost, or worse than lost, on my audience. I fail to get even the attention of the mass. I should suit them better if I suited myself less. I feel that the public demand an average man,—average thoughts and manners,—not originality, not even absolute excellence. You cannot interest them except as you are like them and sympathize with them. I would rather that my audience come to me than that I should go to them and so they be sifted, i.e. I would rather write books than lectures.

He felt a little better after giving his lecture on "Walking" in a church in Amherst, New Hampshire. Afterward he wrote:

▶ At my lecture the audience attended to me closely, and I was satisfied; that is all I ask or expect generally. Not one spoke to me afterward, nor needed they. I have no doubt that they liked it, in the main, though few of them would have dared say so, provided they were conscious of it. Generally, if I can only get the ears of an audience, I do not care whether they say they like my lecture or not. I think I know as well as they can tell. At any rate, it is none of my business, and it would be impertinent for me to inquire. The stupidity of most of these country towns, not to include the cities, is in its innocence infantile. Lectured in basement (vestry) of the orthodox church, and I trust helped to undermine it.

After the out-of-town lecture there was always the problem of where to sleep. On this New Hampshire trip, he continues:

▶ I was told to stop at the U.S. Hotel, but an old inhabitant had never heard of it and could not tell me where to find it, but I found the letters on a sign without help. It was the ordinary unpretending [?] desolate-looking country tavern. The landlord apologized to me because there was to be a ball there that night which would keep me awake, and it did. He and others there, horrible to relate, were in the habit of blowing their noses with their fingers and wiping them on their boots! Champney's U.S. Hotel was an ordinary team tavern and the letters U.S., properly enough, not very conspicuous on the sign.

As the fall of 1854 came on, the prospect of another season of lecturing was weighed by Thoreau:

I GO ABROAD LECTURING

▶ Thinking this afternoon of the prospect of my writing lectures and going abroad to read them the next winter, I realized how incomparably great the advantages of obscurity and poverty which I have enjoyed so long (and may still perhaps enjoy). I thought with what more than princely, with what poetical, leisure I had spent my years hitherto, without care or engagement, fancy-free. I have given myself up to nature; I have lived so many springs and summers and autumns and winters as if I had nothing else to do but live them, and imbibe whatever nutrient they had for me; I have spent a couple of years, for instance, with the flowers chiefly, having none other so binding engagement as to observe when they opened; I could have afforded to spend a whole fall observing the changing tints of the foliage. Ah, how I have thriven on solitude and poverty! I cannot overstate this advantage. I do not see how I could have enjoyed it, if the public had been expecting as much of me as there is danger now that they will. If I go abroad lecturing, how shall I ever recover the lost winter?

That winter of 1854-55 found Thoreau busier lecturing than at any other season. He spoke in Plymouth, Philadelphia, Providence, New Bedford, Nantucket, Worcester, and Concord. The record of the Philadelphia trip (the farthest south he was to venture), shows how he spent his time on these days away from home:

▶ To Philadelphia. . . . 9 A.M., Boston to New York by express train, land route. . . . Started for Philadelphia from foot of Liberty Street at 6 P.M. via Newark, etc., etc., Bordentown, etc., etc., Camden Ferry, to Philadelphia, all in the dark. Saw only the glossy panelling of the cars reflected out into the dark, like the magnificent lit facade of a row of edifices reaching all the way to Philadelphia, except when we stopped and a lanthorn or two showed us a ragged boy and the dark buildings of some New Jersey town. Arrive at 10 P.M.; time, four hours from New York, thirteen from Boston, fifteen from Concord. Put up at Jones's Exchange Hotel, 77 Dock Street; lodgings thirty-seven and a half cents per night, meals separate; not to be named with French's in New York; next door to the fair of the Franklin Institute, then open, and over against the Exchange, in the neighborhood of the printing-offices.

The next morning:

▶ Looked from the cupola of the Statehouse, where the Declaration of Independence was declared. The best view of the city I got. Was interested in the squirrels, gray and black, in Independence and Washington Squares. Heard that they have, or have had, deer in Logan Square. The squirrels are fed, and live in boxes in the trees in the winter. Fine view from Fairmount water-works. The line of the hypothenuse of the gable end of Girard College was apparently deflected in the middle six inches or more, reminding me of the anecdote of the church of the Madeleine in Paris.

Was admitted into the building of the Academy of Natural Sciences by a Mr. Durand of the botanical department, Mr. Furness applying to him. The carpenters were still at work adding four stories (!) of galleries to the top. These four (Furness thought all of them, I am not sure but Durand referred to one side only) to be devoted to the birds. It is said to be the largest collection of birds in the world. They belonged to the son of Massena (Prince of Essling?), and were sold at auction, and bought by a Yankee for $22,000, over all the crowned heads of Europe, and presented to the Academy. Other collections, also, are added to this. The Academy has received great donations. There is Morton's collection of crania, with (suppose a cast from) an Indian skull found in an Ohio mound; a polar bear killed by Dr. Kane; a male moose not so high as the female which we shot; a European elk (a skeleton) about seven feet high, with horns each about five feet long and tremendously heavy; grinders, etc., of the Mastodon giganteum from Barton County, Missouri; etc., etc. Zinzinger was named as of the geological department.

In Philadelphia and also New York an ornamental tree with bunches of seed-vessels supplying the place of leaves now. I suppose it the ailanthus, or Tree of Heaven. What were those trees with long, black sickle-shaped pods? I did not see Steinhauser's Burd family at St. Stephen's Church. The American Philosophical Society is described as a company of old women.

In the narrow market-houses in the middle of the streets, was struck by the neat-looking women marketers with full cheeks. Furness described a lotus identical with an Egyptian one as found somewhere down the river below Philadelphia; also spoke of a spotted chrysalis which he had also seen in Massachusetts. There was a mosquito about my head at night. Lodged at the United States Hotel, opposite the Girard (formerly United States) Bank.

On the way back to Concord, he stopped in New York:

▶ Went to Crystal Palace; admired the houses on Fifth Avenue, the specimens of coal at the Palace, one fifty feet thick as it was cut from the mine, in the form of a square column, iron and copper ore, etc. Saw sculptures and paintings innumerable, and armor from the Tower of London, some of the Eighth Century. Saw Greeley; Snow, the commercial editor of the Tribune; Solon Robinson; Fry, the musical critic,

Mr. Thoreau, of Concord, delivered a second lecture on Wednesday evening upon his life in the woods. The first lecture was upon the economy of that life; this was upon its object and some of its enjoyments. Judging from the remarks which we have heard concerning it, Mr. Thoreau was even less successful this time in suiting all, than on the former occasion. The diversity of opinion is quite amusing. Some persons are unwilling to speak of his lecture as any better than "tom-foolery and nonsense," while others think they perceived, beneath the outward sense of his remarks, something wise and valuable. It is undoubtedly true that Mr. Thoreau's style is rather too allegorical for a popular audience. He "peoples the solitudes" of the woods too profusely, and gives voices to their "dim aisles" not recognized by the larger part of common ears.

Some parts of this lecture—which on the whole we thought less successful than the former one—were generally admitted to be excellent. He gave a well-considered defence of classical literature, in connection with some common sense remarks upon books; and also some ingenious speculations suggested by the inroads of railroad enterprise upon the quiet and seclusion of Walden Pond; and told how he found nature a counsellor and companion, furnishing

"Tongues in the trees, books in the running brooks,
Sermons in stones, and good in everything."

We take the purpose of Mr. T.'s lecture to have been, the elucidation of the poetical view of life—showing how life may be made poetical, the apprehensive imagination clothing all things with divine forms, and gathering from them a divine language.

"He went to the gods of the wood
To bring their word to men."

And here we may remark that the public are becoming more critical. The standard of Lyceum lectures has been raised very ... and shows that Lyceums have accomplished an important work. We doubt if twenty years ago such lecturers as Professors Agassiz, Guyon, and Rogers, would have been appreciated by popular audiences.— But now they instruct and delight great multitudes.

In regard to Mr. Thoreau, we are glad to hear that he is about issuing a book, which will contain these lectures, and will enable us perhaps to judge better of their merit.

Thoreau lectured again in Salem on February 28, 1849, and the local reviewer found his style "rather too allegorical for a popular audience." He was preparing *Walden* for the press, as the last paragraph notes, but it was not published for another four years.

LIFE IN THE WOODS. A sylvan philosopher, (Mr Thoreau of Concord,) delivered a lecture at the City Hall Friday evening. His discourse was intended as an autobiography of two years of life in the woods;—an experiment by the lecturer to illustrate, not perhaps so much the absurdity of the present organization and customs of society, as the ease with which a man of resolution and stern expedients may have ample leisure for the cultivation of his intellectual powers and the acquisition of knowledge. This sylvan philosopher, after leaving college, (perhaps a little charmed by some "representative," man) betook himself to the woods, where they slope down to the margin of a lakelet, of clear water resting upon a fine gravelly bottom. There, with a little aid from a brawny Emeralder, the young man Thoreau erected a house of ample accommodations for himself. Around his house he planted corn, beans, and other esculents, which at a trifling cost furnished him the means of living. At the end of the time he found that he had lived at the expense of about $27 a year, and that his income exceeded his outgoes $13 a year; and that most of his time had been given to study, to reading, and to reflection. His lecture was a history of his experience; and is said to have been witty, sarcastic, and amusing.

Such philosophers illustrate the absurdities the human mind is capable of. What would a forest full of them be good for? Nothing but curiosities for people to look after, as they pay their shilling to see a menagerie. They are watches without any pointers; their springs and wheels are well adjusted, and perform good service; but nobody is the wiser for it, as they do not tell the time of day. They are a train of car-wheels; they run well, and in good time, but can carry no passengers or luggage. A wheelbarrow, with an Irishman for its vitals, renders the world a far better service.

In Worcester, the *Palladium* reported (above) that "a sylvan philosopher" had lectured at City Hall on April 20, 1849, on his life in the woods. He was said to have been "witty, sarcastic, and amusing," but the paper thought him not much better than a curiosity people pay to see in a menagerie. *The Daily Spy,* however, went out of its way (below) to call attention to Thoreau's second lecture given a week later.

The Daily Spy.
WORCESTER:
THURSDAY, APRIL 26, 1849.

☞ HENRY D. THOREAU. This sylvan philosopher will deliver the second of his very agreeable lectures, in Brinley Hall, to-morrow evening. It will be an intellectual entertainment that should not be neglected.— We would suggest that the attendance of a numerous audience will give no offence to the lecturer.

A news account of Thoreau's lecture on "Misspent Lives" at the Boston Music Hall, October 9, 1859.

etc.; and others. Greeley carried me to the new opera house where I heard Grisi and her troupe. First, at Barnum's Museum, I saw the camelopards, said to be one eighteen the other sixteen feet high. I should say the highest stood about fifteen feet high at most (twelve or thirteen ordinarily). The body was only about five feet long. Why has it horns, but for ornament? Looked through his diorama, and found the houses all over the world much alike. Greeley appeared to know and be known by everybody; was admitted free to the opera, and we were led by a page to various parts of the house at different times. Saw at Museum some large flakes of cutting arrowhead stone made into a sort of wide cleavers, also a hollow stone tube, probably from mounds.

Two months later he was in Worcester, lecturing on "The connection between man's employment and his higher life." The town offered an opportunity he would not miss:

▶ Visited the Antiquarian Library of twenty-two or twenty-three thousand volumes. It is richer in pamphlets and newspapers than Harvard. One alcove contains Cotton Mather's library, chiefly theological works, reading which exclusively you might live in his days and believe in witchcraft. Old leather-bound tomes, many of them as black externally as if they had been charred with fire. Time and fire have the same effect. Haven said that the Rev. Mr. Somebody had spent almost every day the past year in that alcove.

Saw after my lecture a young negro who introduced himself as a native of Africa, Leo L. Lloyd, who lectures on "Young Africa!!" I never heard of anything but old Africa before.

Once in Worcester, where he often lectured in the parlors of his friends, Thoreau tried out his new piece on "Autumnal Tints." One member of the

[*130*]

small audience wrote to her friend that "It was a beautiful and, I doubt not, a faithful report of the colours of leaves in October." She found Thoreau "quaint and observing and humorous withal," but apparently others disagreed this time, too. "All the criticism which I got on my lecture on Autumnal Tints," the Journal reports, "was that I assumed that my audience had not seen so much of them as they had. But after reading it I am more than ever convinced that they have not seen much of them,—that there are few persons who do see much of nature."

What made a lecture good? Thoreau developed his own notion quite early:

▶ I require of any lecturer that he will read me a more or less simple and sincere account of his own life, of what he has done and thought,—not so much what he has read or heard of other men's lives and actions, but some such account as he would send to his kindred from a distant land, —and if he has lived sincerely, it must have been in a distant land to me,—describing even his outward circumstances and what adventures he has had, as well as his thoughts and feelings about them. He who gives us only the results of other men's lives, though with brilliant temporary success, we may in some measure justly accuse of having defrauded us of our time. We want him to give us that which was most precious to him,—not his life's blood but even that for which his life's blood circulated, what he has got by living. If anything ever yielded him pure pleasure or instruction, let him communicate it. Let the money-getter tell us how much he loves wealth, and what means he takes to accumulate it. He must describe those facts which he knows and loves better than anybody else. He must not write on foreign missions. The mechanic will naturally lecture about his trade, the farmer about his farm, and every man about that which he, compared with other men, knows best.

A man once came a considerable distance to ask Thoreau to lecture on slavery:

▶ But on conversing with him [Thoreau said] I found that he and his clique expected seven eighths of the lecture to be theirs, and only one eighth mine; so I declined. I take it for granted, when I am invited to lecture anywhere,—for I have had a little experience in that business,— that there is a desire to hear what I think on some subject, though I may be the greatest fool in the country,—and not that I should say pleasant things merely, or such as the audience will assent to; and I resolve, accordingly, that I will give them a strong dose of myself. They have sent for me, and engaged to pay for me, and I am determined that they shall have me, though I bore them beyond all precedent.

Thoreau felt it was "no compliment" to be invited to lecture before the rich Institutes and Lyceums, those who could afford the fees of what Mark Twain called the "big guns" of the system.

▶   The settled lecturers are as tame as the settled ministers. The audiences do not want to hear any prophets; they do not wish to be stimulated and instructed, but entertained. They, their wives and daughters, go to the Lyceum to suck a sugar-plum. The little of medicine they get is disguised with sugar. It is never the reformer they hear there, but a faint and timid echo of him only. They seek a pastime merely. Their greatest guns and sons of thunder are only wooden guns and great-grandsons of thunder, who give them smooth words well pronounced from manuscripts well punctuated,—they who have stolen the little fire they have from prophets whom the audience would quake to hear. They ask for orators that will entertain them and leave them where they found them. The most success-ful lecturing on Washington, or what-not, is an awful scratching of backs to the tune, it may be, of fifty thousand dollars. Sluggards that want to have a lullaby sung to them! Such manikins as I have described are they, alas, who have made the greatest stir (and what a shallow stir) in the church and Lyceum, and in Congress. They want a medicine that will not interfere with their daily meals.

There is the Lowell Institute with its restrictions, requiring a certain faith in the lectures. How can any free-thinking man accept its terms? It is as if you were to resolve that you would not eat oysters that were not of a particular faith,—that, for instance, did not believe the Thirty-Nine Articles,—for the faith that is in an oyster is just as valuable as the faith referred to in Mr. Lowell's will. These popular lecturers, our preachers, and magazines are for women and children in the bad sense.

The curators have on their lists the names of the men who came before the Philomathean Institute in the next large town and did no harm; left things in statu quo, so that all slept the better for it; only confirmed the audience in their previous badness; spoke a good word for God; gave the clergy, that heavy set, a lift; told the youngsters to be good boys. A man may have a good deal to say who has not any desk to thump on, who does not thunder in bad air.

They want all of a man but his truth and independence and manhood.

One who spoke to their condition would of course make them wince, and they would retaliate, i.e. kick him out, or stop their ears.

In Thoreau's mind, it took two to make a good lecture—the talker and the listener. The greatest compliment ever paid him, he said, was when someone asked him what he thought—and attended to his answer. A good lecturer? That depends on how he is heard.

▶ There may be elocution and pronunciation (recitation, say) to satiety, but there can be no good reading unless there is good hearing also. It takes two at least for this game, as for love, and they must cooperate.

An audience will draw out of a lecture, or enable a lecturer to read, only such parts of his lecture as they like. A lecture is like a barrel half full of some palatable liquor. You may tap it at various levels,—in the sweet liquor or in the froth or in fixed air above. If it is pronounced good, it is partly to the credit of the hearers; if bad, it is partly their fault. Sometimes a lazy audience refuses to cooperate and pull on the ropes with a

the latter part of November, 1854, Thoreau delivered a lecture in Philadelphia. It was not a marked success. Emerson's friend W. H. Furness reported, "Miss Caroline Haven heard him, & from her report I judge the audience was stupid & did not appreciate him." But the occasion did result in an amusing caricature of Thoreau by Furness in a letter reporting the lecture to Emerson. Seeing it, we can understand Hawthorne's comment that Thoreau was "as ugly as sin, long-nosed, queer-mouthed." (Fortunately Hawthorne added, "But his ugliness is of an honest and agreeable fashion, and becomes him much better than beauty.") We can also understand why some of his friends said that the two biggest things about Henry Thoreau were his thoughts—and his nose.

Phila. Nov 26.54

My dear friend,
We depend upon hearing the NY Lecture here.

I was glad to see Mr Thoreau. He was full of interesting talk for the little while that we saw him, & it was amusing to hear your intonations and then he looked so differently from my idea of him [something so]. He had a glimpse of the Academy as he was like you—I could not hear him lecture for which I was sorry. Miss Caroline Haven heard him, & from her report I judge the audience was stupid & did not appreciate him

With much love

R. W. E.   W H Furness

will, simply because the hogshead is full and therefore heavy, when if it were empty, or had only a little sugar adhering to it, they would whisk it up the slope in a jiffy. The lecturer, therefore, desires of his audience a long pull, a strong pull, and all pull together. I have seen a sturdy truckman, or lecturer who had nearly broken his back with shoving his lecture up such an inclined plane while the audience were laughing at him, at length, as with a last effort, set it a-rolling in amid the audience and upon their toes, scattering them like sheep and making them cry out with pain, while he drove proudly away. Rarely it is a very heavy freight of such hogsheads stored in a vessel's hold that is to be lifted out and deposited on the public wharf, and this is accomplished only after many a hearty pull all together and a good deal of heave-yo-ing.

Thoreau listened to other lecturers, hundreds of them as they came through Concord in the thirty-odd years he was a member of the Lyceum. In his own Journal the critic had his say about Thomas Wentworth Higginson, the young minister:

▶   Heard Higginson lecture to-night on Mohammed. Why did I not like it better? Can I deny that it was good? Perhaps I am bound to account to myself at least for any lurking dislike for what others admire and I am not prepared to find fault with. Well, I did not like it, then, because it did not make me like it, it did not carry me away captive. He is not simple enough. For the most part the manner overbore, choked off, and stifled, put out of sight and hearing, the matter. I was inclined to forget that he was speaking, conveying ideas; thought there had been an intermission. Never endeavor consciously to supply the tone which you think proper for certain sentences. It is as if a man whose mind was at ease should supply the tones and gestures for a man in distress who found only the words; as when one makes a speech and another behind him makes gestures. Then he reminded me of Emerson, and I could not afford to be reminded of Christ himself. Yet who can deny that it was good? But it was that intelligence, that way of viewing things (combined with much peculiar talent), which is the common property of this generation. A man does best when he is most himself.

A week later, Ellery Channing was on the rostrum:

▶   Heard C. lecture to-night. It was a bushel of nuts. Perhaps the most original lecture I ever heard. Ever so unexpected, not to be foretold, and so sententious that you could not look at him and take his thought at the same time. You had to give your undivided attention to the thoughts, for you were not assisted by set phrases or modes of speech intervening.

There was no sloping up or down to or from his points. It was all genius, no talent. It required more close attention, more abstraction from surrounding circumstances, than any lecture I have heard. For, as well as I know C., he more than any man disappoints my expectation. When I see him in the desk, hear him, I cannot realize that I ever saw him before. He will be strange, unexpected, to his best acquaintance. I cannot associate the lecturer with the companion of my walks. It was from so original and peculiar a point of view, yet just to himself in the main, that I doubt if three in the audience apprehended a tithe that he said. It was so hard to hear that doubtless few made the exertion. A thick succession of mountain passes and no intermediate slopes and plains. Other lectures, even the best, in which so much space is given to the elaborate development of a few ideas, seemed somewhat meagre in comparison. Yet it would be how much more glorious if talent were added to genius, if there were a just arrangement and development of the thoughts, and each step were not a leap, but he ran a space to take a yet higher leap!

For his lectures to the Concord Lyceum—he gave nineteen of these—Thoreau was paid nothing. He and the other local citizens donated their services, and the town heard free an Emerson lecture which other people might pay $50 for. Thoreau's fees, however, were small; he never could command the high and highly publicized sums the stars of the lecture circuit were paid.

He wasn't interested in fees, but others were:

▶   Men's minds run so much on work and money that the mass instantly associate all literary labor with a pecuniary reward. They are mainly curious to know how much money the lecturer or author gets for his work. They think that the naturalist takes so much pains to collect plants or animals because he is paid for it. An Irishman who saw me in the fields making a minute in my note-book took it for granted that I was casting up my wages and actually inquired what they came to, as if he had never dreamed of any other use for writing. I might have quoted to him that the wages of sin is death, as the most pertinent answer. "What do you get for lecturing now?" I am occasionally asked. It is the more amusing since I only lecture about once a year out of my native town, often not at all; so that I might as well, if my objects were merely pecuniary, give up the business. Once, when I was walking on Staten Island, looking about me as usual, a man who saw me would not believe me when I told him that I was indeed from New England but was not looking at that region with a pecuniary view,—a view to speculation; and he offered me a handsome bonus if I would sell his farm for him.

12

Pencil-Maker

PROBABLY ONE of the most common stories about Henry Thoreau is that he succeeded in making the best pencil in America and when he found he could not improve on it, never made another one.

There is an element of truth in it, but the full story is of greater interest and not as well known. It was another Concord man, William Munroe, who seems to have made the first American pencils. In 1812, when the War with England brought a slump in Munroe's cabinet-making trade, he turned to hand manufacture of pencils. He pounded plumbago with a hammer, mixed it in a spoon with an adhesive, and stuffed the compound into cedar wood cases. His pencils found a ready market in nearby Boston and a new industry was under way. It lasted only a couple of years, however, for the same war interfered with his supply of raw materials.

A little later, in 1819-20, the inventor, Joseph Dixon, experimenting with graphite in Salem, began making pencils by hand. European pencils dominated the market, and when Dixon carried his to Boston for peddling door-to-door, he was told he would have to put foreign labels on them if he expected to make sales. Infuriated, he turned to other fields. But it was from Dixon in his Salem shop that Henry's father John Thoreau learned the art of making lead pencils.

The Thoreaus moved back to Concord in 1823, when Henry was six, and John Thoreau Senior quit the manufacture of stove polish to take up the pencil business. His first pencils were gritty, greasy, brittle, and inefficient —no better than other American makes. He sought to improve them, and found Henry helpful. In the Harvard Library, Henry unearthed an Edinburgh encyclopedia, which revealed that the graphite in the famed Faber pencils of Germany was mixed with a fine Bavarian clay. In the United States, however, glue and spermaceti or bayberry wax were used to form a black and malleable paste.

Following the German formula, the Thoreaus imported the same clay, baked it with the graphite (graphite had been discovered in land owned by Uncle Charles Dunbar, in New Hampshire), and produced the hardest,

Pencil made by J. Thoreau & Son, Concord, Mass.

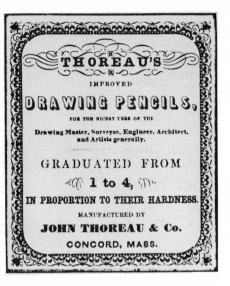

Wrappers for the Thoreau pencils. They show their market included drawing masters, surveyors, engineers, mechanics, architects, and "artists generally."

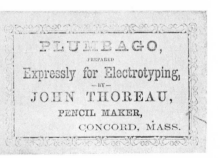

Announcement of a new Thoreau product, which was to replace pencil-making.

The Thoreau pencil factory, sketched by Mary C. Wheeler.

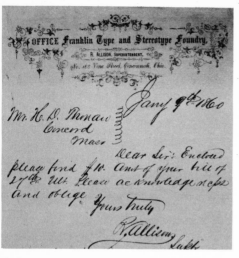

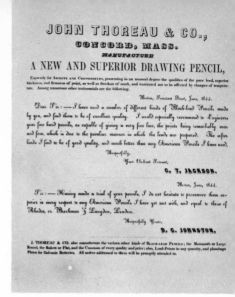

A letter addressed to Henry Thoreau by a Cincinnati firm, enclosing $10 in payment for a graphite bill.

A circular advertising the new and superior drawing pencil of John Thoreau & Co., and bearing testimonials dated June, 1844, from Messrs. Jackson and Johnston.

In 1824, only a year after he began to make pencils, John Thoreau (misspelled "Thorough" in the news item) won this special notice from the *New England Farmer* at an exhibition of the Massachusetts Agricultural Society.

A bundle of Thoreau pencils in the wrapper which originally contained them.

blackest pencil in America. It was still gritty, but so much of an improvement that sales began to go up. Not content, father and son worked out a simple flotation process that gave their pencils a premium fineness. Art teachers in Boston, the story goes, would instruct their pupils to ask for a Thoreau pencil at the supply store because they were the best. A single Thoreau pencil cost 25 cents, while a dozen of any other brand sold for 50 cents.

The Thoreau formula and air blast method were kept secret. Henry went on to devise still further improvements. He invented a new type of saw for stripping the graphite, and a machine to drill a round hole through solid cedar sticks so that round and not square leads could be inserted. This replaced the old way of having two pieces of wood glued together around a square lead. Production was speeded up too by Henry's labor-saving machinery.

In 1849, with the invention of electrotyping, the Thoreaus found a new market for their superior graphite. A Boston electrotyper tried it to coat his plate surfaces and promptly contracted for it at $10 a pound. (In a few years the price dropped to $2.) Since pencils were now selling at $6 a gross, this was a better outlet. Sales reached 500 pounds a year, and brought the family a good income. At first the Thoreaus did not know the use to which their finely ground graphite was put. When they discovered it, they extended their sales to other customers. The shop was in an annex to the rear of the Yellow House on Main Street, to which the Thoreaus had moved in August, 1850. To conceal their markets from the men in the shop, Sophia and Thoreau packed and addressed the bulk material from an upstairs room.

The graphite powder was so fine it pervaded the house, and may have contributed to Thoreau's early death from tuberculosis. After 1852 it was no longer profitable to make pencils, and Thoreau's remark about his perfect pencil, while certainly in character, may also have been a blind to throw competitors off. With the death of his father in 1859, he took complete responsibility for running the graphite business.

13

I Lived Alone,
in the Woods...

THOREAU HAD LONG BEEN INTERESTED in the philosophy of the simple life. At his graduation exercises at Harvard in 1837, as has already been pointed out, he had read a paper in which he advocated reversing the Biblical formula by working one day a week and resting six. While still in college his classmate Charles Stearns Wheeler had built a cabin on Flint's Pond in nearby Lincoln and spent many vacations there. According to tradition Thoreau joined him there for several weeks. And later he considered building a cabin for himself on Flint's Pond but could not get the necessary permission of the owner. In the early 1840's, as he tells us in *Walden,* he very nearly purchased the old Hollowell Farm on the outskirts of Concord, but the owner—or more precisely, the owner's wife—changed his mind and the purchase was not completed.

On April 5, 1841, he wrote in his Journal, "I will build my lodge on the southern slope of some hill, and take there the life the gods send me. Will it not be employment enough to accept gratefully all that is yielded me between sun and sun?" And again, on December 24, "I want to go soon and live away by the pond, where I shall hear only the wind whispering among the reeds. It will be success if I shall have left myself behind. But my friends ask what I will do when I get there. Will it not be employment enough to watch the progress of the seasons?"

In the late fall of 1844 Thoreau's opportunity came. Emerson purchased much of the land around the shore of Walden Pond, a beautiful glacial lake less than two miles from Concord village, to preserve it from the woodchopper's axe. On March 5, 1845, Thoreau received a letter from his old friend Ellery Channing, saying in part:

It seems to me you are the same old sixpence you used to be, rather rusty, but a genuine piece. I see nothing for you in this earth but that field which I once christened "Briars" [near Walden Pond]; go out upon

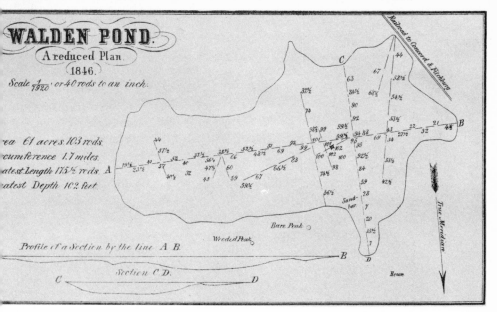

WALDEN POND.
A reduced Plan
1846.
Scale $\frac{1}{7920}$ or 40 rods to an inch.

ea 61 acres 103 rods
cumference 1.7 miles.
atest Length 175½ rods. A
atest Depth 102 feet

Profile of a Section by the line A B.

Section C.D.

Thoreau's own map of Walden Pond, which was included in the original editions of *Walden,* but dropped later. The pond is three quarters of a mile long and half a mile wide. Although recent research attests to the map's scientific accuracy, Thoreau's contemporaries refused to take it seriously. Thoreau's Journal for January 5, 1855, reports that "R. W. E. told of Mr. Hill, his classmate, of Bangor, who was much interested in my 'Walden' but relished it merely as a capital satire and joke, and even thought that the survey and map of the pond were not real, but a caricature of the Coast Survey."

that, build yourself a hut, & there begin the grand process of devouring yourself alive. I see no alternative, no other hope for you. Eat yourself up; you will eat nobody else, nor anything else.

Thoreau quickly made an agreement with Emerson. In return for clearing some of the scrub land at the pond and reforesting it with pines, he might build a cabin on the land and live there rent free.

Thoreau's motives for "taking to the woods" were not mere escapism. He went there because he realized that living such a simple life would give him the economic freedom to devote himself to writing. He had thought of himself as a professional writer for some years, but a lack of money had prevented his devoting the time he wished to his career. Now by eliminating the need for money he could have that time.

And Thoreau had a particular writing task in mind. Ever since the death of his brother John in 1842, Henry had wished to write as a memorial tribute an account of their vacation voyage together on the Concord and Merrimack Rivers in 1839. Living at Walden Pond gave him the opportunity to write that book.

The account of his actual experiment should be told only in his own words:

▶ Near the end of March, 1845, I borrowed an axe and went down to the woods by Walden Pond, nearest to where I intended to build my house, and began to cut down some tall, arrowy white pines, still in their youth, for timber. It is difficult to begin without borrowing, but perhaps it is the most generous course thus to permit your fellow-men to have an interest in your enterprise. The owner of the axe, as he released his hold on it, said that it was the apple of his eye; but I returned it sharper than I received it. It was a pleasant hillside where I worked, covered with pine woods, through which I looked out on the pond, and a small open field in the woods where pines and hickories were springing up. The ice in the pond was not yet dissolved, though there were some open spaces, and it was all dark-colored and saturated with water. There were some slight flurries of snow during the days that I worked there; but for the most part when I came out on to the railroad, on my way home, its yellow sand-heap stretched away gleaming in the hazy atmosphere, and the rails shone in the spring sun, and I heard the lark and pewee and other birds already come to commence another year with us. They were pleasant spring days, in which the winter of man's discontent was thawing as well as the earth, and the life that had lain torpid began to stretch itself. . . .

I hewed the main timbers six inches square, most of the studs on two sides only, and the rafters and floor timbers on one side, leaving the rest of the bark on, so that they were just as straight and much stronger than sawed ones. Each stick was carefully mortised or tenoned by its stump, for I had borrowed other tools by this time. My days in the woods were not very long ones; yet I usually carried my dinner of bread and butter, and read the newspaper in which it was wrapped, at noon, sitting amid the green pine boughs which I had cut off, and to my bread was imparted some of their fragrance, for my hands were covered with a thick coat of pitch. Before I had done I was more the friend than the foe of the pine tree, though I had cut down some of them, having become better acquainted with it. Sometimes a rambler in the wood was attracted by the sound of my axe, and we chatted pleasantly over the chips which I had made.

By the middle of April, for I made no haste in my work, but rather made the most of it, my house was framed and ready for the raising. I had already bought the shanty of James Collins, an Irishman who worked on the Fitchburg Railroad, for boards. James Collins' shanty was considered an uncommonly fine one. When I called to see it he was not at home. I walked about the outside, at first unobserved from within, the window was so deep and high. It was of small dimensions, with a peaked cottage roof, and not much else to be seen, the dirt being raised five feet all around as if it were a compost heap. The roof was the soundest part, though a good deal warped and made brittle by the sun. Doorsill there was none, but a perennial passage for the hens under the door-board. Mrs. C. came to the door and asked me to view it from the inside. The hens were driven in by my approach. It was dark, and had a dirt floor for the most part, dank, clammy, and aguish, only here a board and there a board which would not bear removal. She lighted a lamp to show me the inside of the roof and the walls, and also that the board floor extended under the bed, warning me not to step into the cellar, a sort of dust hole two feet deep. In her own words, they were "good boards overhead, good boards all around, and a good window,"—of two whole squares originally, only the cat had passed out that way lately. There was a stove, a bed, and a place to sit, an infant in the house where it was born, a silk parasol, gilt-framed looking-glass, and a patent new coffee-mill nailed to an oak sapling, all told. The bargain was soon concluded, for James had in the meanwhile returned. I to pay four dollars and twenty-five cents to-night, he to vacate at five to-morrow morning, selling to nobody else meanwhile: I to take possession at six. It were well, he said, to be there early, and anticipate certain indistinct but wholly unjust claims on the score of ground rent and fuel. This he assured me was the only encumbrance. At six I passed him and his family on the road. One large bundle held their all,—bed, coffee-mill, looking-glass, hens,—all but the cat; she took to the woods and became a wild cat, and, as I learned afterward, trod in a trap set for woodchucks, and so became a dead cat at last.

I took down this dwelling the same morning, drawing the nails, and removed it to the pond-side by small cartloads, spreading the boards on the grass there to bleach and warp back again in the sun. One early thrush gave me a note or two as I drove along the woodland path. I was informed treacherously by a young Patrick that neighbor Seeley, an Irishman, in the intervals of the carting, transferred the still tolerable, straight, and drivable nails, staples, and spikes to his pocket, and then stood when I came back to pass the time of day, and look freshly up, unconcerned, with spring thoughts, at the devastation; there being a dearth of work, as he said. He was there to represent spectatordom, and help make this seemingly insignificant event one with the removal of the gods of Troy.

I dug my cellar in the side of a hill sloping to the south, where a woodchuck had formerly dug his burrow, down through sumach and blackberry roots, and the lowest stain of vegetation, six feet square by seven deep, to a fine sand where potatoes would not freeze in any

The foundations of the chimney and fireplace of Thoreau's hut were uncovered on November 12, 1945, by Roland W. Robbins, after months of archaeological work at Walden Pond. By chance the date was 100 years to the day Thoreau's Journal recorded he had finished the cabin. This stone (right) was set in place in 1947 to mark the site. The winter view shows the cairn by Walden which had been piled up over many years by visitors who thought it was the site of Thoreau's cabin. Robbins' probings revealed the hut had been built just behind the cairn, some 12 rods up the slope.

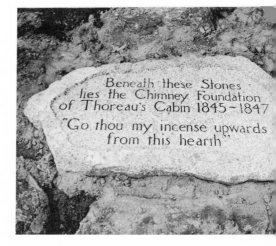

Beneath these Stones
lies the Chimney Foundation
of Thoreau's Cabin 1845–1847
"Go thou my incense upwards
from this hearth"

winter. The sides were left shelving, and not stoned; but the sun having never shone on them, the sand still keeps its place. It was but two hours' work. I took particular pleasure in this breaking of ground, for in almost all latitudes men dig into the earth for an equable temperature. Under the most splendid house in the city is still to be found the cellar where they store their roots as of old, and long after the superstructure has disappeared posterity remark its dent in the earth. The house is still but a sort of porch at the entrance of a burrow.

A drawing of Thoreau's hut made by Mrs. Baker, who visited it.

Henry's sister Sophia made this drawing to be used on the title page of *Walden*. Thoreau complained of it to the printer: "I would suggest a little alteration, chiefly in the door, in the wide projection of the roof at the front; and that the bank more immediately about the house be brought out more distinctly."

This drawing of Thoreau's hut was made from memory in 1880 by Joseph Hosmer, one of Thoreau's contemporaries who had often visited Thoreau at Walden.

Another sketch of the Walden cabin made by May Alcott.

At length, in the beginning of May, with the help of some of my acquaintances, rather to improve so good an occasion for neighborliness than from any necessity, I set up the frame of my house. No man was ever more honored in the character of his raisers than I. They are destined, I trust, to assist at the raising of loftier structures one day. I began to occupy my house on the 4th of July, as soon as it was boarded and roofed, for the boards were carefully feather-edged and lapped, so that it was perfectly impervious to rain, but before boarding I laid the foundation of a chimney at one end, bringing two cartloads of stones up the hill from the pond in my arms. I built the chimney after my hoeing in the fall, before a fire became necessary for warmth, doing my cooking in the meanwhile out of doors on the ground, early in the morning: which mode I still think is in some respects more convenient and agreeable than the usual one. When it stormed before my bread was baked, I fixed a few boards over the fire, and sat under them to watch my loaf, and passed some pleasant hours in that way. In those days, when my hands were much employed, I read but little, but the least scraps of paper which lay on the ground, my holder, or tablecloth, afforded me as much entertainment, in fact answered the same purpose as the Iliad. . . .

Before winter I built a chimney, and shingled the sides of my house, which were already impervious to rain, with imperfect and sappy shingles made of the first slice of the log, whose edges I was obliged to straighten with a plane.

I have thus a tight shingled and plastered house, ten feet wide by fifteen long, and eight-feet posts, with a garret and a closet, a large window on each side, two trap-doors, one door at the end, and a brick fireplace opposite. The exact cost of my house, paying the usual price for such materials as I used, but not counting the work, all of which was done by myself, was as follows; and I give the details because very few

May Alcott's drawing of the Walden hut, with Thoreau in the boat below. Although she was familiar with the site, she grossly exaggerated the height of the cabin above the water.

are able to tell exactly what their houses cost, and fewer still, if any, the separate cost of the various materials which compose them:—

Boards	$8 03½	, mostly shanty boards	
Refuse shingles for roof and sides	4 00		
Laths	1 25		
Two second-hand windows with glass	2 43		
One thousand old brick	4 00		
Two casks of lime	2 40	That was high	
Hair	0 31	More than I needed	
Mantle-tree iron	0 15		
Nails	3 90		
Hinges and screws	0 14		
Latch	0 10		
Chalk	0 01		
Transportation	1 40	I carried a good part on my back.	
In all	28 12½		

These are all the materials, excepting the timber, stones, and sand, which I claimed by squatter's right. I have also a small woodshed adjoining me, made chiefly of the stuff which was left after building the house. . . .

Before I finished my house, wishing to earn ten or twelve dollars by some honest and agreeable method, in order to meet my unusual expenses, I planted about two acres and a half of light and sandy soil near it chiefly with beans, but also a small part with potatoes, corn, peas, and turnips. The whole lot contains eleven acres, mostly growing up to pines and hickories, and was sold the preceding season for eight dollars and eight cents an acre. One farmer said that it was "good for nothing but to raise cheeping squirrels on." I put no manure whatever on this land, not being the owner, but merely a squatter, and not expecting to cultivate so much again, and I did not quite hoe it all once. I got out several cords of stumps in plowing, which supplied me with fuel for a long time, and left small circles of virgin mould, easily distinguishable through the summer by the greater luxuriance of the beans there. The dead and for the most part unmerchantable wood behind my house, and the driftwood from the pond, have supplied the remainder of my fuel. I was obliged to hire a team and a man for the plowing, though I held the plow myself. My farm outgoes for the first season were, for implements, seed, work, etc., $14.72½. The seed corn was given me. This never costs anything

Many of Thoreau's belongings are gathered in this room in the Concord Antiquarian Society. In the Walden hut were the desk, rocker, and the bed he caned himself. His surveyor's chain is on the table at left, and beneath are his father's fire buckets. On the smaller table near the bed is his flute and the statuette of Uncle Tom and Little Eva that was said to have been sent to him by a fugitive slave he helped to escape to Canada.

to speak of, unless you plant more than enough. I got twelve bushels of beans, and eighteen bushels of potatoes, beside some peas and sweet corn. The yellow corn and turnips were too late to come to anything. My whole income from the farm was

$$
\begin{array}{lr}
 & \$23 \ 44 \\
\text{Deducting the outgoes} \ \ldots \ldots & 14 \ 72\frac{1}{2} \\
\hline
\text{There are left} \ \ldots \ldots \ldots \ldots & 8 \ 71\frac{1}{2},
\end{array}
$$

beside produce consumed and on hand at the time this estimate was made of the value of $4.50,—the amount on hand much more than balancing a little grass which I did not raise. All things considered, that is, considering the importance of a man's soul and of today, notwithstanding the short time occupied by my experiment, nay, partly even because of its transient character, I believe that that was doing better than any farmer in Concord did that year.

The next year I did better still, for I spaded up all the land which I required, about a third of an acre, and I learned from the experience of both years, not being in the least awed by many celebrated works on husbandry, Arthur Young among the rest, that if one would live simply and eat only the crop which he raised, and raise no more than he ate, and not exchange it for an insufficient quantity of more luxurious and expensive things, he would need to cultivate only a few rods of ground, and that it would be cheaper to spade up that than to use oxen to plow it, and to select a fresh spot from time to time than to manure the old, and he could do all his necessary farm work as it were with his left hand at odd hours in the summer; and thus he would not be tied to an ox, or horse, or cow, or pig, as at present. I desire to speak impartially on this point, and as one not interested in the success or failure of the present economical and social arrangements. I was more independent than any farmer in Concord, for I was not anchored to a house or farm, but could follow the bent of my genius, which is a very crooked one, every moment. Beside being better off than they already, if my house had been burned or my crops had failed, I should have been nearly as well off as before. . . .

By surveying, carpentry, and day-labor of various other kinds in the village in the meanwhile, for I have as many trades as fingers, I had earned $13.34. The expense of food for eight months, namely, from July 4th to March 1st, the time when these estimates were made, though I lived there more than two years,—not counting potatoes, a little green corn, and some peas, which I had raised, nor considering the value of what was on hand at the last date,—was

Rice	$1 73½	
Molasses	1 73	Cheapest form of the saccharine.
Rye meal	1 04¾	
Indian meal	0 99¾	Cheaper than rye.
Pork	0 22	
Flour	0 88	Costs more than Indian meal, both money and trouble.
Sugar	0 80	
Lard	0 65	
Apples	0 25	
Dried apple	0 22	
Sweet potatoes	0 10	
One pumpkin	0 6	
One watermelon	0 2	
Salt	0 3	

All experiments which failed

Yes, I did eat $8.74, all told; but I should not thus unblushingly publish my guilt, if I did not know that most of my readers were equally guilty with myself, and that their deeds would look no better in print. The next year I sometimes caught a mess of fish for my dinner, and once I went so far as to slaughter a woodchuck which ravaged my bean-field,— effect his transmigration, as a Tartar would say,—and devour him, partly for experiment's sake; but though it afforded me a momentary enjoyment, notwithstanding a musky flavor, I saw that the longest use would not make that a good practice, however it might seem to have your wood-chucks ready dressed by the village butcher.

Clothing and some incidental expenses within the same dates, though little can be inferred from this item, amounted to

$8 40¾

Oil and some household utensils 2 00

So that all the pecuniary outgoes, excepting for washing and mending, which for the most part were done out of the house, and their bills have not yet been received,—and these are all and more than all the ways by which money necessarily goes out in this part of the world,—were

House	$28	12½
Farm one year	14	72½
Food eight months	8	74
Clothing, etc., eight months	8	40¾
Oil, etc., eight months	2	00
In all	$61	99¾

I address myself now to those of my readers who have a living to get. And to meet this I have for farm produce sold $23 44
Earned by day-labor 13 34

In all $36 78,

which subtracted from the sum of the outgoes leaves a balance of $25.21¾ on the one side,—this being very nearly the means with which I started, and the measure of expenses to be incurred,—and on the other, beside the leisure, and independence and health thus secured, a comfortable house for me as long as I choose to occupy it.

These statistics, however accidental and therefore uninstructive they may appear, as they have a certain completeness, have a certain value also. Nothing was given me of which I have not rendered some account.

It appears from the above estimate, that my food alone cost me in money about twenty-seven cents a week. It was, for nearly two years after this, rye and Indian meal without yeast, potatoes, rice, a very little salt pork, molasses, and salt; and my drink, water. It was fit that I should live on rice, mainly, who loved so well the philosophy of India. To meet the objections of some inveterate cavillers, I may as well state, that if I dined out occasionally, as I always had done, and I trust shall have opportunities to do again, it was frequently to the detriment of my domestic arrangements. But the dining out, being, as I have stated, a constant element, does not in the least affect a comparative statement like this.

I learned from my two years' experience that it would cost incredibly little trouble to obtain one's necessary food, even in this latitude; that a man may use as simple a diet as the animals, and yet retain health and strength. I have made a satisfactory dinner, satisfactory on several accounts, simply off a dish of purslane (Portulaca oleracea) which I gathered in my cornfield, boiled and salted. I give the Latin on account of the savoriness of the trivial name. And pray what more can a reasonable man desire, in peaceful times, in ordinary noons, than a sufficient number of ears of green sweet corn boiled, with the addition of salt? Even the little variety which I used was a yielding to the demands of appetite, and not of health. Yet men have come to such a pass that they frequently starve, not for want of necessaries, but for want of luxuries; and I know a good woman who thinks that her son lost his life because he took to drinking water only. . . .

When first I took up my abode in the woods, that is, began to spend my nights as well as days there, which, by accident, was on Independence Day, or the Fourth of July, 1845, my house was not finished for winter, but was merely a defence against the rain, without plastering or chimney, the walls being of rough, weather-stained boards, with wide chinks, which made it cool at night. The upright white hewn studs and freshly planed door and window casings gave it a clean and airy look, especially in the morning, when its timbers were saturated with dew, so that I fancied that by noon some sweet gum would exude from them. To my imagination it retained throughout the day more or less of this auroral character, reminding me of a certain house on a mountain which I had visited a year before. This was an airy and unplastered cabin, fit to entertain a travelling god, and where a goddess might trail her garments. The winds which passed over my dwelling were such as sweep over the ridges of mountains, bearing the broken strains, or celestial parts only, of terrestrial music. The morning wind forever blows, the poem of creation is uninterrupted; but few are the ears that hear it. Olympus is but the outside of the earth everywhere.

The only house I had been the owner of before, if I except a boat, was

Walden Pond in May.

Walden Pond in winter.

a tent, which I used occasionally when making excursions in the summer, and this is still rolled up in my garret; but the boat, after passing from hand to hand, has gone down the stream of time. With this more substantial shelter about me, I had made some progress toward settling in the world. This frame, so slightly clad, was a sort of crystallization around me, and reacted on the builder. It was suggestive somewhat as a picture in outlines. I did not need to go outdoors to take the air, for the atmosphere within had lost none of its freshness. It was not so much within-doors as behind a door where I sat, even in the rainiest weather. The Harivansa says, "An abode without birds is like a meat without seasoning." Such was not my abode, for I found myself suddenly neighbor to the birds; not by having imprisoned one, but having caged myself near them. I was not only nearer to some of those which commonly frequent the garden and the orchard, but to those wilder and more thrilling song-sters of the forest which never, or rarely, serenade a villager,—the wood thrush, the veery, the scarlet tanager, the field sparrow, the whip-poor-will, and many others.

I was seated by the shore of a small pond, about a mile and a half south of the village of Concord and somewhat higher than it, in the midst of an extensive wood between that town and Lincoln, and about two miles south of that our only field known to fame, Concord Battle Ground; but I was so low in the woods that the opposite shore, half a mile off, like the rest, covered with wood, was my most distant horizon. For the first week, whenever I looked out on the pond it impressed me like a tarn high up on the side of a mountain, its bottom far above the surface of other lakes, and, as the sun rose, I saw it throwing off its nightly clothing of mist, and here and there, by degrees, its soft ripples or its smooth reflecting surface was revealed, while the mists, like ghosts, were stealthily withdrawing in every direction into the woods, as at the breaking up of some nocturnal conventicle. The very dew seemed to hang upon the trees later into the day than usual, as on the sides of mountains.

This small lake was of most value as a neighbor in the intervals of a gentle rain-storm in August, when, both air and water being perfectly still, but the sky overcast, mid-afternoon had all the serenity of evening, and the wood thrush sang around, and was heard from shore to shore. A lake like this is never smoother than at such a time; and the clear portion of the air above it being shallow and darkened by clouds, the water, full of light and reflections, becomes a lower heaven itself so much the more important. From a hill-top near by, where the wood had been recently cut off, there was a pleasing vista southward across the pond, through a wide indentation in the hills which form the shore there, where their opposite side sloping toward each other suggested a stream flowing out in that direction through a wooded valley, but stream there was none.

That way I looked between and over the near green hills to some distant and higher ones in the horizon, tinged with blue. Indeed, by standing on tiptoe I could catch a glimpse of some of the peaks of the still bluer and more distant mountain ranges in the northwest, those true-blue coins from heaven's own mint, and also of some portion of the village. But in other directions, even from this point, I could not see over or beyond the woods which surrounded me. It is well to have some water in your neighborhood, to give buoyancy to and float the earth. One value even of the smallest well is, that when you look into it you see that earth is not continent but insular. This is as important as that it keeps butter cool. When I looked across the pond from this peak toward the Sudbury meadows, which in time of flood I distinguished elevated perhaps by a mirage in their seething valley, like a coin in a basin, all the earth beyond the pond appeared like a thin crust insulated and floated even by this small sheet of intervening water, and I was reminded that this on which I dwelt was but dry land.

Though the view from my door was still more contracted, I did not feel crowded or confined in the least. There was pasture enough for my imagination. The low shrub oak plateau to which the opposite shore arose stretched away toward the prairies of the West and the steppes of Tartary, affording ample room for all the roving families of men. "There are none happy in the world but beings who enjoy freely a vast horizon,"—said Damodara, when his herds required new and larger pastures. . . .

I went to the woods because I wished to live deliberately, to front only the essential facts of life, and see if I could not learn what it had to teach, and not, when I came to die, discover that I had not lived. I did not wish to live what was not life, living is so dear; nor did I wish to practise resignation, unless it was quite necessary. I wanted to live deep and suck out all the marrow of life, to cut a broad swath and shave close, to drive life into a corner, and reduce it to its lowest terms, and, if it proved to be mean, why then to get the whole and genuine meanness of it, and publish its meanness to the world; or if it were sublime, to know it by experience, and be able to give a true account of it in my next excursion. For most men, it appears to me, are in a strange uncertainty about it, whether it is of the devil or of God, and have somewhat hastily concluded that it is the chief end of man here to "glorify God and enjoy him forever."

Despite popular opinion to the contrary, Thoreau did not live the life of a hermit at Walden Pond. Rarely a day went by that he did not visit his friends and relatives in Concord village or that they did not come out to the pond to see him. Indeed, as one of his aunts wrote at the time, "Going to see Henry [is] one of Concord's first recreations."

Fortunately we can see Thoreau through the eyes of some of his Concord friends: Joseph Hosmer recalled a Sunday early in September, 1845, which he spent at the lakeside retreat on Thoreau's invitation:

The building was not then finished, the chimney had no beginning—the sides were not battened, or the walls plastered. It stood in the open field, some thirty rods from the lake, and the "Devil's Bar" and in full view of it.

Upon its construction he had evidently bestowed much care, and the proportions of it, together with the work, were very much better than would have been expected of a novice, and he seemed well pleased with his effort.

The entrance to the cellar was thro' a trap door in the center of the room. The king-post was an entire tree, extending from the bottom of the cellar to the ridge-pole, upon which we descended, as the sailors do into the hold of a vessel.

His hospitality and manner of entertainment were unique, and peculiar to the time and place.

The cooking apparatus was primitive and consisted of a hole made in the earth and inlaid with stones, upon which the fire was made, after the manner at the sea-shore, when they have a clam-bake.

When sufficiently hot remove the smoking embers and place on the fish, frog, etc. Our bill of fare included roasted horn pout, corn, beans, bread, salt, etc. Our viands were nature's own, "sparkling and bright."

I gave the bill of fare in English and Henry rendered it in French, Latin and Greek.

The beans had been previously cooked. The meal for our bread was mixed with lake water only, and when prepared it was spread upon the surface of a thin stone used for that purpose and baked. It was according to the old Jewish law and custom of unleavened bread, and of course it was very, very primitive.

When the bread had been sufficiently baked the stone was removed, then the fish placed over the hot stones and roasted—some in wet paper and some without—and when seasoned with salt, were delicious.

He was very much disappointed in not being able to present to me one of his little companions—a mouse.

He described it to me by saying that it had come upon his back as he leaned against the wall of the building, ran down his arm to his hand, and ate the cheese while holding it in his fingers; also, when he played the flute, it would come and listen from its hiding place, and remain there while he continued to play the same tune, but when he changed the tune, the little visitor would immediately disappear.

Owing perhaps to some extra noise, and a stranger present, it did not put in an appearance, and I lost that interesting part of the show—but I had enough else to remember all my life.

The land where he raised his beans and other vegetables had been so continuously cropped with rye in the years preceding that the weeds had a stunted and sickly look; this however was favorable, as the crops needed but little cultivation.

Perhaps it was in this "field of glory," strewn with the bones and fur of the wood-chucks and rabbits, that he took his first lessons in combativeness: as he had to contend with the woodchucks by day, and the owls (his faithful allies,) stood sentry by night to keep away the rabbits, (literal fact,) otherwise he would not have harvested a bean.

One of the axioms of his philosophy had been to take the life of nothing that breathed, if he could avoid it: but, it had now become a serious question with him, whether to allow the wood-chucks and rabbits to destroy his beans, or fight.

Having determined on the latter, he procured a steel trap, and soon caught a venerable old fellow to the "manor born," and one who had held undisputed possession there for all time.

After retaining the enemy of all beans in "durance vile" for a few hours, he pressed his foot on the spring of the trap and let him go—expecting and hoping never to see him more. Vain delusion!

In a few days after, on returning from the village post-office, on looking in the direction of the bean field, to his disgust and apprehension he saw the same old grey-back disappear behind some brush just outside the field.

On a reconnaissance he discovered that the enemy had taken up a strategic position covered by some brush near his beans, and had entrenched himself by digging a "rifle pit," and otherwise made preparations for a determined siege. Accordingly he again set the trap and again caught the thief.

Now it so happened that those old knights of the shot gun, hook and line, Wesson, Pratt and Co., were on a piscatorial visit to the "devil's bar," equipped with all the necessary appliances to allure the finny tribe to destruction. A council of war was held at the "Bar," to determine what should be done with the wood-chuck.

A decision was rendered immediately by that old and popular landlord of the Middlesex, in his terse and laconic manner "knock his brains out."

This however was altogether too severe on the wood-chuck, thought Henry; even woodchucks had some rights that "Squatter Sovereigns" should respect. Was he not the original occupant there? and had he not "jumped" the "wood-chuck's claim," destroyed his home, and built his "hut" upon the ruins? After considering the question carefully he took the woodchuck in his arms and carried him some two miles away; and then with a severe admonition at the end of a good stick, he opened the trap, and again let him "depart in peace"; and he never saw him more.

Two years, two months, and two days after going to live at Walden Pond Thoreau left there. Ostensibly the reason for leaving was that Emerson, who planned to go abroad for a lecture tour in England, asked that in his absence Thoreau look after his house and family. And this Thoreau, with fond recollections of his happy days with the Emersons before he went to Staten Island, was happy to do.

But the real reason for leaving the pond was that he had not only written his book—*A Week on the Concord and Merrimack Rivers*—and a large part of a second book—*Walden*—but also he had other lives to live:

▶ I left the woods for as good a reason as I went there. Perhaps it seemed to me that I had several more lives to live, and could not spare any more time for that one. It is remarkable how easily and insensibly we fall into a particular route, and make a beaten track for ourselves. I had not lived there a week before my feet wore a path from my door to the pond-side; and though it is five or six years since I trod it, it is still quite distinct. It is true, I fear, that others may have fallen into it, and so helped to keep it open. The surface of the earth is soft and impressible by the feet of men; and so with the paths which the mind travels. How worn and dusty, then, must be the highways of the world, how deep the ruts of tradition and conformity! I did not wish to take a cabin passage, but rather to go before the mast and on the deck of the world, for there I could best see the moonlight amid the mountains. I do not wish to go below now.

I learned this, at least, by my experiment: that if one advances confidently in the direction of his dreams, and endeavors to live the life which he has imagined, he will meet with a success unexpected in common hours. He will put some things behind, will pass an invisible boundary; new, universal, and more liberal laws will begin to establish themselves around and within him; or the old laws be expanded, and interpreted in his favor in a more liberal sense, and he will live with the license of a higher order of beings. In proportion as he simplifies his life, the laws of the universe will appear less complex, and solitude will not be solitude, nor poverty poverty, nor weakness weakness. If you have built castles in the air, your work need not be lost; that is where they should be. Now put the foundations under them.

14

My Night in Prison

EARLY ONE JULY EVENING in 1846, on his way into Concord from his Walden cabin to get a shoe that was being repaired, Thoreau was arrested. The charge was nonpayment of the poll-tax, a tax he had not paid since 1842.

"As I stood considering the walls of solid stone, two or three feet thick," Thoreau wrote, "the door of wood and iron, a foot thick, and the iron grating which strained the light, I could not help being struck with the foolishness of that institution which treated me as if I were mere flesh and blood and bones, to be locked up. I wondered that it should have concluded at length that this was the best use it could put me to, and had never thought to avail itself of my services in some way."

Thoreau's jailer was neighbor Sam Staples. "Henry knew that I had a warrant for him," Staples said, "but I didn't go to hunt for him, 'cause I knew I could git him when I wanted to."

With Thoreau locked up, Staples went into town to take care of some other business. While he was gone, someone rapped at the door of his apartment in the jail. When his daughter opened it, a veiled woman said, "Here is the money to pay Mr. Thoreau's tax," and immediately left, without identifying herself. Now that the tax matter was cleared up, Thoreau should have been let out at once, but by the time his daughter told him, Staples remembered, he "had got his boots off and was sittin' by the fire, and I wasn't goin' to take the trouble to unlock after I'd got the boys all fixed for the night, so I kep' him in till after breakfast next mornin' and then I let him go."

His night in prison, Thoreau reported,

▶ . . . was novel and interesting enough. The prisoners in their shirt-sleeves were enjoying a chat and the evening air in the doorway, when I entered. But the jailer said, "Come, boys, it is time to lock up;" and so they dispersed, and I heard the sound of their steps returning into the hollow apartments. My roommate was introduced to me by the jailer as "a first-rate fellow and a clever man." When the door was locked, he showed me where to hang my hat, and how he managed matters there. The rooms were whitewashed once a month; and this one, at least, was the whitest, most simply furnished, and probably the neatest apartment in the town. He naturally wanted to know where I came from, and what brought me there; and, when I had told him, I asked him in my turn how he came

ourselves better. ... . y in
happy way of making his guests feel at home. w
wl
☞ While the Bostonians are complaining re
of the extreme hot weather, we, the priviledg- co
ed people of old Concord, are as cool as cu-
cumbers. All our public houses are abun- ya
dantly provided with ice-houses, and if the of
sun gets to be a little *heateriferous*, and his in
favors become too profuse,—we immediately th
adjourn to some one of them and take up our
lodgings for the time being—bid defiance to o'
his scorching rays—and come out real Ice- st
landers. Trot up here, ye unsophisticated ce
youths, and see how *we* live ! . h
g

ALL THE GO IN CONCORD—Chowder par- cc
ties, Sleepy-Hollow parties, blackberry par- s
ties, whortleberry parties, horseback parties, av
Egg-rock parties, dog-fighting parties, not-to- th
be-mentioned parties, Bedford Spring parties, p
temperance parties, anti-temperance parties, a
non-committal parties, cool-off parties, and st
stay-at-home parties. The latter class is the i'
most numerous—and the recent hot weather o
has somewhat increased the number. p
h

☞ The morning salutation now is, in- w
stead of "Good morning."—"Did you get k
any sleep last night ?" The answer usually s
is, " No—it was hotter than ——'s kitchen." y
The people are getting to be very wicked— w
very—they are. n

What was Concord doing while Thoreau was paying his brief penalty in jail for his act of civil disobedience? These notes from the Concord *Freeman* show most of the townsfolk had their minds on other matters.

Sam Staples, the Concord jailer who took Thoreau in for that night in July, 1846. Five years later, Thoreau's Journal recorded this sidelight on himself and Sam: "There is some advantage in being the humblest, cheapest, least dignified man in the village, so that the very stable boys shall damn you. Methinks I enjoy that advantage to an unusual extent. There is many a coarsely well-meaning fellow, who knows only the skin of me, who addresses me familiarly by my Christian name. I get the whole good of him and lose nothing myself. There is 'Sam,' the jailer,—whom I never call Sam, however,—who exclaimed last evening: 'Thoreau, are you going up the street pretty soon? Well, just take a couple of these handbills along and drop one in at Hoar's piazza and one at Holbrook's, and I'll do as much for you another time.' I am not above being used, aye abused, sometimes."

N.	POLL TAX.	R. ESTATE	P. ESTATE.		No.	POLL TAX.	R. ESTATE.	P. ESTATE			TAX.	T No. TAX
	Polls.	Dolls.	Cts.	Dolls.	Cts.	Dolls.	Cts.	Polls	Dolls	Cts.	Dolls	Cts.	Dolls	Cts.	Dolls	Cts.

Named

John Thoreau	1	1 50	6 00	3 57	1	1 50	1 24	11	3 41	11 07 6
Henry D. Thoreau	1	1 55								1 50
Hike P.& M. Thoreau		8 50								8 8 6

The Concord tax register for 1849 reveals that Thoreau's poll tax—$1.50—was paid for 1849, as were the taxes of his father and his aunts Jane and Maria. This did not mean he had abandoned his principles, since he states specifically in "Civil Disobedience" that someone else continued to pay his taxes for him— over his protest—to prevent his being arrested.

there, presuming him to be an honest man, of course; and, as the world goes, I believe he was. "Why," said he, "they accuse me of burning a barn; but I never did it." As near as I could discover, he had probably gone to bed in a barn when drunk, and smoked his pipe there; and so a barn was burnt. He had the reputation of being a clever man, had been there some three months waiting for his trial to come on, and would have to wait as much longer; but he was quite domesticated and contented, since he got his board for nothing, and thought that he was well treated.

He occupied one window, and I the other; and I saw that if one stayed there long, his principal business would be to look out the window. I had soon read all the tracts that were left there, and examined where former prisoners had broken out, and where a grate had been sawed off, and heard the history of the various occupants of that room; for I found that even here there was a history and a gossip which never circulated beyond the walls of the jail. Probably this is the only house in the town where verses are composed, which are afterward printed in a circular form, but not published. I was shown quite a long list of verses which were composed by some young men who had been detected in an attempt to escape, who avenged themselves by singing them.

I pumped my fellow-prisoner as dry as I could, for fear I should never see him again; but at length he showed me which was my bed, and left me to blow out the lamp.

It was like traveling into a far country, such as I had never expected to behold, to lie there for one night. It seemed to me that I never had heard the town clock strike before, nor the evening sounds of the village; for we slept with the windows open, which were inside the grating. It was to see my native village in the light of the Middle Ages, and our Concord was turned into a Rhine stream, and visions of knights and castles passed before me. They were the voices of old burghers that I heard in the streets. I was an involuntary spectator and auditor of whatever was done and said in the kitchen of the adjacent village inn,—a wholly new and rare experience to me. It was a closer view of my native town. I was fairly

[*160*]

inside of it. I never had seen its institutions before. This is one of its peculiar institutions; for it is a shire town. I began to comprehend what its inhabitants were about.

In the morning, our breakfasts were put through the hole in the door, in small oblong-square tin pans, made to fit, and holding a pint of chocolate, with brown bread, and an iron spoon. When they called for the vessels again, I was green enough to return what bread I had left; but my comrade seized it, and said that I should lay that up for lunch or dinner. Soon after he was let out to work at haying in a neighboring field, whither he went every day, and would not be back till noon; so he bade me good-day, saying that he doubted if he should see me again.

When I came out of prison,—for some one interfered, and paid that tax,—I did not perceive that great changes had taken place on the common, such as he observed who went in a youth and emerged a tottering and gray-headed man; and yet a change had to my eyes come over the scene,—the town, and State, and country,—greater than any that mere time could effect. I saw yet more distinctly the State in which I lived. I saw to what extent the people among whom I lived could be trusted as good neighbors and friends; that their friendship was for summer weather only; that they did not greatly propose to do right; that they were a distinct race from me by their prejudices and superstitions, as the Chinamen and Malays are; that in their sacrifices to humanity they ran no risks, not even to their property; that after all they were not so noble but they treated the thief as he had treated them, and hoped, by a certain outward observance and a few prayers, and by walking in a particular straight though useless path from time to time, to save their souls. This may be to judge my neighbors harshly; for I believe that many of them are not aware that they have such an institution as the jail in their village.

It was formerly the custom in our village, when a poor debtor came out of jail, for his acquaintances to salute him, looking through their fingers, which were crossed to represent the grating of a jail window, "How do ye do?" My neighbors did not thus salute me, but first looked at me, and then at one another, as if I had returned from a long journey. I was put into jail as I was going to the shoemaker's to get a shoe which was mended. When I was let out the next morning, I proceeded to finish my errand, and, having put on my mended shoe, joined a huckleberry party, who were impatient to put themselves under my conduct; and in half an hour,—for the horse was soon tackled,—was in the midst of a huckleberry field, on one of our highest hills, two miles off, and then the State was nowhere to be seen.

A story is widely told that Emerson visited Thoreau in jail, asking "Henry, why are you here?"

"Waldo, why are you *not* here?" Thoreau is said to have replied.

There is no certain evidence for this exchange, but it has often been repeated. Probàbly the conversation took place, but not until a day or two later. In his Journal, however, Emerson commented: "Mr. Webster told them how much the war cost . . . and sends his son to it. They calculated rightly on Mr. Webster. My friend Mr. Thoreau has gone to jail rather than to pay his tax. On him they could not calculate."

As for the mysterious lady who paid the tax—it made Thoreau "mad as the devil," Staples said—she has been identified as Elizabeth Hoar or, more probably, Thoreau's Aunt Maria.

Thoreau was not the first or only man in Concord to go to jail for refusal to pay taxes. The significance of his act lay rather in what his pen did with the experience. Three years earlier both Bronson Alcott and Charles Lane had been jailed for the same principle. It was the same year the poll tax itself had become a party issue in Massachusetts politics.

Thoreau's arrest, however, inspired him to write what was to become the most widely read of all his works. In February 1848, under the title of "The Rights and Duties of the Individual in Relation to Government," he lectured about his experience to the Concord Lyceum, repeating the talk three weeks later.

In 1849, on invitation from Elizabeth Peabody, Thoreau submitted his lecture-essay for publication in the first—and only—number of her new journal, *Aesthetic Papers*. It appeared in May—the same month in which James Munroe published Thoreau's first book, *A Week on the Concord*

The table of contents of Miss Peabody's *Aesthetic Papers* magazine. Hawthorne and Emerson also appeared in what was to be the first and last issue.

and Merrimack Rivers. "Resistance to Civil Government" was now the title of the essay. In 1866, after Thoreau's death, it was published a second time in his *A Yankee in Canada, With Anti-Slavery and Reform Papers,* retitled "Civil Disobedience," the name under which it has been often reprinted.

Thoreau's refusal to pay his poll tax as a protest against slavery was consistent with his refusal to take part in abolitionist or political organizations. First he decided what was right.

Then he acted upon it:

▶   I meet this American government, or its representative, the state government, directly, and face to face, once a year—no more—in the person of its tax-gatherer; this is the only mode in which a man situated as I am necessarily meets it; and it then says distinctly, Recognize me; and the simplest, the most effectual, and, in the present posture of affairs, the indispensablest mode of treating with it on this head, of expressing your little satisfaction with and love for it, is to deny it them. My civil neighbor, the tax-gatherer, is the very man I have to deal with,—for it is, after all, with men and not with parchment that I quarrel,—and he has voluntarily chosen to be an agent of the government. How shall he ever know well what he is and does as an officer of the government, or as a man, until he is obliged to consider whether he shall treat me, his neighbor, for whom he has respect, as a neighbor and well-disposed man, or as a maniac and disturber of the peace, and see if he can get over this obstruction to his neighborliness without a ruder and more impetuous thought or speech corresponding with his action. I know this well, that if one thousand, if one hundred, if ten men whom I could name,—if ten honest men only,—ay, if one HONEST man, in this State of Massachusetts, ceasing to hold slaves, were actually to withdraw from this copartnership, and be locked up in the county jail therefor, it would be the abolition of slavery in America. For it matters not how small the beginning may seem to be; what is once well done is done forever.

It was 1846 when Thoreau went to jail. The War with Mexico was beginning, a war Thoreau believed to be started by the United States on behalf of slaveholders who wished to extend their slave territory.

"How does it become a man to behave toward this American government today?" Thoreau asked.

▶   I answer, that he cannot without disgrace be associated with it. I cannot for an instant recognize that political organization as my government which is the slave's government also.

All men recognize the right of revolution; that is, the right to refuse allegiance to, and to resist, the government, when its tyranny or its inefficiency are great and unendurable. But almost all say that such is not the case now. But such was the case, they think, in the Revolution of '75. If one were to tell me that this was a bad government because it taxed certain foreign commodities brought to its ports, it is most probable that I should not make an ado about it, for I can do without them. All machines have their friction; and possibly this does enough good to counterbalance the evil. At any rate, it is a great evil to make a stir about it. But when the friction comes to have its machine, and oppression and robbery are organized, I say, let us not have such a machine any longer. In other words, when a sixth of the population of a nation which has undertaken to be the refuge of liberty are slaves, and a whole country is unjustly overrun and conquered by a foreign army, and subjected to military law, I think that it is not too soon for honest men to rebel and revolutionize. What makes this duty the more urgent is the fact that the country so overrun is not our own, but ours is the invading army.

The blame for the government's war policy in Mexico should not be laid exclusively at the door of the slavocracy, he continued.

▶ Practically speaking, the opponents to a reform in Massachusetts are not a hundred thousand politicians at the South, but a hundred thousand merchants and farmers here, who are more interested in commerce and agriculture than they are in humanity, and are not prepared to do justice to the slave and to Mexico, cost what it may. I quarrel not with far-off foes, but with those who, near at home, cooperate with, and do the bidding of, those far away, and without whom the latter would be harmless. We are accustomed to say, that the mass of men are unprepared; but improvement is slow, because the few are not materially wiser or better than the many. It is not so important that many should be as good as you, as that there be some absolute goodness somewhere; for that will leaven the whole lump. There are thousands who are in opinion opposed to slavery and to the war, who yet in effect do nothing to put an end to them; who, esteeming themselves children of Washington and Franklin, sit down with their hands in their pockets, and say that they know not what to do, and do nothing; who even postpone the question of freedom to the question of free-trade, and quietly read the prices-current along with the latest advices from Mexico, after dinner, and, it may be, fall asleep over them both. What is the price-current of an honest man and patriot to-day? They hesitate, and they regret, and sometimes they petition; but they do nothing in earnest and with effect. They will wait, well disposed, for others to remedy the evil, that they may no longer have it to regret. At most, they give only a cheap vote, and a feeble countenance and God-speed, to the right, as it goes by them. There are nine hundred and ninety-nine patrons of virtue to one virtuous man. But it is easier to deal with the real possessor of a thing than with the temporary guardian of it.

Unjust laws exist: shall we be content to obey them, or shall we endeavor to amend them, and obey them until we have succeeded, or shall we transgress them at once? Men generally, under such a government as this, think that they ought to wait until they have persuaded the majority to alter them. They think that, if they should resist, the remedy would be worse than the evil. But it is the fault of the government itself that the remedy is worse than the evil. It makes it worse. Why is it not more apt to anticipate and provide for reform? Why does it not cherish its wise minority? Why does it cry and resist before it is hurt? Why does it not encourage its citizens to be on the alert to point out its faults, and do better than it would have them? Why does it always crucify Christ, and excommunicate Copernicus and Luther, and pronounce Washington and Franklin rebels?

I do not hesitate to say, that those who call themselves Abolitionists should at once effectively withdraw their support, both in person and property, from the government of Massachusetts, and not wait till they constitute a majority of one before they suffer the right to prevail through them. I think that it is enough if they have God on their side, without waiting for that other one. Moreover, any man more right than his neighbors constitutes a majority of one already.

Then, speaking as he might have to Emerson in their conversation about what he was doing in jail, Thoreau said:

▶ Under a government which imprisons any unjustly, the true place for a just man is also a prison. The proper place to-day, the only place which Massachusetts has provided for her freer and less desponding spirits, is in her prisons, to be put out and locked out of the State by her own act, as they have already put themselves out by their principles. It is there that the fugitive slave, and the Mexican prisoner on parole, and the Indian come to plead the wrongs of his race should find them; on that separate, but more free and honorable ground, where the State places those who are not with her, but against her,—the only house in a slave State in which a free man can abide with honor. If any think that their influence would be lost there, and their voices no longer afflict the ear of the State, that they would not be as an enemy within its walls, they do not know by how much truth is stronger than error, nor how much more eloquently and effectively he can combat injustice who has experienced a little in his own person. Cast your whole vote, not a strip of paper merely, but your whole influence. A minority is powerless while

Mahatma Gandhi, who became acquainted with Thoreau's essay while fighting for the rights of Indians in South Africa in the early 1900's. He adopted some of Thoreau's ideas and took the name of his movement in India from Thoreau's "Civil Disobedience."

Martin Luther King, Jr., a leader in the nonviolent resistance movement to desegregate American life and win equal rights for the Negro. He read Thoreau's "Civil Disobedience" while in college and was "fascinated by the idea of refusing to cooperate with an evil system."

it conforms to the majority; it is not even a minority then; but it is irresistible when it clogs by its whole weight. If the alternative is to keep all just men in prison, or give up war and slavery, the State will not hesitate which to choose. If a thousand men were not to pay their tax-bills this year, that would not be a violent and bloody measure, as it would be to pay them, and enable the State to commit violence and shed innocent blood. This is, in fact, the definition of a peaceable revolution, if any such is possible. If the tax-gatherer, or any other public officer, asks me, as one has done, "But what shall I do?" my answer is, "If you really wish to do anything, resign your office." When the subject has refused allegiance, and the officer has resigned his office, then the revolution is accomplished. But even suppose blood should flow. Is there not a sort of blood shed when the conscience is wounded? Through this wound a man's real manhood and immortality flow out, and he bleeds to an everlasting death. I see this blood flowing now.

The authority of government, even such as I am willing to submit to, —for I will cheerfully obey those who know and can do better than I, and in many things even those who neither know nor can do so well,— is still an impure one: to be strictly just, it must have the sanction and consent of the governed. It can have no pure right over my person and property but what I concede to it. The progress from an absolute to a limited monarchy, from a limited monarchy to a democracy, is a progress toward a true respect for the individual. Even the Chinese philosopher was wise enough to regard the individual as the basis of the empire. Is a democracy, such as we know it, the last improvement possible in government? Is it not possible to take a step further towards recognizing and organizing the rights of man? There will never be a really free and enlightened State until the State comes to recognize the individual as a higher and independent power, from which all its own power and authority are derived, and treats him accordingly. I please myself with imagining a State at last which can afford to be just to all men, and to treat the individual with respect as a neighbor; which even would not think it inconsistent with its own repose if a few were to live aloof from it, not meddling with it, nor embraced by it, who fulfilled all the duties of neighbors and fellowmen. A State which bore this kind of fruit, and suffered it to drop off as fast as it ripened, would prepare the way for a still more perfect and glorious State, which also I have imagined, but not yet anywhere seen.

15

Monarch of All
I Survey

IN THE SPRING of 1847 Emerson noted in his account book that he had paid Thoreau one dollar for surveying the newly acquired Warren lot. That transaction is the earliest record of another occupation taken up by Thoreau the schoolmaster, lecturer, pencil-maker, writer, and odd-jobsman.

For one who loved tramping over the woods and fields surveying must have seemed a good way to piece out a living and still leave some of the year and even part of the day free. Thoreau soon became the leading land surveyor in Concord, with a reputation, Emerson's son Edward later reported, for doing the best possible work. "Exceedingly particular," he took more offsets than any other surveyors in the county, often correcting bounds carelessly placed by others. The man who succeeded Thoreau in local leadership of the profession said he soon learned that by following Thoreau's lines he was sure to find his plans minutely accurate.

Edward Emerson believed Thoreau enjoyed the work of surveying, although Thoreau said it was "quite trivial" and only more "grinding at the mill of the Philistines."

▶ The ways by which you may get money [he wrote] almost without exception lead downward. To have done anything by which you earned money merely is to have been truly idle or worse. If the laborer gets no more than the wages which his employer pays him, he is cheated, he cheats himself. If you would get money as a writer or lecturer, you must be popular, which is to go down perpendicularly. Those services which the community will most readily pay for, it is most disagreeable to render. You are paid for being something less than a man. The state does not commonly reward a genius any more wisely. Even the poet laureate would rather not have to celebrate the accidents of royalty. He must be bribed with a pipe of wine; and perhaps another poet is called away from his muse to gauge that very pipe.

Thoreau's drawing instruments. His first surveying equipment seems to have been bought in 1840, and was used to teach the pupils in his and brother John's school some applications of mathematics. In 1846, still as an amateur, he made the survey of Walden Pond published later in *Walden*. The next year he made his first professional dollar at surveying and listed himself as "a Surveyor"—among many other occupations—in his Harvard class's tenth anniversary record.

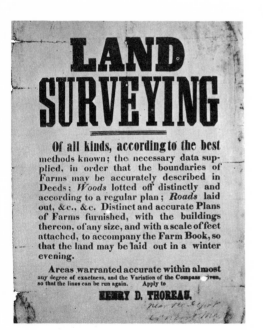

This handbill is the only known record of Thoreau publicly advertising himself as a surveyor. In the lower right corner, beneath his printed name, is penciled "near the Depot Concord Mass." This address probably refers to the Texas House. The handbill may therefore have been circulated before August, 1850, when the Thoreaus moved into the Yellow House. It is not known whether Thoreau wrote the text himself.

This page from the "Reports of the Selectmen" of Concord for 1851-52 has three entries for surveying jobs Thoreau had done for the village. They are the second, fifth, and last items, showing payments to Thoreau totaling $64.

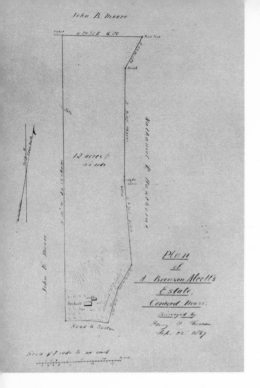

Thoreau surveyed Alcott's Orchard House property for him on September 22, 1857. After two years of living rent-free in Walpole, New Hampshire, the Alcott family had moved back to Concord and bought this house next to Hawthorne's "Wayside."

As for his own business of surveying,

▶ . . . even that kind of surveying which I could do with most satisfaction my employers do not want. They would prefer that I should do my work coarsely and not too well, ay, not well enough. When I observe that there are different ways of surveying, my employer commonly asks which will give him the most land, not which is most correct.

▶ One day [he said] a man came "just to get me to run a line in the woods." This is the usual request. "Do you know where one end of it is?" I asked. (It was the Stratton lot.) "No," said he, "I don't know either end; that is what I want to find." "Do you know either of the next sides of the lot?" Thinking a moment, he answered, "No." "Well, do you know any one side of the whole lot, or any corner?" After a little hesitation he said that he did not. Here, then, was a wood-lot of half a dozen acres, well enough described in a deed dated 1777, courses and distances given, but he could not tell exactly in what part of the universe any particular part of it was, but he expected me to find out. This was what he understood by "running." On the strength of this deed he had forbidden a man to chop wood somewhere.

Frequently, when my employer does not know where his land lies, and has put into my hands an ancient and tattered piece of paper called his deed, which throws no light at all on the question, he turns away, saying, "I want you to make it all right. Give me all that belongs to me."

For his work Thoreau was apparently not paid much more than he usually got as a handyman. Once he wrote his friend Blake that he had just earned a dollar a day for 76 days past, at surveying, adding "it is long since I have spent so many days so profitably in a pecuniary sense."
But on another occasion, he reported, he did some surveying for a man

▶ . . . who remarked, but not till the job was done, that he did not know when he should pay me. I did not pay much heed to this, though it was unusual, supposing that he meant to pay me some time or other. But after a while he sent to me a quart of red huckleberries, and this I thought was ominous and he distinguished me altogether too much by this gift, since I was not his particular friend. I saw it was the first installment, which would go a great way toward being the last. In course of years he paid a part of the debt in money, and that is the last I have heard of it.

Sometimes Thoreau complained about the routine of surveying—the people he had to work with, the food he had to eat. He had been three days on a job, he wrote in his Journal:

▶ . . . they have not yielded much that I am aware of. All I find is old boundmarks, and the slowness and dullness of farmers reconfirmed. They even complain that I walk too fast for them. Their legs have become stiff from toil. This coarse and hurried outdoor work compels me to live grossly or be inattentive to my diet; that is the worst of it. Like work, like diet; that, I find, is the rule. Left to my chosen pursuits, I should never drink tea nor coffee, nor eat meat. The diet of any class or generation is the natural result of its employment and locality. It is remarkable how unprofitable it is for the most part to talk with farmers. They commonly stand on their good behavior and attempt to moralize or philosophize in a serious conversation. Sportsmen and loafers are better company. For society a man must not be too good or well-disposed, to spoil his natural disposition. The bad are frequently good enough to let you see how bad they are, but the good as frequently endeavor to get between you and themselves.
I have dined out five times and tea'd once within a week. Four times there was tea on the dinner-table, always meat, but once baked beans, always pie, but no puddings. I suspect tea has taken the place of cider with farmers. I am reminded of Haydon the painter's experience when he went about painting the nobility. I go about to the houses of the farmers and squires in like manner. This is my portrait-painting,—

when I would fain be employed on higher subjects. I have offered myself much more earnestly as a lecturer than a surveyor. Yet I do not get any employment as a lecturer; was not invited to lecture once last winter, and only once (without pay) this winter. But I can get surveying enough, which a hundred others in this country can do as well as I, though it is not boasting much to say that a hundred others in New England cannot lecture as well as I on my themes.

Into the Journal went quick sketches of the people with whom surveying brought him together. "There was a cross-eyed fellow used to help me survey,—he was my stake-driver,—and all he said was, at every stake he drove, 'There, I shouldn't like to undertake to pull that up with my teeth.'"

On the last day of 1857, Thoreau took stock of his December experience:

▶ I have been surveying most of the time for a month past and have associated with various characters:—

First there was Staples, quick, clear, downright, and on the whole a good fellow, especially good to treat with rougher and slower men than himself, always meaning well.

An Irishman, rather slow and dull but well-meaning.

A rustic innkeeper, evidently rather close-fisted.

George Heywood, a quiet, efficient man, very gentlemanly and agreeable to deal with; no pretense nor bluster, but simple, direct, and even sweet.

————— —————, a crooked stick, not readily apprehending your drift, referring to old deeds or places which he can't find, thinking he is entitled to many more acres than belong to him, but never leaving his work or his cattle to attend to you. To be found commonly in his barn, if you come upon him suddenly before he can hide. Has some complaint or injury which deforms him somewhat,—has crooked his body, so that when you meet him in the street he looks as if he was going across the road.

Another Irishman, one of the worst of his race, full of blarney, one of the would-be gentlemen, who, when treated according to his deserts, having complained unreasonably of my price, apologizes by saying that he meant nothing. "What's the use of having a tongue in your head if you don't use it?"

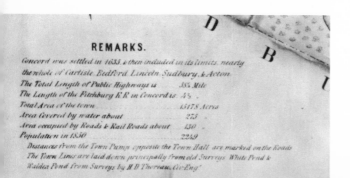

For an 1852 map of Concord, Thoreau made surveys of White Pond and Walden Pond. In the lower left corner, shown here, he was given credit for his work, and designated as H. D. Thoreau, Civil Engineer, a title he used now and then on his surveys.

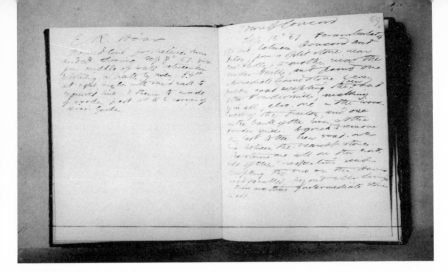

Pages opened out in Thoreau's "Field Notes of Surveys," a small manuscript notebook in which he kept a running account of his jobs. The left page records finding a line for E. R. Hoar between his and a neighbor's land, and the right notes perambulation of the line between Concord and Acton. In 1859 Thoreau was hired to survey the bridges and study water depths on the Concord and Sudbury Rivers, as well as to investigate the history of their flowage. His findings were needed to help settle a controversy involving flooding of haying land valuable to the river-meadow proprietors. By 1860 Thoreau was surveyor-in-chief for Concord.

A common specimen of the Yankee, who commonly answers me with "exactly" or "just so."

—————— ————, who was so afraid he should lose some land belonging to him that, though he had employed Rice to survey his small wood-lot of three acres, within a year, he working two or three days at it and setting at least fifty stakes about it, having also two plans of it, yet, seeing that I had by chance set a stake a foot or two one side of his line, thought there was some mistake and would have me measure his lot anew. It was but little labor, the lines were so open,—for a path was actually worn round the whole lot. He appears to go round it every day or two. When I wanted a straight pole, he was very scrupulous not to cut it from his neighbor's side of the line. He did not seem able to understand a plan or deed, and had sold some of his land because he did not know that he had a good title to it. Everything I told him about his deed and plan seemed to surprise him infinitely and make him laugh with excess of interest. When I pointed out anything in the plan, he did not look at it, only at my finger and at me, and took my word for it. I told him that I wondered his last surveyor had not set a stake and stone in one place, according to his plan and deed, a perfectly plain case, the stump of the pitch pine referred to being left. He said he didn't want to make bounds, and asked me if I should have set it there, to which I answered, "Yes, of course," that was what I had been doing all my life, making bounds, or rather finding them, remaking what had been unmade, where they were away. He listened to me as if I were an oracle. He did not in the least understand my instrument, or "spy-glass," as he called it, but had full faith that it knew the way straight through the thickest wood to missing bounds. He was so deaf I had to shout to him, and there were two more in his house deafer than he,—and I think only one other. The passers-by commonly hear them talking to one another within. I could never communicate with him when setting a stake or carrying the chain but by signs, and must first get his attention to the signs. This I accomplished, when he had hold of the chain, by giving it several smart jerks. When he paid me at his house, I observed that all his money was in silver. He said he told H_____ that we had been cutting off some of his land, and H_____ said, "Is that right?" H_____ has a good deal of large old wood which he will not cut. _____ says that he goes into it with his axe, and striking on an old tree says, "That's sound," and so lets it stand, though when cut it turns out to be false-hearted.

_____ says that Rice worked two days on only two sides of his lot, but that he told him he would not charge him but two dollars if it took him a week. I found and used one of Rice's poles, left on the ground all planed for the purpose, for he worked not without tools.

When Thoreau became surveyor-in-chief for Concord, he laid out roads, walked the bounds with the selectmen, and supplied the technical documentation for lawsuits involving his craft. He soon knew more about his neighbors' property than they did. Sometimes he took his tools abroad, as when he laid out house lots in Haverhill or the streets for Marcus Spring's experimental colony near Perth Amboy in New Jersey.

Coming home after three or four weeks in the field, he would make a fire in his room and try to return to himself,

▶ . . . to dive into some deep stream of thoughtful and devoted life, which meandered through retired and fertile meadows far from towns. I wished to do again, or for once, things quite congenial to my highest inmost and most sacred nature, to lurk in crystalline thought like the trout under verdurous banks, where stray mankind should only see my bubble come to the surface. I wished to live, ah! as far away as a man can think. I wished for leisure and quiet to let my life flow in its proper channels, with its proper currents; when I might not waste the days, might establish daily prayer and thanksgiving in my family; might do my own work and not the work of Concord and Carlisle, which would yield me better than money.

16

A Week

Although Thoreau had spent his "Week on the Concord and Merrimack Rivers" with his brother John in 1839 and had written most of the text of the book while he was at Walden Pond from 1845 to 1847, the book itself was not published until 1849. As early as 1847 he was circulating the manuscript to various publishers, but receiving no solid indication of any interest on their part. On January 14, 1847, he wrote to Wiley & Putnam of New York City about the book and submitted the manuscript for their consideration on May 28, 1847. On August 28, having had his manuscript rejected by Wiley & Putnam, he wrote Emerson's then-current publisher, James Munroe & Co. of Boston, offering to pay half the cost of publication if they would accept. But then on December 27 he wrote Munroe again saying that he had decided to postpone publication—probably because he now wished to make further revisions. Early in 1848 he added the memorable section on "Friendship" to the "Wednesday" chapter of the book. Finally, late in 1848 he negotiated terms with Munroe for its publication—apparently guaranteeing to underwrite the cost of the book if it did not sell—and it was issued in May of 1849.

Ostensibly *A Week on the Concord and Merrimack Rivers* is an account of the 1839 voyage with his brother John. Roughly about half the book is devoted to an account of the voyage, telling of their boating and camping experiences and describing the scenery along the way. Many passages are almost idyllic in their beauty, and one can easily understand from them why the English essayist H. M. Tomlinson, himself the author of one of the outstanding travel books of our century, *The Sea and the Jungle,* thought *A Week* to be the greatest travel book ever written.

But *A Week* is not just a travel book. Imbedded in the narrative is a whole series of quotations from Thoreau's favorite reading, a number of Thoreau's own poems, and many, many almost independent essays, ranging in length from a paragraph to many pages, on such varied subjects as friendship, Chaucer, the Christian religion, Oriental literature, Sir Walter Raleigh, geological potholes, Goethe, and cattle shows. Thoreau uses the least provocation (and sometimes no provocation at all) to range off on a digressive essay. Many of the essays are exceptionally good examples of Thoreau's writing, but most readers are somewhat disconcerted at suddenly coming across them in the middle of the travel narrative—as James Russell Lowell said in his review of the book—"like snags, jolting us headforemost out of our places as we are rowing placidly up stream or drifting down."

The book's reception could hardly be termed "rousing." George Ripley, now a reviewer for Horace Greeley's New York *Tribune,* denounced it for its pantheism. James Russell Lowell was mildly enthusiastic in the newly established and small-circulation *Massachusetts Quarterly Review. Godey's Lady's Book* thought it had been written by John Greenleaf Whittier under a pseudonym.

Thoreau sent copies to various literary lights of the day. The one favorable response of which there is any record today was a belated letter from Thomas Carlyle's friend and biographer, J. A. Froude.

Title page of Thoreau's first published book. In addition to a day-by-day account of his 1839 rowboat voyage with his brother John, the book has many digressions—essays, 48 of Thoreau's poems, about 126 quotations, accounts of trips to western Massachusetts and Staten Island. Although he had been sent page proofs in 1848, his insistence on making over 1000 corrections delayed publication until May, 1849.

Page proof, with corrections in Thoreau's hand, from the "Sunday" chapter of his *A Week on the Concord and Merrimack Rivers.* The section on religion in this chapter was what upset his contemporaries.

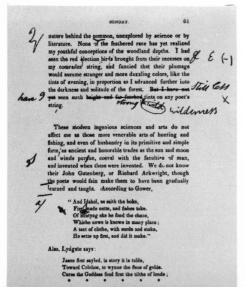

A WEEK

ON THE

CONCORD AND MERRIMACK RIVER

BY

HENRY D. THOREAU.

BOSTON AND CAMBRIDGE·
JAMES MUNROE AND COMPANY
NEW YORK: GEORGE P. PUTNAM.   PHILADELPHIA : LINDS
AND BLACKISTON.   LONDON : JOHN CHAPMAN.
1849

I have long intended to write you, to thank you for that noble expression of yourself you were good enough to send to me. I know not why I have not done so; except from a foolish sense that I should not write till I had thought of something to say which it would be worth your while to read.

What can I say to you except express the honour & the love I feel for you. An honour and a love which Emerson taught me long ago to feel, but which I feel now "not on account of his word, but because I myself have read & know you."

When I think of what you are—of what you have done as well as of what you have written, I have a right to tell you that there is no man living upon this earth at present, whose friendship or whose notice I value more than yours; What are these words? Yet I wished to say something—and I must use words though they serve but seldom in these days for much but lies.

A WEEK ON THE CONCORD AND MERRI-MACK RIVERS. By Henry D. Thoreau. Boston and Cambridge: James Munroe & Co. Those who have read "Margaret Smith's Journal," will be at no loss in settling the authorship of this clever and interesting work. Mr. Whittier touches all his themes with the true poet's wand; all show forms of beauty and gleams of light that, like the sunbeams on the far-off mountain, make the cold and rugged landscape appear soft and charming. It is just the book to read in the idleness of summer, when wishing to enjoy the pleasures of journeying, without the inconvenience which the actual packing up and going off in hot steamboats and dusty cars occasion. Read it, and see.

WILL SOON BE PUBLISHED,

WALDEN,

OR

LIFE IN THE WOODS.

BY

HENRY D. THOREAU.

An advertisement for *Walden* that appeared in the back of *A Week.* In 1862, when Ticknor and Fields reissued what was unsold of the first edition, with new binding and title page, this sheet was mistakenly left in. *Walden,* of course, had been published eight years earlier.

Not Henry Thoreau, but John Greenleaf Whittier, was the true author of that "clever and interesting" work, said *Godey's Lady's Book* in September, 1849.

A Week got few reviews, but Horace Greeley's *Tribune* did not neglect friend Thoreau's book. This is the beginning of the more than two columns of space George Ripley's review got in the June 13, 1849, issue.

REVIEWS OF NEW BOOKS.

H. D. Thoreau's Book.

A WEEK ON THE CONCORD AND MERRIMAC RIVERS By Henry D Thoreau. (pp 413 12mo.) Boston Munroe & Co New York G P Putnam.

A really new book—a fresh, original, thoughtful work—is sadly rare in this age of omniferous publication. Mr. Thoreau's, if not entirely this, is very near it. Its observations of Nature are as genial as Nature herself, and the tones of his harp have an Æolian sweetness. His reflections are always striking, often profoundly truthful, and his scholastic treasures, though a little too ostentatiously displayed, are such as the best instructed reader will enjoy and thank him for. His philosophy, which is the Pantheistic egotism vaguely characterized as Transcendental does not delight us. It seems second-hand, imitative, often exaggerated—a bad specimen of a dubious and dangerous school. But we will speak first of the staple of the work.

Mr Thoreau is a native and resident of Concord Mass—a scholar, a laborer, and in some sort a hermit. He traveled somewhat in his earlier years (he is still young,) generally trusting to his own thoughts for company and his walking-cane for motive power. It would seem a main purpose of his life to demonstrate how slender an impediment is poverty to a man who pampers no super-

Glancing over his own book once again in 1851, Thoreau commented in his journal:

▶ I thought that one peculiarity of my "Week" was its hypaethral character, to use an epithet applied to those Egyptian temples which are open to the heavens above, under the ether. I thought that it had little of the atmosphere of the house about it, but might wholly have been written, as in fact it was to a considerable extent, out-of-doors. It was only at a late period in writing it, as it happened, that I used any phrases implying that I lived in a house or led a domestic life. I trust it does not smell [so much] of the study and library, even of the poet's attic, as of the fields and woods; that it is a hypaethral or unroofed book, lying open under the ether and permeated by it, open to all weathers, not easy to be kept on a shelf.

But the book did not sell and Munroe demanded payment of the cost of publication. Thoreau was driven to what was for him desperate business maneuvers:

▶ I once came near speculating in cranberries. Being put to it to raise the wind to pay for "A Week on the Concord and Merrimack Rivers," and having occasion to go to New York to peddle some pencils which I had made, as I passed through Boston I went to Quincy Market and inquired the price of cranberries. The dealers took me down cellar, asked if I wanted wet or dry, and showed me them. I gave them to understand that I might want an indefinite quantity. It made a slight sensation among them and for aught I know raised the price of the berry for a time. I then visited various New York packets and was told what would be the freight, on deck and in the hold, and one skipper was very anxious for my freight. When I got to New York, I again visited the markets as a purchaser, and "the best of Eastern Cranberries" were offered me by the barrel at a cheaper rate than I could buy them in Boston. I was obliged to manufacture a thousand dollars' worth of pencils and slowly dispose of and finally sacrifice them, in order to pay an assumed debt of a hundred dollars.

But finally, on October 28, 1853, the unsold stock was shipped to Thoreau at Concord and that night he wrote in his Journal:

▶ For a year or two past, my publisher, falsely so called, has been writing from time to time to ask what disposition should be made of the copies of "A Week on the Concord and Merrimack Rivers" still on hand, and at last suggesting that he had use for the room they occupied in his

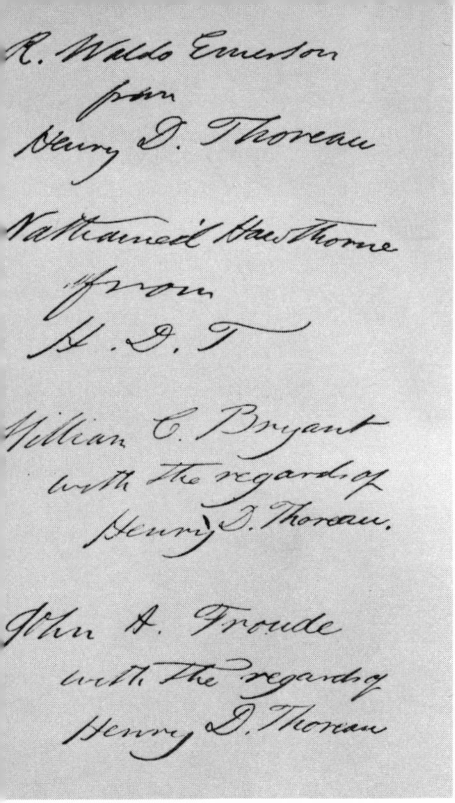

R. Waldo Emerson
from
Henry D. Thoreau

Nathaniel Hawthorne
from
H. D. T

William C. Bryant
with the regards of
Henry D. Thoreau.

John A. Froude
with the regards of
Henry D. Thoreau

Thoreau sent copies of his first book to several distinguished writers, some of them friends, others strangers. These are his inscriptions written in the four copies intended for Emerson, Hawthorne, Bryant, and Froude, the English historian whose response was highly favorable.

Concord Ap. 30th 1855

Gentlemen,

Is it not time to republish "A Week on the Concord & Merrimack Rivers"? You said you would notify me when it was; but I am afraid that it will soon be too late for this season.

I have, with what were sent to you, about 250 bound, and 450 in sheets.

Yrs truly
Henry D. Thoreau

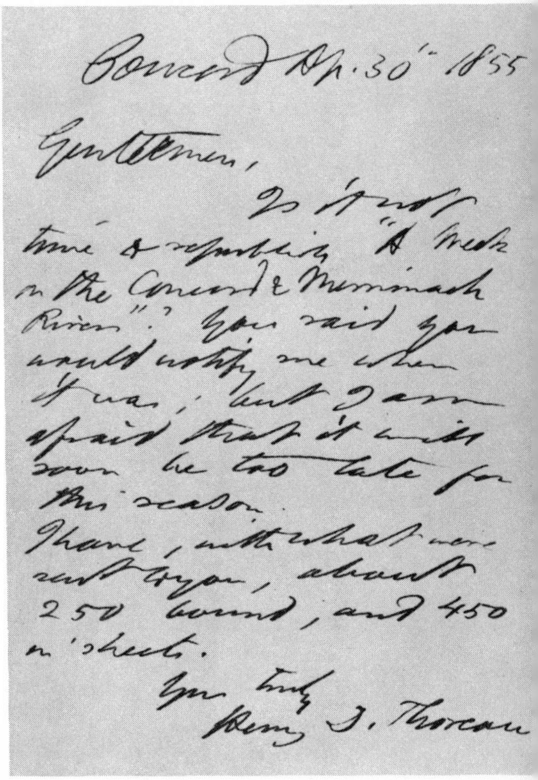

Thoreau prodded Ticknor & Fields to republish *A Week* six years after the miserable failure of the book in the first edition by Munroe.

cellar. So I had them all sent to me here, and they have arrived to-day by express, filling the man's wagon,—706 copies out of an edition of 1000 which I bought of Munroe four years ago and have been ever since paying for, and have not quite paid for yet. The wares are sent to me at last, and I have an opportunity to examine my purchase. They are something more substantial than fame, as my back knows, which has borne them up two flights of stairs to a place similar to that to which they trace their origin. Of the remaining two hundred and ninety and

odd, seventy-five were given away, the rest sold. I have now a library of nearly nine hundred volumes, over seven hundred of which I wrote myself. Is it not well that the author should behold the fruits of his labor? My works are piled up on one side of my chamber half as high as my head, my opera omnia. This is authorship; these are the work of my brain. There was just one piece of good luck in the venture. The unbound were tied up by the printer four years ago in stout paper wrappers, and inscribed,—

H. D. Thoreau's
Concord River
50 cops.

So Munroe had only to cross out "River" and write "Mass." and deliver them to the expressman at once. I can see now what I write for, the result of my labors.

Nevertheless, in spite of this result, sitting beside the inert mass of my works, I take up my pen to-night to record what thought or experience I may have had, with as much satisfaction as ever. Indeed, I believe that this result is more inspiring and better for me than if a thousand had bought my wares. It affects my privacy less and leaves me freer.

Shortly thereafter he added,

▶ Settled with J. Munroe & Co. and on a new account placed twelve of my books with him on sale. I have paid him directly out of pocket since the book was published two hundred and ninety dollars and taken his receipt for it. This does not include postage on proof-sheets, etc., etc. I have received from other quarters about fifteen dollars. This has been the pecuniary value of the book.

For the remaining years of his life Thoreau from time to time sold copies to individuals as they were requested, often adding in his own handwriting three lines of the text that had been dropped on page 396 by a printer's blunder. The book was not officially republished until 1862, a few weeks after Thoreau's death, when Ticknor & Fields, who had bought the remainder of the first edition from Thoreau in April of that year, reissued the first edition in a new binding and with a new title-page, as a "second edition." Through some slip-up they neglected to remove a page of advertisement at the back of the book so that they found themselves announcing the "publication soon" of *Walden,* which had been published eight years before.

Ironically now, a century later, copies of the first edition of *A Week* bring hundreds of dollars on the book market and even the "second edition" brings fifteen or twenty or more dollars a copy.

17

I Have Travelled
a Good Deal...

ALTHOUGH THOREAU said that he "traveled much in Concord" (and travel much in Concord he unquestionably did), he also traveled considerably outside Concord. It was his custom to take what he liked to call "excursions," sometimes alone, and sometimes with a companion or two such as Ellery Channing, Edward Hoar, or H. G. O. Blake and Theo Brown.

Once he had decided upon an excursion, he would make a thorough study of the history, geography, flora, and fauna of the area, arming himself with copious notes for future reference. His second step was to outfit himself, as he suggested to friends who were preparing themselves for a trip in 1858:

▶ For such an excursion . . . carry and wear:—
Three strong check shirts.
Two pairs socks.
Neck ribbon and handkerchief.
Three pocket-handkerchiefs.
One thick waistcoat.
One thin (or half-thick) coat.
One thick coat (for mountain).
A large, broad india-rubber knapsack, with a broad flap.
A flannel shirt.
India-rubber coat.
Three bosoms (to go and come in).
A napkin.
Pins, needles, thread.
A blanket.
A cap to lie in at night.
Tent (or a large simple piece of india-rubber cloth for the mountain tops?).

Veil and gloves (or enough millinet to cover all at night).
Map and compass.
Plant book and paper.
Paper and stamps.
Botany, spy-glass, microscope.
Tape, insect-boxes.
Jack-knife and clasp-knife.
Fish-line and hooks.
Matches.
Soap and dish-cloths.
Waste-paper and twine.
Iron spoon.
Pint dipper with a pail-handle added (not to put out the fire), and perhaps a bag to carry water in.
Frying-pan, only if you ride.
Hatchet (sharp), if you ride, and perhaps in any case on mountain, with a sheath to it.
Hard-bread (sweet crackers good); a moist, sweet plum cake very good and lasting; pork, corned beef or tongue, sugar, tea or coffee, and a little salt.

Then he would set out, often on foot, occasionally if the distance were great by train or stage coach. His favorite method was the beeline hike—setting his compass by the maps and then hiking straight across country. (Legend has it that once he and Ellery Channing walked in through the open front door and out the back of a farmer's house that stood on their path!)

He took more notes while he was hiking and often gathered botanical specimens for his herbarium. Then upon his return he would write up an account of his trip and deliver it as a lecture before the local lyceum. Still later the lecture would be rewritten for periodical or book publication.

Rebecca Thatcher, Thoreau's Bangor cousin, in a portrait painted of her a few years before Thoreau's first Maine trip in 1846. Her husband George, who was in the lumber trade, accompanied Thoreau on the "Ktaadn" expedition.

The Notch House in the White Mountains, a way station for Thoreau on his journey to Mt. Washington in 1839. With his brother John, on foot and by stagecoach, he traveled through the White Mountains after boating up the Concord and Merrimack rivers to Hooksett.

One of his favorite sites for an excursion was the mountains of New Hampshire—Monadnock, Red Hill, or the White Mountains. Typical is this account of an excursion to Monadnock in 1852:

▶ *Sept. 7. Tuesday.*

Went, across lots still, to Monadnock, the base some half-dozen miles in a straight line from Peterboro,—six or seven miles. (It had been eleven miles (by road) from Mason Village to Peterboro.) My clothes sprinkled with ambrosia pollen. Saw near the mountain a field of turnips whose leaves, all but the midribs, were eaten up by grasshoppers and looked white over the field, and sometimes the turnips were eaten also. Joe Eavely's, the house nearest the top, that we saw under the east side, a small red house a little way up. The summit hardly more than a mile distant in a straight line, but about two miles as they go. Bunch-berries everywhere now. Acer Pennsylvanicum, striped maple or moosewood or striped dogwood, but no keys to be seen,—a very large-leaved three-lobed maple with a handsome striped bark. This, I believe, the Indians smoke. Also Acer spicatum, mountain maple, with upright racemes in fruit. Between the rocks on the summit, an abundance of large and fresh blueberries still, apparently Vaccinium Pennsylvanicum, very large, fresh and cooling to eat, supplying the place of water. They said they did not get ripe so early as below, but at any rate they last much longer; both, perhaps, because of the greater coolness of the atmosphere. Though this vegetation was very humble, yet it was very productive of fruit. In one

[*183*]

little hollow between the rocks grew blue-berries, choke-berries, bunch-berries, red cherries, wild currants (Ribes prostratum, with the berry the odor of skunk-cabbage, but a not quite disagreeable wild flavor), a few raspberries still, holly berries, mountain cranberries (Vaccinium Vitis-Idoea), all close together. The little soil on the summit between the rocks was covered with the Potentilla tridentata, now out of bloom, the prevailing plant at the extreme summit. Mountain-ash berries also.

Descending toward Troy, a little after 1 P.M., plucked the Trillium erythrocarpum with the large red berry, painted trillium. The Aster acuminatus, with its leaves in a whorl, white; methinks we may have it. When we had got down, we could see that the mountain had spurs or buttresses on every side, by whose ridge you might ascend. It is an interesting feature in a mountain. I have noticed that they will send out these buttresses every way from their centre.

Were on the top of the mountain at 1 P.M. The cars left Troy, four or five miles off, at three. We reached the depot, by running at last, at the same instant the cars did, and reached Concord at a quarter after five, i.e. four hours from the time we were picking blueberries on the mountain, with the plants of the mountain fresh in my hat.

Or again, in 1860:

▶ *Aug. 4. 8.30 A.M.*
    Start for Monadnock.
    Begins to rain at 9 A.M., and rains from time to time thereafter all day, the mountain-top being constantly enveloped in clouds.

Old prints of lumbering in the Maine woods. Thoreau went there primarily to study the Indians, in 1846 (while he was at Walden), 1853, and 1857. The travel pieces that came out of these trips he was editing for *The Maine Woods* volume at the time of his death. The book contains much Indian lore and language.

Notice in Troy much of the cyperinus variety of wool-grass, now done, of various heights. Also, by roadside, the Ribes Cynosbati, with its prickly berries now partly reddened but hardly ripe. Am exhilarated by the peculiar raspberry scent by the roadside this wet day—and of the dicksonia fern. Raspberries still quite common, though late. The high blackberries, the mulberry kind, all still green and red; and also on the 9th, except one berry on a rock.

There was a little sunshine on our way to the mountain, but the cloud extended far down its sides all day, so that one while we mistook Gap Monadnock for the true mountain, which was more to the north.

According to the guide-board it is two and one fourth miles from Troy to the first fork in the road near the little pond and schoolhouse, and I should say it was near two miles from there to the summit,—all the way uphill from the meadow.

We crossed the immense rocky and springy pastures, containing at first raspberries, but much more hardhack in flower, reddening them afar, where cattle and horses collected about us, sometimes came running to us, as we thought for society, but probably not. I told Bent of it,—how they gathered about us, they were so glad to see a human being,—but he said I might put it in my book so, it would do no harm, but then the fact was they came about me for salt. "Well," said I, "it was probably because I had so much salt in my constitution." Said he, "If you had had a little salt with you [you] could hardly have got away from them." "Well," said I, "[I] had some salt in my pocket." "That's what they smelt," said he. Cattle, young and old, with horns in all stages of growth, —young heifers with budding horns,—and horses with a weak [?] Sleepy-David look, though sleek and handsome. They gathered around us while we took shelter under a black spruce from the rain.

We were wet up to our knees before reaching the woods or steep ascent where we entered the cloud. It was quite dark and wet in the woods, from which we emerged into the lighter cloud about 3 P.M., and proceeded to construct our camp, in the cloud occasionally amounting to rain, where I camped some two years ago.

Choosing a place where the spruce was thick in this sunken rock yard, I cut out with a little hatchet a space for a camp in their midst, leaving two stout ones six feet apart to rest my ridge-pole on, and such limbs of these as would best form the gable ends. I then cut four spruces as rafters for the gable ends, leaving the stub ends of the branches to rest the cross-beams or girders on, of which there were two or three to each slope; and I made the roof very steep. Then cut an abundance of large flat spruce limbs, four or five feet long, and laid them on, shingle-fashion, beginning at the ground and covering the stub ends. This made a foundation for two or three similar layers of smaller twigs. Then made a bed of the same, closed up the ends somewhat, and all was done. All these twigs and boughs, of course, were dripping wet, and we were wet through up to our middles. But we made a good fire at the door, and in an hour or two were completely dried.

The most thickly leaved and flattest limbs of the spruce are such as spread flat over the rocks far and wide (while the upper ones were more bushy and less flat); not the very lowest, which were often partly under the surface and but meagerly leafed, but those close above them.

Standing and sitting before the fire which we kindled under a shelving rock, we could dry us much quicker than at any fireside below, for, what with stoves and reduced fireplaces, they could not have furnished such blaze or heat in any inn's [?] kitchen or parlor. This fire was exactly on the site of my old camp, and we burned a hole deep into the withered remain of its roof and bed.

It began to clear up and a star appeared at 8 P.M. Lightning was seen far in the south. Cloud, drifting cloud, alternated with moonlight all the rest of the night. At 11.30 P.M. I heard a nighthawk. Maybe it hunted then because prevented by the cloud at evening.

I heard from time to time through the night a distant sound like thunder or a falling of a pile of lumber, and I suspect that this may have been the booming of nighthawks at a distance.

Aug. 5.

The wind changed to northerly toward morning, falling down from over the summit and sweeping through our camp, open on that side, and we found it rather cold!

About an hour before sunrise we heard again the nighthawk; also the robin, chewink, song sparrow Fringilla hyemalis; and the wood thrush from the woods below.

Had a grand view of the summit on the north now, it being clear. I set my watch each morning by sunrise, and this morning the lichens on the rocks of the southernmost summit (south of us), just lit by the rising sun, presented a peculiar yellowish or reddish brown light (being wet) which they did not any morning afterward. The rocks of the main summit were olive-brown, and C. called it the Mount of Olives.

Another favorite locale for his excursions was the woods of Northern Maine, which he visited in 1846, 1853, and 1857. Bangor, the jumping-off place for such trips, was the home of his cousins the Thatchers. Here he could see the true wilderness at first hand, exploring vast areas that few white men had seen. Indeed he was one of the earliest white men to reach the top of Maine's lofty Mount Katahdin.

He went often to Cape Cod—in 1849, 1850, 1855, and 1857. Before

A northeast view of Provincetown on Cape Cod, as it looked in Thoreau's day. He made four excursions there: 1849, 1850, 1855, 1857. The first three are woven into his *Cape Cod* book (edited after his death by Sophia Thoreau and Ellery Channing), which is a delightful picture of the place before the tourist invasion began.

The Wellfleet oysterman's house, the scene of one of the best chapters in *Cape Cod*. Thoreau's sketch of the Rabelaisian oysterman, "the merriest old man and one of the best preserved" he had ever seen, is one of the many memorable portraits he drew.

his death he was able to combine the accounts of the first three of these journeys into a series of essays that was published posthumously as *Cape Cod,* Thoreau's sunniest, most light-hearted book—as witnessed by his account of his breakfast with the Wellfleet Oysterman:

▶   Before sunrise the next morning they let us out again, and I ran over to the beach to see the sun come out of the ocean. The old woman of eighty-four winters was already out in the cold morning wind, bareheaded, tripping about like a young girl, and driving up the cow to milk. She got the breakfast with dispatch, and without noise or bustle; and meanwhile the old man resumed his stories, standing before us, who were sitting, with his back to the chimney, and ejecting his tobacco-juice right and left into the fire behind him, without regard to the various dishes which were there preparing. At breakfast we had eels, buttermilk cake, cold bread, green beans, doughnuts, and tea. The old man talked a steady stream; and when his wife told him he had better eat his breakfast, he said, "Don't hurry me; I have lived too long to be hurried." I ate of the apple-sauce and the doughnuts, which I thought had sustained the least detriment from the old man's shots, but my companion refused the apple-sauce, and ate of the hot cake and green beans, which had appeared to him to occupy the safest part of the hearth. But on comparing notes afterward, I told him that the buttermilk cake was particularly exposed, and I saw how it suffered repeatedly, and therefore I avoided it; but he declared that, however that might be, he witnessed that the apple-sauce was seriously injured, and had therefore declined that. After breakfast we looked at his clock, which was out of order, and oiled it with some "hen's grease," for want of sweet oil, for he scarcely could believe that we were not tinkers or pedlers; meanwhile, he told a story about visions, which had reference to a crack in the clock-case made by frost one night. He was curious to know to what religious sect we belonged. He said that he had been to hear thirteen kinds of preaching in one month, when he was young, but he did not join any of them,—he stuck to his Bible. There was nothing like any of them in his Bible. While I was shaving in the next room, I heard him ask my companion to what sect he belonged, to which he answered,—

"Oh, I belong to the Universal Brotherhood."

"What's that?" he asked, "Sons o'Temperance?"

And his description of the sands and people of Provincetown:

▶   The sand is the great enemy here. The tops of some of the hills were inclosed and a board put up forbidding all persons entering the inclosure, lest their feet should disturb the sand, and set it a-blowing or a-sliding.

The inhabitants are obliged to get leave from the authorities to cut wood behind the town for fish-flakes, bean-poles, pea-brush, and the like, though, as we were told, they may transplant trees from one part of the township to another without leave. The sand drifts like snow, and sometimes the lower story of a house is concealed by it, though it is kept off by a wall. The houses were formerly built on piles, in order that the driving sand might pass under them. We saw a few old ones here still standing on their piles, but they were boarded up now, being protected by their younger neighbors. There was a schoolhouse, just under the hill on which we sat, filled with sand up to the tops of the desks, and of course the master and scholars had fled. Perhaps they had imprudently left the windows open one day, or neglected to mend a broken pane. Yet in one place was advertised "Fine sand for sale here,"—I could hardly believe my eyes,—probably some of the street sifted,—a good instance of the fact that a man confers a value on the most worthless thing by mixing himself with it, according to which rule we must have conferred a value on the whole back side of Cape Cod; but I thought that if they could have advertised "Fat Soil," or perhaps "Fine sand got rid of," ay, and "Shoes emptied here," it would have been more alluring. As we looked down on the town, I thought that I saw one man, who probably lived beyond the extremity of the planking, steering and tacking for it in a sort of snowshoes, but I may have been mistaken. In some pictures of Provincetown the persons of the inhabitants are not drawn below the ankles, so much being supposed to be buried in the sand. Nevertheless, natives of Provincetown assured me that they could walk in the middle of the road without trouble even in slippers, for they had learned how to put their feet down and lift them up without taking in any sand. One man said that he should be surprised if he found half a dozen grains of sand in his pumps at night, and stated, moreover, that the young ladies had a dexterous way of emptying their shoes at each step, which it would take a stranger a long time to learn. The tires of the stage-wheels were about five inches wide; and the wagon-tires generally on the Cape are an inch or two wider, as the sand is an inch or two deeper than elsewhere. I saw a baby's wagon with tires six inches wide to keep it near the surface. The more tired the wheels, the less tired the horses. Yet all the time that we were in Provincetown, which was two days and nights, we saw only one horse and cart, and they were conveying a coffin. They did not try such experiments there on common occasions. The next summer I saw only the two-wheeled horse-cart which conveyed me thirty rods into the harbor on my way to the steamer. Yet we read that there were two horses and two yoke of oxen here in 1791, and we were told that there were several more when we were there, beside the stage team. In Barber's "Historical Collections," it is said, "so rarely are wheel-carriages seen in the place that they are a matter of some curiosity to the younger part of the community. A lad who understood navigating the ocean much better than land travel, on seeing a man driving a wagon in the street, expressed his surprise at his being able to drive so straight without the assistance of a rudder." There was no rattle of carts, and there would have been no rattle if there had been any carts. Some saddle horses that passed the hotel in the evening merely made the sand fly with a rustling sound like a writer sanding his paper copiously, but there was no sound of their tread. No doubt there are more horses and carts there at present. A sleigh is never seen, or at least is a great novelty on the Cape, the snow being either absorbed by the sand or blown into drifts.

In 1850, Thoreau also made an excursion to Quebec which he later wrote up as *A Yankee in Canada*. It is the least successful of all his books—a fact which Thoreau apparently realized at the time, for he opened the book with the statement, "What I got by going to Canada was a cold."

Although some of Thoreau's "excursions" were published in various periodicals during his lifetime, they were not published in book form until after his death. He did some preparation and polishing of the texts in the last few months before he died, but none—*The Maine Woods, Cape Cod, A Yankee in Canada,* or any of the shorter pieces—had the full benefit of his editorial hand. Therefore all quite understandably suffer somewhat from a lack of unity or polish. But nonetheless they do have a fascination all their own. They are lighter-hearted, less philosophical, and more humorous—often even slapstick—than his better known works. And each one captures the essential flavor of the area visited. We can almost taste the salt as we turn the pages of *Cape Cod* and smell the fragrance of the pine trees as we leaf through *The Maine Woods.*

18

Steering for the North Star

THOREAU SAW SLAVERY as the central issue of his time. So did his family and some of his neighbors. The Woman's Anti-Slavery Society was organized in Concord shortly after Garrison unfurled his *Liberator*. Mrs. Joseph Ward and her daughter Prudence, living with the Thoreaus, were members, as were Thoreau's sister Helen and his Aunt Maria. A neighbor, Mrs. Mary Merrick Brooks, was president. But Thoreau, feeling himself "too Transcendental," never joined any abolitionist society. He kept to his belief that all reforms must come from within. That did not, however, prevent his speaking out against slavery and acting, too, when the issue came to his door. If the individual worked to perfect himself, then by his actions he would help reform society. One of Thoreau's first protests against slavery was his refusal to pay his poll tax, a defiance of the failure of Massachusetts to resist the national government's extension of slave territory. He made no attempt to organize popular support for his position; he simply acted as his individual conscience dictated.

Another New Englander who, like Thoreau, was a "no organization" abolitionist, was Nathaniel Peabody Rogers, the New Hampshire editor. His *Herald of Freedom* was read regularly in the Thoreau household. In April, 1844, *The Dial* carried Thoreau's brief tribute to one of the few men he was able to praise without stint:

▶ We had occasionally, for several years, met with a number of this spirited journal, edited, as abolitionists need not to be informed, by Nathaniel P. Rogers, once a counselor-at-law in Plymouth, still farther up the Merrimack, but now, in his riper years, come down the hills thus far, to be the Herald of Freedom to these parts. We had been refreshed not a little by the cheap cordial of his editorials, flowing like his own mountain-torrents, now clear and sparkling, now foaming and gritty, and always spiced with the essence of the fire and the Norway pine; but never

An abolitionist song book of 1842 which belonged to Thoreau. His signature is at the top.

dark nor muddy, nor threatening with smothered murmurs, like the rivers of the plain. The effect of one of his effusions reminds us of what the hydropathists say about the electricity in fresh spring-water, compared with that which has stood over night, to suit weak nerves. We do not know of another notable and public instance of such pure, youthful, and hearty indignation at all wrong. The Church itself must love it, if it have any heart, though he is said to have dealt rudely with its sanctity. His clean attachment to the right, however, sanctions the severest rebuke we have read.

Mr. Rogers seems to us to have occupied an honorable and manly position in these days, and in this country, making the press a living and breathing organ to reach the hearts of men, and not merely "fine paper and good type," with its civil pilot sitting aft, and magnanimously waiting for the news to arrive,—the vehicle of the earliest news, but the latest intelligence,—recording the indubitable and last results, the marriages and deaths, alone. This editor was wide awake, and standing on the beak of his ship; not as a scientific explorer under government, but a Yankee sealer rather, who makes those unexplored continents his harbors in which to refit for more adventurous cruises. He was a fund of news and freshness in himself,—had the gift of speech, and the knack of writing; and if anything important took place in the Granite State, we might be sure that we should hear of it in good season. No other paper that we know kept pace so well with one forward wave of the restless public thought and sentiment of New England, and asserted so faithfully and ingenuously the largest liberty in all things. There was beside more unpledged poetry in his prose than in the verses of many an accepted rhymer; and we were occasionally advertised by a mellow hunter's note from his trumpet, that, unlike most reformers, his feet were still where they should be, on the turf, and that he looked out from a serener natural life into the turbid arena of politics. Nor was slavery always a sombre theme with him, but invested with the colors of his wit and fancy, and an evil to be abolished by other means than sorrow and bitterness of complaint. He will fight this fight with what cheer may be.

A few months later, on August 1, 1844, a meeting to commemorate the anniversary of the Emancipation of the Negroes in the British West Indies was held in Concord. It rained in the morning, and the outdoor plans had to be changed. When the churches, as usual, refused their rooms, the abolitionists simply took over the courthouse. Thirteen towns were reported to have delegations in the audience to hear an address Emerson had been induced to make by Mrs. Brooks. The selectmen would not permit the sexton to ring the assembly bell in the meetinghouse so Thoreau "took hold of it with a strong arm" and "the bell pealed forth its summons right merrily," a Concord correspondent wrote in the *Herald of Freedom*.

In November another episode in antislavery history touched Concord. Squire Samuel Hoar, a former Congressman from Massachusetts, bound South on a winter vacation, was appointed by the state to negotiate a friendly settlement with South Carolina of an old dispute. The Southern state for some years had been taking free Negro sailors off Massachusetts ships that sailed into Charleston to load cotton. Under a state law forbidding free Negroes entry as a safeguard against a slave uprising, the sailors had been fined, flogged, and often jailed. The conservative Concord lawyer was

DLESEX CO. ANTI-SLAVERY SOCIETY.
HE Middlesex County Anti-Slavery Society will hold its annual Meeting, the 4th Tuesday of January (24th) e Rev. Dr. Ripley's Meeting-house in Concord. The ty will meet for business at Wesson's Hotel at 11 ck, A. M. Public services in the meeting-house at 2, at 6 o'clock, P. M. Abolitionists generally, and friends e cause in the County are particularly and respectfully ed to attend. Local Societies will please send large gations.   J. W. CROSS, *Sec'y*.
c. 17, 1836.   50

The county society calls all abolitionists to the 1837 annual meeting in Concord.

The Concord *Freeman* gave this terse and somewhat unfriendly notice to the 1851 convention of the Middlesex society.

☞ The Middlesex County Anti-Slavery Society held their annual convention in this town yesterday, at the Orthodox Church. Wendell Phillips, Edmund Quincy, and other lesser lights of the Garrisonian school were present. The speeches were characterized with the usual wildness of imagination, which generally emanates from their gatherings.

In the evening the ladies gave a Tea Party, which was well attended, and passed off to the satisfaction of all interested.

expected to work out a peaceful solution that would not injure commercial relations between the two states. To the horror of Hoar, and Massachusetts, he was thrust back on a ship under threat of being lynched if he dared stay in Charleston. When the Concord town meeting heard his story, the cause of abolition gained new friends.

That winter the slavery question erupted on the floor of the Concord Lyceum. Thoreau, very much in the center of the fight over free discussion of slavery, told the story in a letter printed in the *Liberator* on March 28, 1845:

▶ We have now, for the third winter, had our spirits refreshed, and our faith in the destiny of the Commonwealth strengthened, by the presence and the eloquence of Wendell Phillips; and we wish to tender to him our thanks and our sympathy. The admission of this gentleman into the Lyceum has been strenuously opposed by a respectable portion of our fellow-citizens, who themselves, we trust,—whose descendants, at least, we know,—will be as faithful conservers of the true order, whenever that shall be the order of the day,—and in each instance the people have voted that they would hear him, by coming themselves and bringing their friends to the lecture-room, and being very silent that they might hear. We saw some men and women, who had long ago come out, going in once more through the free and hospitable portals of the Lyceum; and many of our neighbors confessed that they had had a "sound season" this once.

It was the speaker's aim to show what the State, and above all the Church, had to do, and now, alas! have done, with Texas and slavery, and how much, on the other hand, the individual should have to do with Church and State. These were fair themes, and not mistimed, and his words were addressed to "fit audience, and not few."

We must give Mr. Phillips the credit of being a clean, erect, and what was once called a consistent man. He at least is not responsible for slavery, nor for American Independence; for the hypocrisy and superstition of the Church, nor the timidity and selfishness of the State; nor for the indifference and willing ignorance of any. He stands so distinctly, so firmly, and so effectively alone, and one honest man is so much more than a host, that we cannot but feel that he does himself injustice when he reminds us of "the American Society, which he represents." It is rare that we have the pleasure of listening to so clear and orthodox a speaker, who obviously has so few cracks or flaws in his moral nature,—who, having words at his command in a remarkable degree, has much more than words, if these should fail, in his unquestionable earnestness and integrity,—and, aside from their admiration at his rhetoric, secures the genuine respect of his audience. He unconsciously tells his biography as he proceeds, and we see him early and earnestly deliberating on these subjects, and wisely and bravely, without counsel or consent of any, occupying a ground at first from which the varying tides of public opinion cannot drive him.

We would fain express our appreciation of the freedom and steady wisdom, so rare in the reformer, with which he declared that he was not born to abolish slavery, but to do right. We have heard a few, a very few, good political speakers, who afforded us the pleasure of great intellectual power and acuteness, of soldier-like steadiness, and of a graceful and natural oratory; but in this man the audience might detect a sort of moral principle and integrity, which was more stable than their firmness, more discriminating than his own intellect, and more graceful than his rhetoric, which was not working for temporary or trivial ends. It is so rare and encouraging to listen to an orator who is content with another alliance than with the popular party, or even with the sympathizing school of the martyrs, who can afford sometimes to be his own auditor if the mob stay away, and hears himself without reproof, that we feel ourselves in danger of slandering all mankind by affirming that here is one who is at the same time an eloquent speaker and a righteous man.

Perhaps, on the whole, the most interesting fact elicited by these addresses, is the readiness of the people at large, of whatever sect or party, to entertain, with good will and hospitality, the most revolutionary and heretical opinions, when frankly and adequately, and in some sort cheerfully, expressed. Such clear and candid declaration of opinion served like an electuary to whet and clarify the intellect of all parties, and furnished each one with an additional argument for that right he asserted.

We consider Mr. Phillips one of the most conspicuous and efficient champions of a true Church and State now in the field, and would say to him, and such as are like him, "God speed you." If you know of any champion in the ranks of his opponents, who has the valor and courtesy even of Paynim chivalry, if not the Christian graces and refinement of this knight, you will do us a service by directing him to these fields forthwith, where the lists are now open, and he shall be hospitably entertained. For as yet the red-cross knight has shown us only the gallant device upon his shield, and his admirable command of his steed, prancing and curveting in the empty lists; but we wait to see who, in the actual breaking of lances, will come tumbling upon the plain.

Concord seems to have long been a center for Underground Railroad activity. Townspeople engaged as "stationmasters" included Mr. and Mrs. Francis E. Bigelow, Mrs. Brooks of course, Miss Mary E. Rice, Ephraim Allen, Alcott, and Thoreau. In *Walden,* describing the visitors he had at his hut beside the pond, Thoreau wrote of "runaway slaves with plantation

THE

EMANCIPATION OF THE NEGROES

IN THE

BRITISH WEST INDIES.

AN ADDRESS DELIVERED AT CONCORD, MASSACHUSETTS,
ON 1st AUGUST, 1844

BY

R. W. EMERSON.

" Fetters, chains, monopolies, thefts, sales, statutes, all engines of tyranny,
men have found insufficient to annihilate freedom, for the good reason, that
they cannot annihilate the Soul whose first law of being is freedom. Despite
of lies which the ages have told, of tyrannies which the ages have established,
Freedom lives imperishable."

LONDON:
JOHN CHAPMAN, 121, NEWGATE STREET.

M.DCCC.XLIV.

In 1844, Thoreau rang the meeting-house bell summoning the townspeople to hear Emerson take his first public stand on the issue of slavery. In Thoreau's scrapbook was a clipping from the *Liberator,* which warmly welcomed the end of Emerson's silence, but said, "we had previously, we confess, felt half indignant that, while we were struggling against the popular current, mobbed, hunted, denounced from the legislative forum, cursed from the pulpit, sneered at by wealth and fashion and shallow aristocracy, such a man as Ralph Waldo Emerson should be brooding over his pleasant philosophies, writing his quaint and beautiful essays, in his retirement on the banks of the Concord, unconcerned and 'calm as a summer's morning.' "

manners, who listened from time to time, like the fox in the fable, as if they heard the hounds a-baying on their track, and looked at me beseechingly, as much as to say,—

'O Christian, will you send me back?' "

One real runaway slave, Thoreau added, he "helped to forward toward the north star."

When the Fugitive Slave Bill was adopted by Congress as part of the Missouri Compromise of 1850, it made heavier the penalties for helping slaves to escape. A thousand-dollar fine was levied, and all persons were enjoined to help the slave-catchers. "This filthy enactment was made in the 19th century, by people who could read and write," wrote Emerson in his Journal. "I will not obey it, by God."

Nor did the Concord abolitionists mean to obey it. On Saturday morning, February 15, 1851, Shadrach, an escaped Virginia slave working as a waiter in Boston, was the first Negro to be seized by a Federal Marshal under the new law. Early that afternoon two Negroes rescued the runaway from the Court House and rushed him off toward Cambridge. At 3 on Sunday morning a carriage with drawn blinds pulled up in Concord and Shadrach was

[*196*]

put in the capable hands of Francis Bigelow, the town blacksmith, who sent him on to the next station, toward Canada and freedom.

"I think it the most noble deed done in Boston since the destruction of the tea in 1773," said Theodore Parker. Attempts to enforce the 1850 act pushed more Northern neutrals toward an antislavery position than any event since Lovejoy's lynching, Garrison said.

The next fugitive slave case came swiftly. On April 3 Thomas Sims was arrested in Boston. This time however, the outcome was different. A large police force was mustered, the Court House was girded with heavy chains, and Sims was soon marched from his cell to a ship at the Long Wharf which bore the fugitive back to slavery in Virginia.

The incident roused Thoreau to fury. In his Journal he wrote:

▶ In '75 two or three hundred of the inhabitants of Concord assembled at one of the bridges with arms in their hands to assert the right of three millions to tax themselves, to have a voice in governing themselves. About a week ago the authorities of Boston, having the sympathy of many of the inhabitants of Concord, assembled in the gray of the dawn, assisted by a still larger armed force, to send back a perfectly innocent man, and one whom they knew to be innocent, into a slavery as complete as the world ever knew. Of course it makes not the least difference—I wish you to consider this—who the man was,—whether he was Jesus Christ or another,—for inasmuch as ye did it unto the least of these his brethren ye did it unto him. Do you think he would have stayed here in liberty and let the black man go into slavery in his stead? They sent him back, I say,

Nathaniel P. Rogers, who earned praise from Thoreau for his steadfast opposition to a society and government he couldn't accept. The New Hampshire lawyer gave up his profession to fight for the slave's cause, and became editor of the *Herald of Freedom*. What his contemporaries called his "Yankee style" of writing editorials pleased Thoreau so much he wrote a special article on it for *The Dial*. Like Thoreau, Rogers believed strongly in individual action as the path to all reform, so strongly that by 1844 he was advocating dissolution of the abolitionist societies because he felt they infringed on the rights of their members. That was too much for Garrison who, controlling Rogers' paper, removed him as editor.

to live in slavery with other three millions—mark that—whom the same slave power, or slavish power, North and South, holds in that condition,—three millions who do not, like the first mentioned, assert the right to govern themselves but simply to run away and stay away from their prison.

Just a week afterward, those inhabitants of this town who especially sympathize with the authorities of Boston in this their deed caused the bells to be rung and the cannon to be fired to celebrate the courage and the love of liberty of those men who assembled at the bridge. As if those three millions had fought for the right to be free themselves, but to hold in slavery three million others. Why, gentlemen, even consistency, though it is much abused, is sometimes a virtue. Every humane and intelligent inhabitant of Concord, when he or she heard those bells and those cannon, thought not so much of the events of the 19th of April, 1775, as of the event of the 12th of April, 1851.

I wish my townsmen to consider that, whatever the human law may be, neither an individual nor a nation can ever deliberately commit the least act of injustice without having to pay the penalty for it. A government which deliberately enacts injustice, and persists in it!—it will become the laughing-stock of the world.

When I read the account of the carrying back of the fugitive into slavery, which was read last Sunday evening, and read also what was not read here, that the man who made the prayer on the wharf was Daniel Foster of Concord, I could not help feeling a slight degree of pride because, of all the towns in the Commonwealth, Concord was the only one distinctly named as being represented in that new tea-party, and, as she had a place in the first, so would have a place in this, the last and perhaps next most important chapter of the History of Massachusetts. But my second feeling, when I reflected how short a time that gentleman has resided in this town, was one of doubt and shame, because the men of Concord in recent times have done nothing to entitle them to the honor of having their town named in such a connection.

I hear a good deal said about trampling this law under foot. Why, one need not go out of his way to do that. This law lies not at the level of the head or the reason. Its natural habitat is in the dirt. It was bred and has its life only in the dust and mire, on a level with the feet; and he who walks with freedom, unless, with a sort of quibbling and Hindoo mercy, he avoid treading on every venomous reptile, will inevitably tread on it, and so trample it under foot.

It has come to this, that the friends of liberty, the friends of the slave, have shuddered when they have understood that his fate has been left to the legal tribunals, so-called, of the country to be decided.

The people have no faith that justice will be awarded in such a case.

The judge may decide this way or that; it is a kind of accident at best. It is evident that he is not a competent authority in so important a case. I would not trust the life of my friend to the judges of all the Supreme Courts in the world put together, to be sacrificed or saved by precedent. I would much rather trust to the sentiment of the people, which would itself be a precedent to posterity. In their vote you would get something worth having at any rate, but in the other case only the trammelled judgement of an individual, of no significance, be it which way it will.

I think that recent events will be valuable as a criticism on the administration of justice in our midst, or rather as revealing what are the true sources of justice in any community. It is to some extent fatal to the courts when the people are compelled to go behind the courts. They learn that the courts are made for fair weather and for very civil cases.

Let us entertain opinions of our own; let us be a town and not a suburb, as far from Boston in this sense as we were by the old road which led through Lexington; a place where tyranny may ever be met with firmness and driven back with defeat to its ships.

Concord has several more bridges left of the same sort, which she is taxed to maintain. Can she not raise men to defend them?

Probably he meant these entries to be the basis of a speech, but if so, he was not asked to give it. Hardly six months later Thoreau himself defied the Fugitive Slave Law. At 5:00 P.M. on October 1, he recorded the incident in his Journal:

▶ Just put a fugitive slave, who has taken the name of Henry Williams, into the cars for Canada. He escaped from Stafford County, Virginia, to Boston last October; has been in Shadrach's place at the Cornhill Coffee-House; had been corresponding through an agent with his master, who is his father, about buying himself, his master asking $600, but he having been able to raise only $500. Heard that there were writs out for two Williamses, fugitives, and was informed by his fellow-servants and employer that Augerhole Burns and others of the police had called for him when he was out. Accordingly fled to Concord last night on foot, bringing a letter to our family from Mr. Lovejoy of Cambridge and another which Garrison had formerly given him on another occasion. He lodged with us, and waited in the house till funds were collected with which to forward him. Intended to dispatch him at noon through to Burlington, but when I went to buy his ticket, saw one at the depot who looked and behaved so much like a Boston policeman that I did not venture that time. An intelligent and very well-behaved man, a mulatto.

The slave said he could guide himself by many other stars than the north star, whose rising and setting he knew. They steered for the north star even when it had got round and appeared to them to be in the south. They frequently followed the telegraph when there was no railroad. The slaves bring many superstitions from Africa. The fugitives sometimes superstitiously carry a turf in their hats, thinking that their success depends on it.

It was another such occasion, about a year later, which Moncure Conway, the young liberal son of a Southern slave-owner, observed on a visit to the Thoreau house:

> When I went to the house next morning, I found them all (Thoreau was then living in his father's house) in a state of excitement by reason of the arrival of a fugitive negro from the South, who had come fainting to their door about daybreak and thrown himself on their mercy. Thoreau took me in to see the poor wretch, whom I found to be a man with whose face as that of a slave in the South I was familiar. The negro was much terrified at seeing me, supposing that I was one of his pursuers. Having quieted his fears by the assurance that I too, though in a different sense, was a refugee from the bondage he was escaping, and at the same time being able to attest the negro's genuineness, I sat and watched the singularly tender and lowly devotion of the scholar to the slave. He must be fed, his swollen feet bathed, and he must think of nothing but rest. Again and again this coolest and calmest of men drew near to the trembling negro, and bade him feel at home, and have no fear that any power should again wrong him. He could not walk that day, but must mount guard over the fugitive, for slavehunters were not extinct in those days; and so I went away after a while much impressed by many little traits that I had seen as they had appeared in this emergency, and not much disposed to cavil at their source, whether Bible or Bhaghavat.

His feeling for the slave came out, too, in Thoreau's excavations of ancient Concord history. In 1858 his Journal mentions the Pre-Revolutionary slave called Casey:

> ▶   George Minott tells me that he, when young, used often to go to a store by the side of where Bigelow's tavern was and kept by Ephraim Jones,— the Goodnow store. That was probably the one kept by my old trader. Told me how Casey, who was a slave to a man—Whitney—who lived where Hawthorne owns,—the same house,—before the Revolution, ran off one Sunday, was pursued by the neighbors, and hid himself in the river up to his neck till nightfall, just across the Great Meadows. He ran through Gowing's Swamp and came back that night to a Mrs. Cogswell, who lived where Charles Davis does, and got something to eat; then

cleared far away, enlisted, and was freed as a soldier after the war. Whitney's boy threw snowballs at him the day before, and finally C., who was chopping in the yard, threw his axe at him, and W. said he was an ugly nigger and he must put him in jail. He may have been twenty years old when stolen from Africa; left a wife and one child there. Used to say that he went home to Africa in the night and came back again in the morning; i.e., he dreamed of home. Lived to be old. Called Thanksgiving "Tom Kiver."

We hear the names of the worthies of Concord,—Squire Cuming and the rest,—but the poor slave Casey seems to have lived a more adventurous life than any of them. Squire Cuming probably never had to run for his life on the plains of Concord.

The rescue case that won an army of converts to the abolitionist cause began on the night of May 24, 1854, when the Negro, Anthony Burns, was arrested by a marshal in Boston. Within 48 hours the city was in an uproar. An angry crowd listening to speeches in Faneuil Hall by Wendell Phillips and Theodore Parker rushed out to join a small band under Rev. Thomas Wentworth Higginson, who were trying to batter down the doors of the Court House to free the fugitive jailed within. Officers armed with cutlasses stood off the rescuers, who included Bronson Alcott, until four companies of artillery and troops were called out to keep order. The attack failed. Burns was placed aboard a U.S. revenue cutter and returned to his master in Virginia.

Public anger mounted. On the Fourth of July the abolitionists met at Framingham in their annual celebration. Garrison read from the Scriptures and then, to show his feelings for "the pro-slavery laws and deeds of the nation," he held up the Constitution for all to see, and branding it "a covenant with death and an agreement with Hell," burned it to ashes.

Thoreau was among the speakers on this occasion. His violent speech, "Slavery in Massachusetts," incorporating some of what he had written in response to the Sims case, attacked both press and church as defenders of slavery, and appealed for a higher standard of morality:

▸ I lately attended a meeting of the citizens of Concord, expecting, as one among many, to speak on the subject of slavery in Massachusetts; but I was surprised and disappointed to find that what had called my townsmen together was the destiny of Nebraska, and not of Massachusetts, and that what I had to say would be entirely out of order. I had thought that the house was on fire, and not the prairie; but though several of the citizens of Massachusetts are now in prison for attempting to rescue a slave from her own clutches, not one of the speakers at that meeting expressed regret for it, not one even referred to it. It was only the disposi-

THE LIBERATOR.

SLAVERY IN MASSACHUSETTS.

AN ADDRESS,

Delivered at the Anti-Slavery Celebration at Framingham, July 4th, 1854,

By Henry D. Thoreau, of Concord, (Mass.)

I lately attended a meeting of the citizens of Concord, expecting, as one among many, to speak on the subject of slavery in Massachusetts; but I was surprised and disappointed to find that what had called my townsmen together was the destiny of Nebraska, and not of Massachusetts, and that what I had to say would be entirely out of order. I had thought that the house was on fire, and not the prairie ; but though several of the citizens of Massachusetts are now in prison for attempting to rescue a slave from her own clutches, not one of the speakers at that meeting expressed regret for it, not one even referred to it. It was only the disposition of some wild lands a thousand miles off, which appeared to concern them. The inhabitants of Concord are not prepared to stand by one of their own bridges, but talk only of taking up a position on the highlands beyond the Yellowstone river. Our Buttricks, and Davises, and Hosmers are retreating thither, and I fear that they will have no Lexington Common between them and the enemy. There is not one slave in Nebraska ; there are perhaps a million slaves in Massachusetts.

They who have been bred in the school of politics fail now and always to face the facts. Their measures are half measures and make-shifts, merely. They put off the day of settlement indefinitely, and meanwhile, the debt accumulates. Though the Fugitive Slave Law had not been the subject of discussion on that occasion, it was at length faintly resolved by my townsmen, at an adjourned meeting, as I learn, that the compromise compact of 1820 having been repudiated by one of the parties, 'Therefore, . . . the Fugitive Slave Law must be repealed.' But this is not the reason why an iniquitous law should be repealed. The fact which the politician faces is merely, that there is less honor among thieves than was supposed, and not the fact that they are thieves.

As I had no opportunity...

Thoreau's Fourth of July speech, made in Framingham, was reported in the *Liberator* on July 25 and in the New York *Tribune,* as well. It was the widest audience he had reached up to that time.

THE LIBERATO

WENDELL PHILLIPS BEFORE CORD LYCEUM.

Concord, Mass. March 12th, 1

Mr. Editor:

We have now, for the third winter, had our refreshed, and our faith in the destiny of the monwealth strengthened, by the presence an eloquence of Wendell Phillips ; and we wish der to him our thanks and our sympathy. Th mission of this gentleman into the Lyceum has strenuously opposed by a respectable portion o fellow-citizens,

The opening of Thoreau's letter in the *Liberator,* reporting the happy outcome of the battle in the Concord Lyceum to protect the right of Wendell Phillips and of other abolitionists to speak out on slavery.

THOMAS SIMS, THE SLAVE.

Young Thomas Sims begged for a knife to stab himself through the heart when he was ordered sent back into slavery in Georgia. The fugitive's arrest in Boston in April, 1851, deeply roused Thoreau.

tion of some wild lands a thousand miles off which appeared to concern them. The inhabitants of Concord are not prepared to stand by one of their own bridges, but talk only of taking up a position on the highlands beyond the Yellowstone River. Our Buttricks and Davises and Hosmers are retreating thither, and I fear that they will leave no Lexington Common between them and the enemy. There is not one slave in Nebraska; there are perhaps a million slaves in Massachusetts.

They who have been bred in the school of politics fail now and always to face the facts. Their measures are half measures and makeshifts merely. They put off the day of settlement indefinitely, and meanwhile the debt accumulates. Though the Fugitive Slave Law had not been the subject of discussion on that occasion, it was at length faintly resolved by my towns-men, at an adjourned meeting, as I learn, that the compromise compact of 1820 having been repudiated by one of the parties, "therefore, . . . the Fugitive Slave Law of 1850 must be repealed." But this is not the reason why an iniquitous law should be repealed. The fact which the politician faces is merely that there is less honor among thieves than was supposed, and not the fact that they are thieves.

As I had no opportunity to express my thoughts at that meeting, will you allow me to do so here?

Again it happens that the Boston Court-House is full of armed men, holding prisoner and trying a man, to find out if he is not really a slave. Does any one think that justice or God awaits Mr. Loring's decision? For him to sit there deciding still, when this question is already decided from eternity to eternity, and the unlettered slave himself and the multitude around have long since heard and assented to the decision, is simply to make himself ridiculous. We may be tempted to ask from whom he received his commission, and who he is that received it; what novel statutes he obeys, and what precedents are to him of authority. Such an arbiter's very existence is an impertinence. We do not ask him to make up his mind, but to make up his pack.

I listen to hear the voice of a Governor, Commander-in-Chief of the forces of Massachusetts. I hear only the creaking of crickets and the hum of insects which now fill the summer air. The Governor's exploit is to review the troops on muster days. I have seen him on horseback, with his hat off, listening to a chaplain's prayer. It chances that that is all I have ever seen of a Governor. I think that I could manage to get along without one. If he is not of the least use to prevent my being kidnapped, pray of what important use is he likely to be to me? When freedom is most endangered, he dwells in the deepest obscurity. A distinguished clergyman told me that he chose the profession of a clergyman because it afforded the most leisure for literary pursuits. I would recommend to him the profession of a Governor.

Three years ago, also, when the Sims tragedy was acted, I said to myself, There is such an officer, if not such a man, as the Governor of Massachusetts,—what has he been about the last fortnight? Has he had as much as he could do to keep on the fence during this moral earthquake? It seemed to me that no keener satire could have been aimed at, no more cutting insult have been offered to that man, than just what happened,—the absence of all inquiry after him in that crisis. The worst and the most I chance to know of him is that he did not improve that opportunity to make himself known, and worthily known. He could at least have resigned himself into fame. It appeared to be forgotten that there was such a man or such an office. Yet no doubt he was endeavoring to fill the gubernatorial chair all the while. He was no Governor of mine. He did not govern me.

But at last, in the present case, the Governor was heard from. After he and the United States government had perfectly succeeded in robbing a poor innocent black man of his liberty for life, and, as far as they could, of his Creator's likeness in his breast, he made a speech to his accomplices, at a congratulatory supper!

I have read a recent law of this State, making it penal for any officer of the "Commonwealth" to "detain or aid in the . . . detention," anywhere within its limits, "of any person, for the reason that he is claimed as a fugitive slave." Also, it was a matter of notoriety that a writ of replevin to take the fugitive out of the custody of the United States marshal could not be served for want of sufficient force to aid the officer.

I had thought that the Governor was, in some sense, the executive officer of the State; that it was his business, as a Governor, to see that the laws of the State were executed; while, as a man, he took care that he did not, by so doing, break the laws of humanity; but when there is any special important use for him, he is useless, or worse than useless, and permits the laws of the State to go unexecuted. Perhaps I do not know what are the duties of a Governor; but if to be a Governor requires to subject one's self to so much ignominy without remedy, if it is to put a restraint upon my manhood, I shall take care never to be Governor of Massachusetts. I have not read far in the statutes of this Commonwealth. It is not profitable reading. They do not always say what is true; and they do not always mean what they say. What I am concerned to know is, that that man's influence and authority were on the side of the slaveholder, and not of the slave,—of the guilty, and not of the innocent,—of injustice, and not of justice. I never saw him of whom I speak; indeed, I did not know that he was Governor until this event occurred. I heard of him and Anthony Burns at the same time, and thus, undoubtedly, most will hear of him. So far am I from being governed by him. I do not mean that it was anything to his discredit that I had not heard of him, only that

I heard what I did. The worst I shall say of him is, that he proved no better than the majority of his constituents would be likely to prove. In my opinion, he was not equal to the occasion.

The whole military force of the State is at the service of a Mr. Suttle, a slaveholder from Virginia, to enable him to catch a man whom he calls his property; but not a soldier is offered to save a citizen of Massachusetts from being kidnapped! Is this what all these soldiers, all this training, have been for these seventy-nine years past? Have they been trained merely to rob Mexico and carry back fugitive slaves to their masters?

These very nights I heard the sound of a drum in our streets. There were men training still; and for what? I could with an effort pardon the cockerels of Concord for crowing still, for they, perchance, had not been beaten that morning; but I could not excuse this rub-a-dub of the "trainers." The slave was carried back by exactly such as these; i.e., by the soldier, of whom the best you can say in this connection is that he is a fool made conspicuous by a painted coat.

It is to some extent fatal to the courts, when the people are compelled to go behind them. I do not wish to believe that the courts were made for fair weather, and for very civil cases merely; but think of leaving it to any court in the land to decide whether more than three millions of people, in this case a sixth part of a nation, have a right to be freemen or not! But it has been left to the courts of justice, so called,—to the Supreme Court of the land,—and, as you all know, recognizing no authority but the Constitution, it has decided that the three millions are and shall continue to be slaves. Such judges as these are merely the inspectors of a pick-lock and murderer's tools, to tell him whether they are in working order or not, and there they think that their responsibility ends. There was a prior case on the docket, which they, as judges appointed by God, had no right to skip; which having been justly settled, they would have been saved from this humiliation. It was the case of the murderer himself.

The law will never make men free; it is men who have got to make the law free. They are the lovers of law and order who observe the law when the government breaks it.

Among human beings, the judge whose words seal the fate of a man furthest into eternity is not he who merely pronounces the verdict of the law, but he, whoever he may be, who, from a love of truth, and unprejudiced by any custom or enactment of men, utters a true opinion or sentence concerning him. He it is that sentences him. Whoever can discern truth has received his commission from a higher source than the chiefest justice in the world who can discern only law. He finds himself constituted judge of the judge. Strange that it should be necessary to state such simple truths!

Among measures to be adopted, I would suggest to make as earnest and vigorous an assault on the press as has already been made, and with effect, on the church. The church has much improved within a few years; but the press is, almost without exception, corrupt. I believe that in this country the press exerts a greater and a more pernicious influence than the church did in its worst period. We are not a religious people but we are a nation of politicians. We do not care for the Bible, but we do care for the newspaper. At any meeting of politicians,—like that at Concord the other evening, for instance, how impertinent it would be to quote from the Bible! how pertinent to quote from a newspaper or from the Constitution! The newspaper is a Bible which we read every morning and every afternoon, standing and sitting, riding and walking. It is a Bible which every man carries in his pocket, which lies on every table and counter, and which the mail, and thousands of missionaries, are continually dispersing. It is, in short, the only book which America has printed, and which America reads. So wide is its influence. The editor is a preacher whom you voluntarily support. Your tax is commonly one cent daily, and it costs nothing for pew hire. But how many of these preachers preach the truth? I repeat the testimony of many an intelligent foreigner, as well as my own convictions, when I say, that probably no country was ever ruled by so mean a class of tyrants as, with a few noble exceptions, are the editors of the periodical press in this country. And as they live and rule only by their servility, and appealing to the worse, and not the better, nature of man, the people who read them are in the condition of the dog that returns to his vomit.

The Liberator and the Commonwealth were the only papers in Boston, as far as I know, which made themselves heard in condemnation of the cowardice and meanness of the authorities of that city, as exhibited in '51. The other journals, almost with exception, by their manner of referring to and speaking of the Fugitive Slave Law, and the carrying back of the slave Sims, insulted the common sense of the country, at least. And, for the most part, they did this, one would say, because they thought so to secure the approbation of their patrons, not being aware that a sounder sentiment prevailed to any extent in the heart of the Commonwealth. I am told that some of them have improved of late; but they are still eminently timeserving. Such is the character they have won.

But, thank fortune, this preacher can be even more easily reached by the weapons of the reformer than could the recreant priest. The free men of New England have only to refrain from purchasing and reading these sheets, have only to withhold their cents, to kill a score of them at once. One whom I respect told me that he purchased Mitchell's Citizen in the cars, and then threw it out the window. But would not his contempt have been more fatally expressed if he had not bought it?

Are they Americans? are they New-Englanders? are they inhabitants of Lexington and Concord and Framingham, who read and support the Boston Post, Mail, Journal, Advertiser, Courier, and Times? Are these the Flags of our Union? I am not a newspaper-reader, and may omit to name the worst.

The majority of the men of the North, and of the South and East and West, are not men of principle. If they vote, they do not send men to Congress on errands of humanity; but while their brothers and sisters are being scourged and hung for loving liberty, while—I might here insert all that slavery implies and is—it is the mismanagement of wood and iron and stone and gold which concerns them. Do what you will, O Government, with my wife and children, my mother and brother, my father and sister, I will obey your commands to the letter. It will indeed grieve me if you hurt them, if you deliver them to overseers to be hunted by hounds or to be whipped to death; but, nevertheless, I will peaceably pursue my chosen calling on this fair earth, until perchance, one day, when I have put on mourning for them dead, I shall have persuaded you to relent. Such is the attitude, such are the words of Massachusetts.

Rather than do thus, I need not say what match I would touch, what system endeavor to blow up; but as I love my life, I would side with the light, and let the dark earth roll from under me, calling my mother and my brother to follow.

I would remind my countrymen that they are to be men first, and Americans only at a late and convenient hour. No matter how valuable law may be to protect your property, even to keep soul and body together, if it do not keep you and humanity together.

I am sorry to say that I doubt if there is a judge in Massachusetts who is prepared to resign his office, and get his living innocently, whenever it is required of him to pass sentence under a law which is merely contrary to the law of God. I am compelled to see that they put themselves, or rather are by character, in this respect, exactly on a level with the marine who discharges his musket in any direction he is ordered to. They are just as much tools, and as little men. Certainly, they are not the more to be respected, because their master enslaves their understandings and consciences, instead of their bodies.

The judges and lawyers,—simply as such, I mean,—and all men of expediency, try this case by a very low and incompetent standard. They consider, not whether the Fugitive Slave Law is right, but whether it is what they call constitutional. Is virtue constitutional, or vice? Is equity constitutional, or iniquity? In important moral and vital questions, like this, it is just as impertinent to ask whether a law is constitutional or not, as to ask whether it is profitable or not. They persist in being the servants of the worst of men, and not the servants of humanity. The question is, not whether you or your grandfather, seventy years ago, did not enter into an agreement to serve the devil, and that service is not accordingly now due; but whether you will not now, for once and at last, serve God,—in spite of your own past recreancy, or that of your ancestor,—by obeying that eternal and only just CONSTITUTION, which He, and not any Jefferson or Adams, has written in your being.

The amount of it is, if the majority vote the devil to be God, the minority will live and behave accordingly, and obey the successful candidate, trusting that, some time or other, by some speaker's casting-vote, perhaps, they may reinstate God. This is the highest principle I can get out or invent for my neighbors. These men act as if they believed that they could safely slide down a hill a little way,—or a good way,—and would surely come to a place, by and by, where they could begin to slide up again. This is expediency, or choosing that course which offers the slightest obstacles to the feet, that is, a down-hill one. But there is no such thing as accomplishing a righteous reform by the use of "expediency." There is no such thing as sliding up-hill. In morals the only sliders are backsliders.

Thus we steadily worship Mammon, both school and state and church, and on the seventh day curse God with a tintamar from one end of the Union to the other.

Will mankind never learn that policy is not morality,—that it never secures any moral right, but considers merely what is expedient? chooses the available candidate,—who is invariably the devil,—and what right have his constituents to be surprised, because the devil does not behave like an angel of light? What is wanted is men, not of policy, but of probity,—who recognize a higher law than the Constitution, or the decision of the majority. The fate of the country does not depend on how you vote at the polls,—the worst man is as strong as the best at that game; it does not depend on what kind of paper you drop into the ballot-box once a year, but on what kind of man you drop from your chamber into the street every morning.

What should concern Massachusetts is not the Nebraska Bill, nor the Fugitive Slave Bill, but her own slaveholding and servility. Let the State dissolve her union with the slaveholder. She may wriggle and hesitate, and ask leave to read the Constitution once more; but she can find no respectable law or precedent which sanctions the continuance of such a union for an instant.

Let each inhabitant of the State dissolve his union with her, as long as she delays to do her duty.

The events of the past month teach me to distrust Fame. I see that she does not finely discriminate, but coarsely hurrahs. She considers not the simple heroism of an action, but only as it is connected with its apparent consequences. She praises till she is hoarse the easy exploit of the Boston tea-party, but will be comparatively silent about the braver and more disinterestedly heroic attack on the Boston Court-House, simply because it was unsuccessful!

Covered with disgrace, the State has sat down coolly to try for their lives and liberties the men who attempted to do its duty for it. And this is called justice! They who have shown that they can behave particularly well may perchance be put under bonds for their good behavior. They whom truth requires at present to plead guilty are, of all the inhabitants of the State, preeminently innocent. While the Governor, and the Mayor, and countless officers of the Commonwealth are at large, the champions of liberty are imprisoned.

Only they are guiltless who commit the crime of contempt of such a court. It behooves every man to see that his influence is on the side of justice, and let the courts make their own characters. My sympathies in this case are wholly with the accused, and wholly against their accusers and judges. Justice is sweet and musical; but injustice is harsh and discordant. The judge still sits grinding at his organ, but it yields no music, and we hear only the sound of the handle. He believes that all the music resides in the handle, and the crowd toss him their coppers the same as before.

Do you suppose that that Massachusetts which is now doing these things,—which hesitates to crown these men, some of whose lawyers, and even judges, perchance, may be driven to take refuge in some poor quibble, that they may not wholly outrage their instinctive sense of justice,—do you suppose that she is anything but base and servile? that she is the champion of liberty?

Show me a free state, and a court truly of justice, and I will fight for them, if need be; but show me Massachusetts, and I refuse her my allegiance, and express contempt for her courts.

The effect of a good government is to make life more valuable; of a bad one, to make it less valuable. We can afford that railroad and all merely material stock should lose some of its value, for that only compels us to live more simply and economically; but suppose that the value of life itself should be diminished! How can we make a less demand on man and nature, how live more economically in respect to virtue and all noble qualities, than we do? I have lived for the last month—and I think that every man in Massachusetts capable of the sentiment of patriotism must have had a similar experience—with the sense of having suffered a vast and indefinite loss. I did not know at first what ailed me. At last it occurred to me that what I had lost was a country. I had never respected the government near to which I lived, but I had foolishly thought that I might manage to live here, minding my private affairs, and forget it. For my part, my old and worthiest pursuits have lost I cannot say how much of their attraction, and I feel that my investment in life here is worth many per cent less since Massachusetts last deliberately sent back an innocent man, Anthony Burns, to slavery. I dwelt before, perhaps, in the illusion that my life passed somewhere only between heaven and hell, but now I cannot persuade myself that I do not dwell wholly within hell. The site of that political organization called Massachusetts is to me morally covered with volcanic scoriae and cinders, such as Milton describes in the infernal regions. If there is any hell more unprincipled than our rulers, and we, the ruled, I feel curious to see it. Life itself being worth less, all things with it, which minister to it, are worth less. Suppose you have a small library, with pictures to adorn the walls,—a garden laid out around, —and contemplate scientific and literary pursuits, and discover all at once that your villa, with all its contents, is located in hell, and that the justice of the peace has a cloven foot and a forked tail,—do not these things suddenly lose their value in your eyes?

I feel that, to some extent, the State has fatally interfered with my lawful business. It has not only interrupted me in my passage through Court Street on errands of trade, but it has interrupted me and every man on his onward and upward path, on which he had trusted soon to leave Court Street far behind. What right had it to remind me of Court Street? I have found that hollow which even I had relied on for solid.

I am surprised to see men going about their business as if nothing had happened. I say to myself, "Unfortunates! they have not heard the news." I am surprised that the man whom I just met on horseback should be so earnest to overtake his newly bought cows running away,—since all property is insecure, and if they do not run away again, they may be taken away from him when he gets them. Fool! does he not know this his seed-corn is worth less this year,—that all beneficent harvests fail as you approach the empire of hell? No prudent man will build a stone house under these circumstances, or engage in any peaceful enterprise which it requires a long time to accomplish. Art is as long as ever, but life is more interrupted and less available for a man's proper pursuits. It is not an era of repose. We have used up all our inherited freedom. If we would save our lives, we must fight for them.

I walk toward one of our ponds; but what signifies the beauty of nature when men are base? We walk to lakes to see our serenity reflected in them; when we are not serene, we go not to them. Who can be serene in a country where both the rulers and the ruled are without principle? The remembrance of my country spoils my walk. My thoughts are murder to the State, and involuntarily go plotting against her.

But it chanced the other day that I scented a white water-lily, and a season I had waited for had arrived. It is the emblem of purity. It bursts up so pure and fair to the eye, and so sweet to the scent, as if to show us what purity and sweetness reside in, and can be extracted from, the slime and muck of earth. I think I have plucked the first one that has opened for a mile. What confirmation of our hopes is in the fragrance of this flower! I shall not so soon despair of the world for it, notwithstanding slavery, and the cowardice and want of principle of Northern men. It suggests what kind of laws have prevailed longest and widest, and still prevail, and that the time may come when man's deeds will smell as sweet. Such is the odor which the plant emits. If Nature can compound this fragrance still annually, I shall believe her still young and full of vigor, her integrity and genius unimpaired, and that there is virtue even in man, too, who is fitted to perceive and love it. It reminds me that Nature has been partner to no Missouri Compromise. I scent no compromise in the fragrance of the water-lily. It is not a Nymphoea Douglasii. In it, the sweet, and pure, and innocent are wholly sundered from the obscene and baleful. I do not scent in this the time-serving irresolution of a Massachusetts Governor, nor of a Boston Mayor. So behave that the odor of your actions may enhance the general sweetness of the atmosphere, that when we behold or scent a flower, we may not be reminded how inconsistent your deeds are with it; for all odor is but one form of advertisement of a moral quality, and if fair actions had not been performed, the lily would not smell sweet. The foul slime stands for the sloth and vice of man, the decay of humanity; the fragrant flower that springs from it, for the purity and courage which are immortal.

Slavery and servility have produced no sweet-scented flower annually, to charm the senses of men, for they have no real life: they are merely a decaying and a death, offensive to all healthy nostrils. We do not complain that they live, but that they do not get buried. Let the living bury them; even they are good for manure.

19

An Observer of Nature

AT HEART Thoreau was first and always the naturalist—or better—the poet-naturalist, for his interest in the flora and fauna of his beloved Concord was not so much scientific as poetic. Any day in which he did not spend at least five hours in roaming through the woods and fields or boating on the rivers of Concord he felt to be wasted. He could fall in love, he felt, with a scrub oak—or a woodchuck—or a pinxter flower—or the mysterious night warbler that he was never able to identify.

This love, this enthusiasm for nature flowed over into his writings, making him not only the first outstanding nature writer in our literary history, but also the greatest—the one to whom all other nature writers from Audubon to John Burroughs, from Donald Culross Peattie to Edwin Way Teale, are compared. It was he who perfected the nature essay as such—as distinguished from the "letters," "travels," "journals," "rambles," or episodes of earlier nature writers. And most nature writers since his day have followed the pattern he perfected.

One of the most important qualities of Thoreau's nature writing is his lack of condescension. He does not look down his long nose at the mouse and say, "How cute!" or at the muskrat and say, "How naw-sty." He approaches the fauna—and even the flora—of Concord on its own terms. Because he sees nature as it is, he is able to humanize it without indulging in the pathetic fallacy. Through his eyes we see nature clearly.

Yet it is important to remember that Thoreau's real interest is centered in man, not nature. He studies nature because it is an important part of man's background. He believes strongly that nature is essential to man. Like Antaeus of old, modern man must derive his strength from his contact with the earth and with nature. Deprive man of that contact and he becomes weak physically, spiritually, and morally. Let him commune directly with nature and he becomes sturdy.

In the late 1840's Thoreau became acquainted with Louis Agassiz, then teaching at Harvard, and for a time collected specimens of turtles and fish and mice for him. Unwittingly Agassiz had a profound influence on Thoreau,

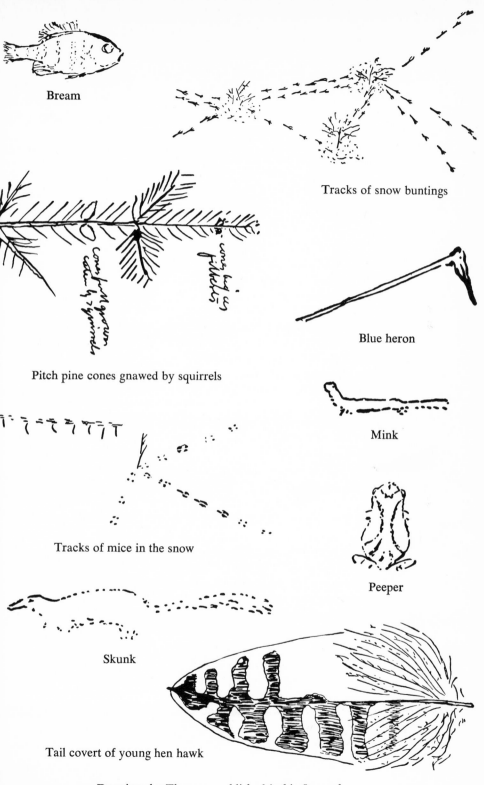

Bream

Tracks of snow buntings

Pitch pine cones gnawed by squirrels

Blue heron

Mink

Tracks of mice in the snow

Peeper

Skunk

Tail covert of young hen hawk

Drawings by Thoreau, published in his *Journal*.

The top entries of a sheet of nature notes kept by Thoreau. It records the earliest flowering of April flowers from 1852 through 1860.

developing Thoreau the scientist at the expense of Thoreau the poet-naturalist. It is interesting to glance through Thoreau's journals chronologically and see the change taking place.

In August, 1851, he wrote:

▶ I fear that the character of my knowledge is from year to year becoming more distinct and scientific; that, in exchange for views as wide as heaven's cope, I am being narrowed down to the field of the microscope. I see details, not wholes nor the shadow of the whole. I count some parts, and say, "I know." The cricket's chirp now fills the air in dry fields near pine woods.

Earlier, in 1850, Thoreau had been elected a corresponding member of the Boston Society of Natural History, for contributing "a fine specimen of an American goshawk" to its museum. In 1853, offered membership in the largest scientific organization in the country, this was his comment:

▶ The secretary of the Association for the Advancement of Science requests me, as he probably has thousands of others, by a printed circular letter from Washington the other day, to fill the blank against certain questions, among which the most important one was what branch of science I was specially interested in, using the term science in the most comprehensive sense possible. Now, though I could state to a select few that department of human inquiry which engages me, and should be rejoiced at an opportunity to do so, I felt that it would be to make myself the laughing-stock of the scientific community to describe or attempt to describe to them that branch of science which specially interests me, inasmuch as they do not believe in a science which deals with the higher law. So I was obliged to speak to their condition and describe to them that poor part of me which alone they can understand. The fact is I am a mystic, a transcendentalist, and a natural philosopher to boot. Now I think of it, I should have told them at once that I was a transcendentalist.

[*214*]

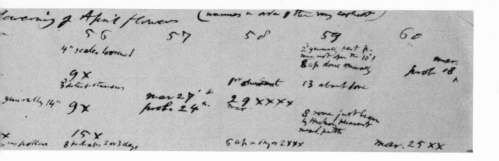

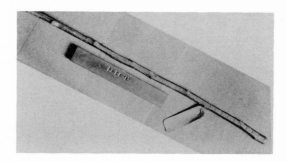

The stick notched for measuring, which Thoreau usually carried with him on his walks. He took the depth of snow with it. His initials—in the original order—are on his school ruler.

That would have been the shortest way of telling them that they would not understand my explanations.

How absurd that, though I probably stand as near to nature as any of them, and am by constitution as good an observer ¹s most, yet a true account of my relation to nature should excite their ridicule only! If it had been the secretary of an association of which Plato or Aristotle was the president, I should not have hesitated to describe my studies at once and particularly.

Although he rejected membership in the AAAS, there were plenty of signs that he was becoming more preoccupied with science and its instruments.

▶   Bought a telescope to-day for eight dollars. Best military spy-glass with six slides, which shuts up to about same size, fifteen dollars, and very powerful. Saw the squares of achromatic glass from Paris which Clark(e?) uses; fifty-odd dollars apiece, the larger. It takes two together, one called the flint. These French glasses all one quality of glass. My glass tried by Clark and approved. Only a part of the object (?) glass available. Bring the edge of the diaphragm against middle of the light, and your nail on object glass in line with these shows what is cut off. Sometimes may enlarge the hole in diaphragm. But, if you do so, you may have to enlarge the hole in diaphragm near small end, which must be exactly as large as the pencil of light there. As the diameter of the pencil is to the diameter of the available portion of the object glass, so is the power,—so many times it magnifies. A good glass because the form of the blurred object is the same on each side of the focus,—i.e., shoved in or drawn out.

A month later, this habit was revealed: "I bought me a spy-glass some weeks since. I buy but few things, and those not till long after I begin to want them, so that when I do get them I am prepared to make a perfect use of them and extract their whole sweet."

On August 18, 1854:

▶ I have just been through the process of killing the cistudo for the sake of science; but I cannot excuse myself for this murder, and see that such actions are inconsistent with the poetic perception, however they may serve science, and will affect the quality of my observations. I pray that I may walk more innocently and serenely through nature. No reasoning whatever reconciles me to this act. It affects my day injuriously. I have lost some self-respect. I have a murderer's experience in a degree.

In January, 1856, Thoreau took to pieces a pensile nest that he found on the south shore of Walden on an oak sapling about fifteen feet from the ground. Here is his detailed observation of the nest, and the conclusions he drew:

▶ Though small, it measures three inches by three in the extreme, and was hung between two horizontal twigs or in a fork forming about a right angle, the third side being regularly rounded without any very stiff material. The twigs extended two or three inches beyond the nest. The bulk of it is composed of fine shreds or fibres, pretty long (say three to six inches), of apparently inner oak (?) bark, judging from some scraps of the epidermis adhering. It looks at first sight like sedge or grass. The bottom, which I accidentally broke off and disturbed the arrangement of, was composed of this and white and pitch pine needles and little twigs about the same size and form, rough, with little leaf-stalks or feet (probably hemlock (?)), and also strips and curls of paper birch epidermis, and some hornet or other wasp nest used like the last. I mention the most abundant material first. Probably the needles and twigs were used on account of their curved form and elasticity, to give shape to the bottom. The sides, which were not so thick, were composed of bark shreds, paper birch, and hornet-nest (the two latter chiefly outside, probably to bind and conceal and keep out the wind), agglutinated together. But most pains was taken with the thin edge and for three quarters of an inch down, where, beside the bark-fibres, birch paper, and hornets' nest, some silky reddish-brown and also white fibre was used to bind all with, almost spun into threads and passed over the twigs and agglutinated to them, or over the bark edge. The shreds of birch paper were smaller there, and the hornets' nest looked as if it had been reduced to a pulp by the bird and spread very thinly here and there over all, mixed with the brown silk. This last looked like cow's hair, but as I found a piece of a small brown cocoon, though a little paler, I suspect it was from that. The white may have been from a cocoon, or else vegetable silk. Probably a vireo's nest, maybe red-eye's.

In our workshops we pride ourselves on discovering a use for what had previously been regarded as waste, but how partial and accidental our economy compared with Nature's. In Nature nothing is wasted. Every decayed leaf and twig and fibre is only the better fitted to serve in some other department, and all at last are gathered in her compost-heap. What a wonderful genius it is that leads the vireo to select the tough fibres of the inner bark, instead of the more brittle grasses, for its basket, the elastic pine-needles and the twigs, curved as they dried to give it form, and, as I suppose, the silk of cocoons, etc., etc., to bind it together with! I suspect that extensive use is made of these abandoned cocoons by the birds, and they, if anybody, know where to find them. There were at least seven materials used in constructing this nest, and the bird visited as many distinct localities many times, always with the purpose or design to find some particular one of these materials, as much as if it had said to itself, "Now I will go and get some old hornets' nest from one of those that I saw last fall down in the maple swamp—perhaps thrust my bill into them—or some silk from those cocoons I saw this morning."

Toward the end of this year, he stopped to think about the changes that had taken place in the way he looked at nature:

▶ My first botany, as I remember, was Bigelow's "Plants of Boston and Vicinity," which I began to use about twenty years ago, looking chiefly for the popular names and the short references to the localities of plants, even without any regard to the plant. I also learned the names of many, but without using any system, and forgot them soon. I was not inclined to pluck flowers; preferred to leave them where they were, liked them best there. I was never in the least interested in plants in the house. But from year to year we look at Nature with new eyes. About half a dozen years ago I found myself again attending to plants with more method, looking out the name of each one and remembering it. I began to bring them home in my hat, a straw one with a scaffold lining to it, which I called my botany-box. I never used any other, and when some whom I visited were evidently surprised at its dilapidated look, as I deposited it on their front entry table, I assured them it was not so much my hat as my botany-box. I remember gazing with interest at the swamps about those days and wondering if I could ever attain to such familiarity with plants that I should know the species of every twig and leaf in them, that I should be acquainted with every plant (excepting grasses and cryptogamous ones), summer and winter, that I saw. Though I knew most of the flowers, and there were not in any particular swamp more than half a dozen shrubs that I did not know, yet these made it seem like a maze to me, of a thousand strange species, and I even thought of commencing at one end and looking it faithfully and laboriously through till I knew it all. I little thought that in a year or two I should have attained to that knowledge without all that labor. Still I never studied botany, and do not to-day systematically, the most natural system is still so artificial. I wanted to know my neighbors, if possible,—to get a little nearer to them. I soon found myself observing when plants first blossomed and leafed, and I followed it up early and late, far and near, several years in succession, running to different sides of the town and into the neighboring towns, often between twenty and thirty miles in a day. I often visited a particular plant four or five miles distant, half a dozen times within a fortnight, that I might know exactly when it opened, beside attending to a great many others in different directions and some of them equally distant, at the same time. At the same time I had an eye for birds and whatever else might offer.

While living at Walden, Thoreau began sending animal specimens to Louis Agassiz (left) at Harvard, where the Swiss scientist was pioneering in the classification of American wild life. Thoreau supplied him with several new specimens. In one package, for instance, he enclosed 15 pouts, 22 perch, 18 shiners, 15 tortoises, 8 breams, a black snake, and a dormouse.

[*218*]

AN OBSERVER OF NATURE

What is the nature of accurate observation? How prepared must the eye be? Thoreau had this answer to make in the fall of 1858:

▶ If, about the last of October, you ascend any hill in the outskirts of the town and look over the forest, you will see, amid the brown of other oaks, which are now withered, and the green of the pines, the bright-red tops or crescents of the scarlet oaks, very equally and thickly distributed on all sides, even to the horizon. Complete trees standing exposed on the edges of the forest, where you have never suspected them, or their tops only in the recesses of the forest surface, or perhaps towering above the surrounding trees, or reflecting a warm rose red from the very edge of the horizon in favorable lights. All this you will see, and much more, if you are prepared to see it,—if you look for it. Otherwise, regular and universal as this phenomenon is, you will think for threescore years and ten that all the wood is at this season sere and brown. Objects are concealed from our view not so much because they are out of the course of our visual ray (continued) as because there is no intention of the mind and eye toward them. We do not realize how far and widely, or how near and narrowly, we are to look. The greater part of the phenomena of nature are for this reason concealed to us all our lives. Here, too, as in political economy, the supply answers to the demand. Nature does not cast pearls before swine. There is just as much beauty visible to us in the landscape as we are prepared to appreciate,—not a grain more. The

The opening page of Thoreau's first published essay on nature, as it appeared in *The Dial* for July, 1842. Drawn chiefly from his Journal of 1837-42, it touched only briefly on the State Reports it was supposed to review, properly crediting their contributions, however, to the study of American flora and fauna.

actual objects which one person will see from a particular hilltop are just as different from those which another will see as the persons are different. The scarlet oak must, in a sense, be in your eye when you go forth. We cannot see anything until we are possessed with the idea of it, and then we can hardly see anything else. In my botanical rambles I find that first the idea, or image, of a plant occupies my thoughts, though it may at first seem very foreign to this locality, and for some weeks or months I go thinking of it and expecting it unconsciously, and at length I surely see it, and it is henceforth an actual neighbor of mine. This is the history of my finding a score or more of rare plants which I could name.

Take one of our selectmen and put him on the highest hill in the township, and tell him to look! What, probably, would he see? What would he select to look at? Sharpening his sight to the utmost, and putting on the glasses that suited him best, aye, using a spy-glass if he liked, straining his optic nerve to its utmost, and making a full report. Of course, he would see a Brocken spectre of himself. Now take Julius Caesar, or Emanuel Swedenborg, or a Fiji-Islander, and set him up there! Let them compare notes afterward. Would it appear that they had enjoyed the same prospect? For aught we know, as strange a man as any of these is always at our elbows. It does not appear that anybody saw Shakespeare when he was about in England looking off, but only some of his raiment.

A year later, he was discussing what "knowing" something means. There was scientific knowledge, yes, but something else, too.

▶   It is only when we forget all our learning that we begin to know. I do not get nearer by a hair's breadth to any natural object so long as I presume that I have an introduction to it from some learned man. To conceive of it with a total apprehension I must for the thousandth time approach it as something totally strange. If you would make acquaintance with the ferns you must forget your botany. You must get rid of what is commonly called knowledge of them. Not a single scientific term or distinction is the least to the purpose, for you would fain perceive something, and you must approach the object totally unprejudiced. You must be aware that no thing is what you have taken it to be. In what book is this world and its beauty described? Who has plotted the steps toward the discovery of beauty? You have got to be in a different state from common. Your greatest success will be simply to perceive that such things are, and you will have no communication to make to the Royal Society. If it were required to know the position of the fruit-dots or the character of the indusium, nothing could be easier than to ascertain it; but if it is required that you be affected by ferns, that they amount to anything, signify anything, to you, that they be another sacred scripture and revelation to you, helping to redeem your life, this end is not so surely accomplished. In the one case, you take a sentence and analyze it, you decide if it is printed in large [sic] primer or small pica; if it is long or short, simple or compound, and how many clauses it is composed of; if the i's are all dotted, or some for variety without dots; what the color and composition of the ink and the paper; and it is considered a fair or mediocre sentence accordingly, and you assign its place among the sentences you have seen and kept specimens of. But as for the meaning of the sentence, that is as completely overlooked as if it had none. This is the Chinese, the Aristotelean, method. But if you should ever perceive the meaning you would disregard all the rest. So far science goes, and it punctually leaves off there,—tells you finally where it is to be found and its synonyms, and rests from its labors.

A year went by, and in October, 1860, he put it another way:

▶ This haste to kill a bird or quadruped and make a skeleton of it, which many young men and some old ones exhibit, reminds me of the fable of the man who killed the hen that laid the golden eggs, and so got no more gold. It is a perfectly parallel case. Such is the knowledge which you may get from the anatomy as compared with the knowledge you get from the living creature. Every fowl lays golden eggs for him who can find them, or can detect alloy and base metal.

But Thoreau was at his best, as he himself realized, when he forgot his science and recorded only his love.

▶ *Jan. 30, 1841.*

Fair Haven Pond is *scored* with the trails of foxes, and you may see where they have gambolled and gone through a hundred evolutions, which testify to a singular listlessness and leisure in nature.

Suddenly, looking down the river, I saw a fox some sixty rods off, making across to the hills on my left. As the snow lay five inches deep, he made but slow progress, but it was no impediment to me. So, yielding to the instinct of the chase, I tossed my head aloft and bounded away, snuffing the air like a fox-hound, and spurning the world and Humane Society at each bound. It seemed the woods rang with the hunter's horn, and Diana and all the satyrs joined in the chase and cheered me on. Olympian and Elean youths were waving palms on the hills. In the meanwhile I gained rapidly on the fox; but he showed a remarkable presence of mind, for, instead of keeping up the face of the hill, which was steep and unwooded in that part, he kept along the slope in the direction of

Thoreau's $8 spyglass, bought in March, 1854, and his flute.

In 1853, a form letter reached Thoreau inviting him to join what is now called the American Association for the Advancement of Science. It prompted a passage in his Journal on March 5 (quoted on these pages). Not until nine months later, however, did he fill out the questionnaire and return it with a letter of refusal. Comparison of the letter with the Journal entry and the remarks on the form shows how troublesome Thoreau found it to explain his real feelings about science to a scientist.

The first page of the last Thoreau piece published before his death. It appeared in the Eighth Annual Report of the Massachusetts Board of Agriculture, 1861, and was given as a lecture in Concord September 20, 1860. It was both first-class ecology and literature.

SUCCESSION OF FOREST TREES.   11

SUCCESSION OF FOREST TREES.

From an Address before the Middlesex Agricultural Society.

BY HENRY D. THOREAU.

I have often been asked, as many of you have been, if I could tell how it happened, that when a pine wood was cut down, an oak one commonly sprang up, and *rice versa*. To which I have answered, and now answer, that I can tell—that it is no mystery to me. As I am not aware that this has been clearly shown by any one, I shall lay the more stress on this point. Let me lead you back into your wood-lots again.

When, hereabouts, a single forest tree or a forest springs up naturally where none of its kind grew before, I do not hesitate to say, though in some quarters still it may sound paradoxical, that it came from a seed. Of the various ways by which trees are *known* to be propagated—by transplanting, cuttings, and the like—this is the only supposable one under these circumstances. No such tree has ever been known to spring from any thing else. If any one asserts that it sprang from something else, or from nothing, the burden of proof lies with him.

It remains, then, only to show how the seed is transported from where it grows to where it is planted. This is done chiefly by the agency of the wind, water and animals. The lighter seeds, as those of pines and maples, are transported chiefly by wind and water; the heavier, as acorns and nuts, by animals.

In all the pines, a very thin membrane, in appearance much like an insect's wing, grows over and around the seed, and independent of it, while the latter is being developed within its base. Indeed this is often perfectly developed, though the seed is abortive, nature being, you would say, more sure to provide the means of transporting the seed, than to provide the seed to be transported. In other words, a beautiful thin sack is woven around the seed, with a handle to it such as the wind can take the forest, though he lost ground by it. Notwithstanding his fright, he took no step which was not beautiful. The course on his part was a series of most graceful curves. It was a sort of leopard canter, I should say, as if he were no-wise impeded by the snow, but were husbanding his strength all the while. When he doubled I wheeled and cut him off, bounding with fresh vigor, and Antaeus-like, recovering my strength each time I touched the snow. Having got near enough for a fair view, just as he was slipping into the wood, I gracefully yielded him the palm. He ran as though there were not a bone in his back, occasionally dropping his muzzle to the snow for a rod or two, and then tossing his head aloft when satisfied of his course. When he came to a declivity he put his fore feet together and slid down it like a cat. He trod so softly that you could not have heard it from any nearness, and yet with such expression that it would not have been quite inaudible at any distance. So, hoping this experience would prove a useful lesson to him, I returned to the village by the highway of the river.

1850.

I have been surprised to discover the amount and the various kinds of life which a single shallow swamp will sustain. On the south side of the pond, not more than a quarter of a mile from it, is a small meadow of ten or a dozen acres in the woods, considerably lower than Walden, and which by some is thought to be fed by the former by a subterranean out-let,—which is very likely, for its shores are quite springy and its supply of water is abundant and unfailing,—indeed tradition says that a sawmill once stood over its outlet, though its whole extent, including its sources, is not more than I have mentioned,—a meadow through which the Fitch-burg Railroad passes by a very high causeway, which required many a carload of sand, where the laborers for a long time seemed to make no progress, for the sand settled so much in the night that by morning they were where they were the day before, and finally the weight of the sand forced upward the adjacent crust of the meadow with the trees on it many feet, and cracked it for some rods around. It is a wet springy place throughout the summer, with a ditch-like channel, and in one part water stands the year round, with cat-o'-nine-tails and tussocks and muskrats' cabins rising above it, where good cranberries may be raked if you are careful to anticipate the frost which visits this cool hollow unexpectedly early. Well, as I was saying, I heard a splashing in the shallow and muddy water and stood awhile to observe the cause of it. Again and again I heard and saw the commotion, but could not guess the cause of it,—what kind of life had its residence in that insignificant pool. We sat down on the hillside. Ere long a muskrat came swimming by as if attracted by the same disturbance, and then another and another, till three had passed, and I began to suspect that they were at the bottom of it. Still ever and anon I observed the same commotion in the waters over the same spot, and at length I observed the snout of some creature slyly raised above the surface after each commotion, as if to see if it were observed by foes, and then but a few rods distant I saw another snout above the water and began to divine the cause of the disturbance. Putting off my shoes and stockings, I crept stealthily down the hill and waded out slowly and noiselessly about a rod from the firm land, keeping behind the tussocks, till I stood behind the tussock near which I had observed the splashing. Then, suddenly stooping over it, I saw through the shallow but muddy water that there was a mud turtle there, and thrusting in my hand at once caught him by the claw, and, quicker than I can tell it, heaved him high and dry ashore; and there came out with him a large pout just dead and partly devoured, which he held in his jaws. It was the pout in his flurry and the turtle in his struggles to hold him fast which had created the commotion. There he had lain, probably buried in the mud at the bottom up to his eyes, till the pout came sailing over, and then this musky lagune had put forth in the direction of his ventral fins, expanding suddenly under the influence of a more than vernal heat,—there are sermons in stones aye and mud turtles at the bottoms of the pools,—in the direction of his ventral fins, his tender white belly, where he kept no eye; and the minister squeaked his last. Oh, what an eye was there, my countrymen! buried in mud up to the lids, meditating on what? sleepless at the bottom of the pool, at the top of the bottom, directed heavenward, in no danger from motes. Pouts expect their foes not from below. Suddenly a mud volcano swallowed him up, seized his midriff; he fell into those relentless jaws from which there is no escape, which relax not their hold even in death. There the pout might calculate on remaining until nine days after the head was cut off. Sculled through Heywood's shallow meadow, not thinking of foes, looking through the water up into the sky. I saw his (the turtle's) brother sunning and airing his broad back like a ship bottom up which had been scuttled,—foundered at sea. I had no idea that there was so much going on in Heywood's meadow.

Aug. 23, 1851.

I saw a snake by the roadside and touched him with my foot to see if he were alive. He had a toad in his jaws, which he was preparing to swallow with his jaws distended to three times his width, but he relinquished his prey in haste and fled; and I thought, as the toad jumped leisurely away with his slime-covered hind-quarters glistening in the sun, as if I, his deliverer, wished to interrupt his meditations,—without a shriek or fainting,—I thought what a healthy indifference he manifested. Is not this the broad earth still? he said.

AN OBSERVER OF NATURE

April 16, 1852.

As I turned round the corner of Hubbard's Grove, saw a woodchuck, the first of the season, in the middle of the field, six or seven rods from the fence which bounds the wood, and twenty rods distant. I ran along the fence and cut him off, or rather overtook him, though he started at the same time. When I was only a rod and a half off, he stopped, and I did the same; then he ran again, and I ran up within three feet of him, when he stopped again, the fence being between us. I squatted down and surveyed him at my leisure. His eyes were dull black and rather inobvious, with a faint chestnut (?) iris, with but little expression and more of resignation than of anger. The general aspect was a coarse grayish brown, a sort of grisel (?). A lighter brown next the skin, then black or very dark brown and tipped with whitish rather loosely. The head between a squirrel and a bear, flat on the top and dark brown, and darker still or black on the tip of the nose. The whiskers black, two inches long. The ears very small and roundish, set far back and nearly buried in the fur. Black feet, with long and slender claws for digging. It appeared to tremble, or perchance shivered with cold. When I moved, it gritted its teeth quite loud, sometimes striking the under jaw against the other chatteringly, sometimes grinding one jaw on the other, yet as if more from instinct than anger. Whichever way I turned, that way it headed. I took a twig a foot long and touched its snout, at which it started forward and bit the stick, lessening the distance between us to two feet, and still it held all the ground it gained. I played with it tenderly awhile with the stick, trying to open its gritting jaws. Ever its long incisors, two above and two below, were presented. But I thought it would go to sleep if I stayed long enough. It did not sit upright as sometimes, but *standing* on its fore feet with its head down, *i.e.* half sitting, half standing. We sat looking at one another about half an hour, till we began to feel mesmeric influences. When I was tired, I moved away, wishing to see him run, but I could not start him. He would not stir as long as I was looking at him or could see him. I walked round him; he turned as fast and fronted me still. I sat down by his side within a foot. I talked to him *quasi* forest lingo, baby-talk, at any rate in a conciliatory tone, and thought that I had some influence on him. He gritted his teeth less. I chewed checkerberry leaves and presented them to his nose at last without a grit; though I saw that by so much gritting of the teeth he had worn them rapidly and they were covered with a fine white powder, which, if you measured it thus, would have made his anger terrible. He did not mind any noise I might make. With a little stick I lifted one of his paws to examine it, and held it up at pleasure. I turned him over to see what color he was beneath (darker or more purely brown), though he turned himself back again sooner than I could have wished. His tail was also all brown, though not very dark, rat-tail like, with loose hairs standing out on all sides like a caterpillar brush. He had a rather mild look. I spoke kindly to him. I reached checkerberry leaves to his mouth. I stretched my hands over him, though he turned up his head and still gritted a little. I laid my hand on him, but immediately took it off again, instinct not being wholly overcome. If I had had a few fresh bean leaves, thus in advance of the season, I am sure I should have tamed him completely. It was a frizzly tail. His is a humble, terrestrial color like the partridge's, well concealed where dead wiry grass rises above darker brown or chestnut dead leaves,—a modest color. If I had had some food, I should have ended with stroking him at my leisure. Could easily have wrapped him in my handkerchief. He was not fat nor particularly lean. I finally had to leave him without seeing him move from the place. A large, clumsy, burrowing squirrel. *Arctomys,* bear-mouse. I respect him as one of the natives. He lies there, by his color and habits so naturalized amid the dry leaves, the withered grass, and the bushes. A sound nap, too, he has enjoyed in his native fields, the past winter. I think I might learn some wisdom of him. His ancestors have lived here longer than mine. He is more thoroughly acclimated and naturalized than I. Bean leaves the red man raised for him, but he can do without them.

July 10, 1852.

There are but few fishes to be seen. They have, no doubt, retreated to the deepest water. In one somewhat muddier place, close to the shore, I came upon an old pout cruising with her young. She dashed away at my approach, but the fry remained. They were of various sizes from a third of an inch to an inch and a half long, quite black and pout-shaped, except that the head was most developed in the smallest. They were constantly moving about in a somewhat circular, or rather lenticular, school, about fifteen or eighteen inches in diameter, and I estimated that there were at least a thousand of them. Presently the old pout came back and took the lead of her brood, which followed her, or rather gathered about her, like chickens about a hen; but this mother had so many children she didn't know what to do. Her maternal yearnings must be on a great scale. When one half of the divided school found her out, they came down upon her and completely invested her like a small cloud. She was soon joined by another smaller pout, apparently her mate, and all, both old and young, began to be very familiar with me; they came round my legs and felt them with their feelers, and the old pouts nibbled my toes, while the fry half concealed my feet. Probably if I had been standing on the bank with my clothes on they would have been more shy. Ever and anon the old pouts dashed aside to drive away a passing bream or perch. The larger one kept circling about her charge, as if to keep them together within a certain

Seed plant specimens gathered by Thoreau. He dried and mounted them in six portfolios, now in the Harvard University Herbarium. The plants he picked he carried in the crown of his soft and battered hat, rather than use a botany-box. In his study (the garret) he stored these specimens, cases of eggs and lichens, Indian arrowheads and hatchets, and piles of nuts "of which he was as fond as squirrels," reported Channing.

compass. If any of her flock were lost or devoured she could hardly have missed them. I wondered if there was any calling of the roll at night,— whether she, like a faithful shepherdess, ever told her tale under some hawthorn in the river's dales. Ever ready to do battle with the wolves that might break into her fold. The young pouts are protected then for a season by the old. Some had evidently been hatched before the others. One of these large pouts had a large velvet-black spot which included the right pectoral fin, a kind of disease which I have often observed on them.

June 16, 1853.

Coming along near the celtis I heard a singular sound as of a bird in distress amid the bushes, and turned to relieve it. Next thought it a squirrel in an apple tree barking at me. Then found that it came from a hole in the ground under my feet, a loud sound between a grunting and a wheezing, yet not unlike the sound a red squirrel sometimes makes, but louder. Looking down the hole, I saw the tail and hind quarters of a woodchuck, which seemed to be contending with another further down. Reaching down carefully, I took hold of the tail, and, though I had to pull very hard indeed, I drew him out between the rocks a bouncing great fat fellow, and tossed him a little way down the hill. As soon as he recovered from his bewilderment he made for the hole again, but, I barring the way, he ran off elsewhere.

Jan. 31, 1855.

As I skated near the shore under Lee's Cliff, I saw what I took to be some scrags or knotty stubs of a dead limb lying on the bank beneath a white oak, close by me. Yet while I looked directly at them I could not but admire their close resemblance to partridges. I had come along with a rapid whir and suddenly halted right against them, only two rods distant, and, as my eyes watered a little from skating against the wind, I was not convinced that they were birds till I had pulled out my glass and deliberately examined them. They sat and stood, three of them, perfectly still with their heads erect, some darker feathers like ears, methinks, increasing their resemblance to scrabs [sic.], as where a small limb is broken off. I was much surprised at the remarkable stillness they preserved, instinctively relying on the resemblance to the ground for their protection, *i.e.* withered grass, dry oak leaves, dead scrags, and broken twigs. I thought at first that it was a dead oak limb with a few stub ends or scrabbs [sic.] sticking up, and for some time after I had noted the resemblance to birds, standing only two rods off, I could not be sure of their character on account of their perfect motionlessness, and it was not till I brought my glass to bear on them and saw their eyes distinctly, steadily glaring on me, their necks and every muscle tense with anxiety, that I was convinced. At length, on some signal which I did not perceive, they went with a whir, as if shot, off over the bushes.

June 10, 1856.

A painted tortoise laying her eggs ten feet from the wheeltrack on the Marlborough road. She paused at first, but I sat down within two feet, and she soon resumed her work. Had excavated a hollow about five inches wide and six long in the moistened sand, and cautiously, with long intervals, she continued her work, resting always on the same spot her fore feet, and never looking round, her eyes shut all but a narrow slit. Whenever I moved, perhaps to brush off a mosquito, she paused. A wagon approached, lumbering afar off, and then there was a pause, till it had passed and long, long after, a tedious, *naturlangsam* pause of the slow-blooded creature, a sacrifice of time such as those animals are up to which slumber half a year and live for centuries. It was twenty minutes before I discovered that she was not making the hole but filling it up slowly, having laid her eggs. She drew the moistened sand under herself, scraping it along from behind with both feet brought together, the claws turned inward. In the long pauses the ants troubled her (as mosquitoes me) by running over her eyes, which made her snap or dart out her head suddenly, striking the shell. She did not dance on the sand, nor finish covering the hollow quite so carefully as the one observed last year. She went off suddenly (and quickly at first), with a slow but sure instinct through the wood toward the swamp.

Sept. 12, 1857.

In an open part of the swamp, started a very large wood frog, which gave one leap and squatted still. I put down my finger, and though it shrank a little at first, it permitted me to stroke it as long as I pleased. Having passed, it occurred to me to return and cultivate its acquaintance. To my surprise, it allowed me to slide my hand under it and lift it up, while it squatted cold and moist on the middle of my palm, panting naturally. I brought it close to my eye and examined it. It was very beautiful seen thus nearly, not the dull dead-leaf color which I had imagined, but its back was like burnished bronze armor defined by a varied line on each side, where, as it seemed, the plates of armor united. It had four or five dusky bars which matched exactly when the legs were folded, showing that the painter applied his brush to the animal when in that position, and reddish-orange soles to its delicate feet. There was a conspicuous dark-brown patch along the side of the head, whose upper edge passed directly through the eye horizontally, just above its centre, so that the pupil and all below were dark and the upper portion of the iris golden. I have since taken up another in the same way.

20

Walden

WALDEN is Thoreau's masterwork. Written, as he tells us in the opening
paragraphs, in reply to the inquiries of his fellow townsmen, it uses as its
unifying theme the story of his two-year adventure in living in his cabin at
Walden Pond. For artistry's sake he combines the experiences of the two
years into one, opening the book with the building of the cabin in the spring,
continuing through his moving into the cabin on July 4th, planting,
weeding, and harvesting his bean patch, winterizing the cabin with plastered
walls and fireplace, watching the ice-harvesting and ice-fishing in the
winter, and ending the book with the return of spring. Such a pattern enables
him to use as his central symbol the theme of rebirth and renewal not only
of the world of nature around one but most importantly of one's own
spiritual development. "There is more day to dawn," he tells us. And in
that new day, if we will but exert the effort, we may achieve spiritual growth
that will overshadow by far man's spiritual and physical growth in the past.

Walden may be read and enjoyed on many levels. It is the account of his
life at the pond and of the world of nature around him. It is the account of
his spiritual growth. It is an exposition of the philosophy of the simple life.
It is a biting criticism of the foibles and follies of modern man and his life
of "quiet desperation." Each reader will find something in it for himself.
It is one of those rare books that it is almost impossible to read without
being personally affected by its philosophy. And it has drastically changed
the life of many a reader.

Thoreau wrote a large part of *Walden* while he lived at the pond. He
had an early version of the book sufficiently ready to promise in an advertisement bound into the back of *A Week on the Concord and Merrimack
Rivers* when it was published in 1849 that *Walden* would "be published
soon." But the failure of *A Week* postponed the publication of *Walden*
for five years. No publisher was willing to take the risk of a second failure.

Thoreau abandoned neither hope for nor work on the manuscript of
Walden. He reworked it, revised it, polished it, cut it and added to it through
eight distinct complete revisions. When one compares the final version with

These advance excerpts from *Walden* appeared in Sartain's *Union Magazine* in July and August, 1852.

On March 29, 1854, before publication of *Walden,* Greeley's *Tribune* ran a lengthy extract (left above) from the first chapter. Then on August 7, page 1 carried this ad (right above) and on August 10 *Walden* was announced at the top of a book-seller's current list.

Title page of the first edition, published August 9, 1854. Ticknor and Fields published *Walden* at a cost of 43 cents per copy. *Walden* was issued in the same year with Maria Cummins' moralistic romance, *The Lamplighter* (it sold 40,000 copies in eight weeks); T. S. Arthur's *Ten Nights in a Bar-Room*, the enormously popular temperance tract; Dickens' *Hard Times*; and B. P. Shillaber's *Life and Sayings of Mrs. Partington*, the Yankee Mrs. Malaprop, which sold 20,000 copies in its first printing.

In a copy of the first edition, Thoreau made several annotations, correcting typographical errors and inserting some additions. Here, on page 201, he wrote "kingfisher dart away from its cover," apparently intending it to be inserted after "skim over it." Some of his revisions were incorporated into later editions, but not this one.

Ellery Channing scribbled these notes on the title page of the copy Thoreau gave him. Angry with Ticknor & Fields, who had refused a book of his, Channing snipped the publisher's name from his copy.

the earliest (as published in J. Lyndon Shanley's *The Making of Walden*), he finds the improvement almost miraculous.

In 1852 Thoreau published two small excerpts from *Walden* in *Sartain's Union Magazine,* portions of the chapters on "Where I Lived, and What I Lived For" and "Sounds." But failure of *Sartain's* that very summer perhaps forestalled further serialization of the book. Finally, in 1854, apparently through Emerson's influence, the rising new firm of Ticknor & Fields (one of their first best sellers had been Hawthorne's *Scarlet Letter* in 1850) was persuaded to publish the book.

Thoreau worked on proofs of *Walden* throughout the spring of 1854, making corrections and additions to the text right up to the last minute. In late July, Horace Greeley, faithful as ever in advancing Thoreau's career, published long extracts from the book in the pages of his New York *Tribune.* The book itself was published early in August. In Thoreau's journal we find two pertinent entries:

▸ Fields to-day sends me a specimen copy of my "Walden." It is to be published on the 12th inst.

That was on August 2. A week later:

▸ Wednesday—To Boston.
"Walden" published. Elder-berries. Waxwork yellowing.

The "American Diogenes" was given a lengthy review in *Chambers's Journal,* November 21, 1857.

The *National Anti-Slavery Standard* carried the most enthusiastic review on December 16, 1854.

CHAMBERS'S JOURNAL

Married — married — parbleu — I understand ! — rnfing !—even Clémence'——
might as well have shaken a log of wood ; and I nped back into my own bed in a state of indescrib-e agitation and dismay.

AN AMERICAN DIOGENES.

ren Philip of Macedon announced his intention to ade Corinth, the inhabitants of that city, overlook-, or feigning not to perceive, their utter incapability resistance, affected to make great preparations for ence ; while Diogenes, who, like many of us, even the present time, delighted to ridicule the follies he not himself commit, rolled about his tub in an eited, bustling manner, by way of deriding the ay, fruitless show of opposition made by the feeble rinthians. The transatlantic Diogenes, however, en he observed the foolish, aimless bustle made by modern Corinthians of the world, in pursuit of the red dollar and its glittering accessories, instead of ling about his tub, quietly sat down in it, and wrote interesting book, replete with pithy, original obser-ions, but strongly tinctured with the inevitable gmatism that ever attends the one *soi-disant* wise n who assumes to be the teacher of all the rest of race. Henry D. Thoreau, the American Diogenes, if may presume to term him so—assuredly we mean offence—is a graduate of Harvard univers e scholar, and a transcendentalist of the ool though he goes much further

this period are ple though, like all soli the importance of h like an obelisk in t means barren expan
The building of tions. He wondere came across a man an occupation as bu he says, ' some of th his own house, as th nest. Who knows l ings with their ow themselves and fan the poetic faculty as birds universally So, as he hewed his as musically, at le bird—

‘ Men say
But lo !
The art:
And a t
The win
Is all th

As Mr Thoreau s glass, ironwork, an

New Publications.

WALDEN ; OR, LIFE IN THE WOODS. By Henry D. Thoreau, Author of "A Week on the Concord and Merrimack Rivers."

These books spring from a depth of thought which will not suffer them to be put by, and are written in a spirit in striking contrast with that which is uppermost in our time and country. Out of the heart of practical, hard-working, progres sive New England come these Oriental utterances. The life exhibited in them teaches us, much more impressively than any number of sermons could, that this Western activity of which we are so proud, these material improvements, this commer-cial enterprise, this rapid accumulation of wealth, even our external, associated philanthropic action, are very easily overrated. The true glory of the human soul is not to be reached by the most rapid travelling in car or steamboat, by the instant transmission of intelligence however far, by the most speedy accumulation of a fortune, and how-ever efficient measures we may adopt for the re-

A YANKEE DIOGENES.

Walden; or, Life in the Woods. By HENRY D.
THOREAU. Boston: Ticknor & Fields. 1854.

THE New England character is essentially anti-Diogenic; the Yankee is too shrewd not to comprehend the advantages of living in what we call the world; there are no bargains to be made in the desert, nobody to be taken advantage of in the woods, while the dwellers in tubs and shanties have slender opportu...... of bettering their condition ......lander...... for his amusement, he liked to go into Concord and listen to the village gossips in the stores and taverns. Mr. Thoreau informs us that he lived alone in the woods, by the shore of Walden Pond, in a shanty built by his own hands, a mile from any neighbor, two years and a half. What he did there besides writing the book before us, cultivating beans, sounding Walden Pond, reading Homer, baking johnny-cakes, studying Brahminical theology, listening to chipping-squirrels,......

The review in *Putnam's Monthly,* October, 1854.

Emerson, a few weeks after the publication of *Walden,* wrote his friend George Partridge Bradford:

All American kind are delighted with "Walden" as far as they have dared say. The little pond sinks in these very days as tremulous at its human fame. I do not know if the book has come to you yet;—but it is cheerful, sparkling, readable, with all kinds of merits, & rising sometimes to very great heights. We account Henry the undoubted King of all American lions. He is walking up & down Concord, firm-looking, but in a tremble of great expectation.

By early fall the reviews began to appear. Although some were unfavorable—one dismissing him as a "rural humbug," another wondering snidely if his experiment were so successful why he hadn't settled down at Walden Pond permanently—many commented favorably and a few showed real insight into the work. The best review of all appeared, anonymously, in the *National Anti-Slavery Standard* for December 16, 1854. Thoreau himself suspected that it was written by his friend H. G. O. Blake, but there is no proof.

These title pages are taken from some of the 150 different editions of *Walden* issued since Thoreau's death. The Danes originally published *Walden* in a small limited edition, which sold out within a week because of the popularity Thoreau won during the Danish resistance movement of World War II when his "Civil Disobedience" was used as a manual of arms. *Walden* has been in print there ever since. Japan has had many editions, a dozen translations into Japanese and several in English. The Dutch experimental colony named "Walden" issued the edition shown here. Russia saw an abridged *Walden* in 1900, and the full text in 1910. There have been at least eight translations into German.

Left to right:
Norwegian edition, Oslo, 1953.
Sanskrit edition, Paynar, India, 1957.
Swedish edition, Stockholm, 1947.
Finnish edition, Helsinki, 1954.
German edition, Jena, Germany, 1922.
Italian edition, Venice, 1928.
Portuguese edition, Rio de Janeiro, 1953.
Greek edition, Athens, 1950.
Danish edition, Copenhagen, 1949.
French edition, Paris, 1922.
Spanish edition, Buenos Aires, 1949.
Japanese edition, Tokyo, 1949.
Dutch edition, Amsterdam, 1902.
Russian edition, Moscow, 1910.

The earliest known authentic portrait of Thoreau was made by Samuel Worcester Rowse, whose crayon drawings made him internationally famous. A frequent visitor to Concord, he boarded with the Thoreau family in the summer of 1854 when *Walden* was published and there made the crayon portrait that now hangs in the Concord Free Public Library. Eben J. Loomis, father of Emily Dickinson's editor, Mabel Loomis Todd, was staying with the Thoreaus at the same time and tells of the creation of the portrait:

"I was very much interested in watching him (Rowse) while he was watching the expression of Henry's face. For two or three weeks he did not put a pencil to paper; but one morning at breakfast, he suddenly jumped up from the table, asked to be excused and disappeared for the rest of the day. The next morning he brought down the crayon, almost exactly in its present form, scarcely another touch was put upon it.

"It is for me, on the whole, the most satisfactory likeness, for it represents Henry just as he was in that summer, so memorable to me, memorable for my intimacy with Henry."

The Rowse crayon unquestionably is romantic in approach. In Sophia Thoreau's words, "It betrays the poet." But she and the other members of the family considered it a good likeness and said they "always like it."

Copies of *Walden* were shipped to England for sale. Nathaniel Hawthorne, then the American consul at Liverpool, did his share to stir up interest in the book by recommending it strongly to his British friends. The best of the reviews to appear there was by Marian Evans, better known as George Eliot, the novelist. Her comments appeared in the *Westminster Review* for January, 1856:

> In a volume called *Walden; or, Life in the Woods,* published last year, but quite interesting enough to make it worth while for us to break our rule by a retrospective notice—we have a bit of pure American life (not the 'go a-head' species, but its opposite pole), animated by that energetic, yet calm spirit of innovation, that practical as well as theoretic independence of formulae, which is peculiar to some of the finer American minds. The writer tells us how he chose, for some years, to be a stoic of the woods; how he built his house; how he earned the necessaries of his simple life by cultivating a bit of ground. He tells his system of diet, his studies, his reflections, and his observations of natural phenomena. These last are not only made by a keen eye, but have their interest enhanced by passing through the medium of a deep poetic sensibility; and, indeed, we feel throughout the book the presence of a refined as well as a hardy mind. People—very wise in their own eyes—who would have every man's life ordered according to a particular pattern, and who are intolerant of every existence the utility of which is not palpable to them, may pooh-pooh Mr. Thoreau and this episode in his history, as unpractical and dreamy. Instead of contesting their opinion ourselves, we will let Mr. Thoreau speak for himself. There is plenty of sturdy sense mingled with his unworldliness.

Sales of the book were not remarkable, but nonetheless much better than those for *A Week*. Ticknor & Fields Cost Books show that 2,000 copies of *Walden* were issued in the first printing. By 1859 the book was out of print. A second printing of 280 copies was made in March and April, 1862, and another 280 in a third printing in November and December of that year. His contract gave Thoreau a ten per cent royalty on the retail price ($1.00) of all copies sold.

Since then *Walden* has never been out of print and has appeared in at least one hundred and fifty different editions, many of the individual editions selling up in the hundreds of thousands of copies. There are probably more copies of it in print than any other American literary work of nonfiction that appeared in the nineteenth century. It has also been translated into Czechoslovakian, Danish, Dutch, Finnish, French, German, Greek, Hebrew, Italian, Japanese, Norse, Portuguese, Russian, Sanskrit, Spanish, and Swedish.

21

Disciples

ALTHOUGH THOREAU never succeeded during his lifetime in attracting a wide audience of readers, he did nonetheless attract a small group of devoted admirers.

Earliest and most devoted of these was Harrison G. O. Blake, a Harvard graduate and former Unitarian minister who lived in the nearby city of Worcester. He was a solemn, conscientious man, one whom Emerson described as the type who would never forget to return a borrowed umbrella. Blake told the story of his friendship with Thoreau for the English biographer Henry Salt:

> I was introduced to him first by Mr. Emerson more than forty years ago, though I had known him by sight before college. I recall nothing of that first interview unless it be some remarks upon astronomy, and his want of interest in the study as compared with studies relating more directly to this world—remarks such as he made here and there in his writings. My first real introduction was from the reading of an article of his in the Dial on "Aulus Persius Flaccus," which appears now in the Week. That led to my first writing to him, and to his reply, which is published in the volume of letters. Our correspondence continued for more than twelve years, and we visited each other at times, he coming here to Worcester, commonly to read something in public, or being on his way to read somewhere else.
>
> As to the outward incidents of our intercourse, I think of little or nothing that it seems worth while to write. Our conversation, or rather his talking, when we were together, was in the strain of his letters and of his books. Our relation, as I look back on it, seems almost an impersonal one, and illustrates well his remark that "our thoughts are the epochs in our lives: all else is but as a journal of the winds that blew while we were here." His personal appearance did not interest me particularly, except as the associate of his spirit, though I felt no discord between them. When together, we had little inclination to talk of personal matters.

Daniel Ricketson first met Thoreau on December 25, 1854. When Ricketson had read *Walden* immediately upon its publication in the summer of 1854, he had written Thoreau a letter of enthusiastic praise and extended an invitation to Thoreau to visit him whenever he was in the vicinity of New Bedford. Finding that he was to lecture in New Bedford on December 26, he wrote Ricketson that he would visit him on the 25th. Ricketson wrote of that first meeting:

"My first interview with him was so peculiar that I will venture to state it. The season was winter, a snow had lately fallen, and I was engaged in shovelling the accumulated mass from the entrance to my house, when I perceived a man walking towards me bearing an umbrella in one hand and a leather travelling-bag in the other. So unlike my ideal Thoreau, whom I had fancied, from the robust nature of his mind and habits of life, to be a man of unusual vigor and size, that I did not suspect, although I had expected him in the morning, that the slight, quaint-looking person before me was the Walden philosopher. There are few persons who had previously read his works that were not disappointed by his personal appearance. As he came near to me I gave him the usual salutation, and supposing him to be either a peddler or some way-traveller, he at once remarked, 'You don't know me.' The truth flashed on my mind, and concealing my own surprise I at once took him by the hand and led him to the room already prepared for him, feeling a kind of disappointment—a disappointment, however, which soon passed off, and never again obtruded itself to the philosopher's disadvantage. In fact, I soon began to see that Nature had dealt kindly by him, and that this apparently slender personage was physically capable of enduring far more than the ordinary class of men, although he had then begun to show signs of failure of strength in his knees."

Ricketson made this sketch of Thoreau to accompany the above description and pasted the sketch in his copy of *Walden*. It is the only full-length drawing from life that we have of Thoreau.

His aim was directed so steadily and earnestly towards what is essential in our experience, that beyond all others of whom I have known, he made but a single impression on me. Geniality, versatility, personal familiarity are, of course, agreeable in those about us, and seem necessary in human intercourse, but I did not miss them in Thoreau, who was, while living, and is still in my recollection and in what he has left to us, such an effectual witness to what is highest and almost precious in life. As I re-read his letters from time to time, which I never tire of doing, I am apt to find new significance in them, am still warned and instructed by them, with more force occasionally than ever before; so that in a sense they are still in the mail, have not altogether reached me yet, and will not probably before I die. They may well be regarded as addressed to those who can read them best.

Blake later inherited Thoreau's manuscript journals from Sophia Thoreau and in the 1880's helped to popularize Thoreau as a naturalist by editing a series of selections from the journals, issuing them in four volumes, one for each season of the year.

Next in importance among Thoreau's followers was Daniel Ricketson, a New Bedford Quaker who read *Walden* when it appeared in August of 1854 and immediately wrote Thoreau of his admiration of the book. At Ricketson's invitation Thoreau visited him in New Bedford the next Christmas and the two corresponded and visited back and forth for the remainder of Thoreau's life. Ricketson was a man of independent means, but he affected a "shanty" in the backyard of his estate where he did his own reading and writing. Thoreau tells of a visit to the Shanty in April, 1857:

▶ D. R.'s shanty is about half a dozen rods southwest of his house (which may be forty rods from the road), nearly between his house and

One of Thoreau's first disciples, Harrison Gray Otis Blake, a Worcester teacher. The two men took many excursions together between 1848 and Thoreau's last illness. The popular notion of Thoreau as primarily a naturalist stems from the four volumes on the seasons that Blake quarried from the journal manuscripts after Thoreau's death.

Theophilus Brown, the tailor and "wit of Worcester" whose "Emporium of Fashion" was a rendezvous for the local intelligentsia. He helped organize lectures for Thoreau to give before small audiences in the Blake parlor. T. W. Higginson, the Worcester minister and abolitionist, spoke of Brown as "the freshest and most original mind in Worcester, by vocation a tailor, and sending out more sparkles of wit and humor over his measuring tape and scissors than any one else would extract from Rabelais or Montaigne."

barn; is twelve by fourteen feet, with seven-feet posts, with common pentroof. In building it, he directed the carpenter to use Western boards and timber, though some Eastern studs (spruce?) were inserted. He had already occupied a smaller shanty at "Woodlee" about a mile south. The roof is shingled and the sides made of matched boards and painted a light clay-color with chocolate (?)-colored blinds. Within, it is not plastered and is open to the roof, showing the timbers and rafters and rough boards and cross-timbers overhead as if ready for plastering. The door is at the east end with a small window on each side of it; a similar window on each side the building, and one at the west end, the latter looking down the garden walk. In front of the last window is a small box stove with a funnel rising to a level with the plate, and there inserted in a small brick chimney which rests on planks. On the south side the room, against the stove, is a rude settle with a coarse cushion and pillow; on the opposite side, a large low desk, with some book-shelves above it; on the same side, by the window, a small table covered with books; and in the northeast corner, behind the door, an old-fashioned secretary, its pigeonholes stuffed with papers. On the opposite side as you enter, is place for fuel, which the boy leaves each morning, a place to hang greatcoats. There were two small pieces of carpet on the floor, and Ricketson or one of his guests swept out the shanty each morning. There was a small kitchen clock hanging in the southwest corner and a map of Bristol County behind the settle.

The west and northwest side is well-nigh covered with slips of paper, on which are written some sentence or paragraph from R.'s favorite books. I noticed, among the most characteristic, Dibdin's "Tom Tackle," a translation of Anacreon's "Cicada," lines celebrating tobacco, Milton's "How charming is divine philosophy," etc., "Inveni requiem: Spes et

Fortuna valete. Nil mihi vobiscum est: ludite nunc alios" (is it Petrarch?) (this is also over the door), "Mors aequo pulsat," etc., some lines of his own in memory of A. J. Downing, "Not to be in a hurry," over the desk, and many other quotations celebrating retirement, country life, simplicity, humanity, sincerity, etc., etc., from Cowper and other English poets, and similar extracts from newspapers. There were also two or three advertisements,—one of a cattle-show exhibition, another warning not to kill birds contrary to law (he being one of the subscribers ready to enforce the act), advertisement of a steamboat on Lake Winnepiseogee, etc., cards of his business friends. The size of different brains from Hall's Journal of Health, and "Take the world easy." A sheet of blotted blotting-paper tacked up, and of Chinese character from a tea-chest. Also a few small pictures and pencil sketches, the latter commonly caricatures of his visitors or friends, as "The Trojan" (Channing) and "Van Best." I take the more notice of these particulars because his peculiarities are so commonly unaffected. He has long been accustomed to put these scraps on his walls and has a basketfull somewhere, saved from the old shanty. Though there were some quotations which had no right there, I found all his peculiarities faithfully expressed,—his humanity, his fear of death, love of retirement, simplicity, etc.

The more characteristic books were Bordley's "Husbandry," Drake's "Indians," Barber's "Historical Collections," Zimmermann on Solitude,

Daniel Ricketson, about 1850, four years before Thoreau became the New Bedford family's friend.

Calvin Greene, who as a young man from Rochester, Michigan, began corresponding with Thoreau in 1856. They never met. Thoreau wrote him: "You may rely on it that you have the best of me in my books, and that I am not worth seeing personally— the stuttering, blundering, clodhopper that I am."

Bigelow's "Plants of Boston, etc.," Farmer's Register of the First Settlers of New England," Marshall's "Gardening," Nicol's "Gardener," John Woolman, "The Modern Horse Doctor," Downing's "Fruits, etc.," "The Farmer's Library," "Walden," Dymond's Essays, Job Scott's Journal, Morton's Memorial, Bailey's Dictionary, Downing's "Landscape Gardening, etc.," "The Task," Nuttall's Ornithology, Morse's Gazetteer, "The Domestic Practice of Hydropathy," "John Buncle," Dwight's Travels, Virgil, Young's "Night Thoughts," "History of Plymouth," and other "Shanty Books."

There was an old gun, hardly safe to fire, said to be loaded with an inextractable charge, and also an old sword over the door, also a tin sign "D. Ricketson's Office" (he having set up for a lawyer once) and a small crumpled horn there. I counted more than twenty rustic canes scattered about, a dozen or fifteen pipes of various patterns, mostly the common, two spyglasses, an open paper of tobacco, an Indian's jaw dug up, a stuffed blue jay and pine grosbeak, and a rude Indian stone hatchet, etc., etc. There was a box with fifteen or twenty knives, mostly very large and old-fashioned jack-knives, kept for curiosity, occasionally given away to a boy or friend. A large book full of pencil sketches to be inspected by whomsoever, containing countless sketches of his friends and acquaintances and himself and of wayfaring men whom he had met, Quakers, etc., etc., and now and then a vessel under full sail or an old-fashioned house, sketched on a peculiar pea-green paper. A pail of water stands behind the door, with a peculiar tin cup for drinking made in France.

One of the most devoted of Thoreau's disciples was Thomas Cholmondeley (pronounced "Chum-ley"), a wealthy young Englishman who made a pilgrimage to Concord in the fall of 1854 to see Emerson, shocking the plain-living Transcendentalists by arriving with a personal valet. But when he met Thoreau (Emerson had suggested that he might board at Mrs. Thoreau's), he much to Emerson's amusement lost all interest in Emerson and proceeded to devote himself entirely to Thoreau. When he returned to England, he sent Thoreau a magnificent collection of more than forty volumes of Oriental works (at that time probably the largest collection of Orientalia in the United States). Thoreau, deeply grateful, announced their arrival in a letter to Daniel Ricketson saying "I send you information of this as I might of the birth of a child."

Cholmondeley often tried—but always unsuccessfully—to persuade Thoreau to visit him in England. He visited Thoreau once again briefly in 1858 in Concord and they continued to correspond until Thoreau's death.

There were other disciples—B. B. Wiley, a Providence businessman who later moved to Chicago, where Thoreau visited him in 1860; Calvin Greene, a young free-thinker from Rochester, Michigan, who never met Thoreau but corresponded at length with him; and Theo Brown, a Worcester tailor, who met Thoreau often at Blake's house and who occasionally skated down the rivers to visit Thoreau in Concord.

These men were disciples; they believed in Thoreau's philosophy of the simple life and in his love of nature. But significantly none of them was an imitator. They each took to heart Thoreau's caution:

▶ I would not have any one adopt *my* mode of living on any account; for, beside that before he has fairly learned it I may have found out another for myself, I desire that there may be as many different persons in the world as possible; But I would have each one be very careful to find out and pursue *his own way,* and not his father's or his mother's or his neighbor's instead.

The young Englishman, Thomas Cholmondeley, who met Thoreau in Concord in 1854. Cholmondeley was an author, a mountaineer, and later a soldier in the Crimean War. He tried many times to get Thoreau to visit him in England, but when Thoreau refused, came to Concord for another visit in 1858. Cholmondeley died young.

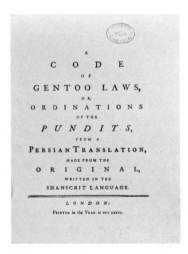

The title page of one of the 44 Oriental volumes Cholmondeley sent Thoreau in November, 1855, and his inscription.

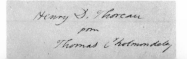

22

The Greatest Democrat

In the fall of 1856 Thoreau spent a month at Eagleswood, New Jersey; it was, after the Staten Island period, his longest stay away from home and it was on this occasion that he met Walt Whitman. The invitation had come from Marcus Spring, the New York businessman and abolitionist who had financed a "Union" for communal living in the little village at the edge of Perth Amboy. Workshops, artists' studios, apartments, and a school primarily for the children of the members were planned to encourage "a freer, larger, more harmonious form of human existence." But like so many other experimental communities of the day, Eagleswood soon went under. From an Association it turned into a close circle of congenial friends, centered around the school which alone survived, under the direction of Theodore Weld.

It was Bronson Alcott, then making a conversational tour of the New York region, who had suggested to Marcus Spring that Thoreau be invited to give lectures at the school and to survey Spring's estate nearby. Thoreau accepted, and came down by way of Norwich to New York in a steamer. He missed the early boat for Perth Amboy, he wrote Sophia:

▶ . . . so I spent the forenoon there, called on Greeley, (who was not in) met [F.A.T.] Bellew in Broadway and walked into his workshop, read at the Astor Library &c &c—I arrived here about 30 miles from N.Y. about 5 pm Saturday, in company with Miss E. Peabody, who was returning in the same covered wagon from the Landing to Eagleswood, which last place she has just left for the winter. This is a queer place— There is one large long stone building, which cost some $40000, in which I do not know exactly who or how many work—(one or two familiar faces, & more familiar names have turned up)—a few shops & offices, an old farm house and Mr. Spring's perfectly private residence within 20 rods of the main building. "The City of Perth Amboy" is about as big as Concord, and Eagleswood is 1¼ miles S W of it, on the bay side. The central fact here is evidently Mr. Weld's school—recently established—around which various other things revolve. Saturday evening I went to the school room, hall, or what not, to see the children & their teachers & patrons dance. Mr. Weld, a kind looking man with a long white beard, danced with them, & Mr. [E.J.] Cutler his assistant, lately from Cambridge, who is acquainted [with] Sanborn, Mr. Spring— and others. This Sat. eve-dance is a regular thing, & it is thought something strange if you dont attend. They take it for granted that you want society!

Sunday forenoon, I attended a sort of Quaker meeting at the same place—(The Quaker aspect & spirit prevails here—Mrs. Spring says "—does thee not?") where it was expected that the spirit would move me (I having been previously spoken to about it) & it, or something else, did, an inch or so. I said just enough to set them a little by the ears & make it lively. I had excused myself by saying that I could not adapt myself to a particular audience, for all the speaking & lecturing here has reference to the children, who are far the greater part of the audience, & they are not so bright as N.E. children. Imagine them sitting close to the wall all around a hall—with old Quaker looking men & women here & there. There sat Mrs. Weld (Grimke) & her sister, two elderly gray-headed ladies, the former in extreme Bloomer costume, which was what you may call remarkable; Mr. [Arnold] Buffum with broad face & a great white beard, looking like a pier head made of the cork tree with the bark on, as if he could buffet a considerable wave;—James G. Birney,

---

In June of 1856, while on a visit to Worcester, Massachusetts, Thoreau posed for the daguerreotypist Benjamin D. Maxham. Three daguerreotypes were made, but they are so much alike that the differences can be found only upon close examination of such details as the wrinkles in the coat and the smoothness of the hair. Two of them he gave immediately to his Worcester friends H. G. O. Blake and Theo. Brown; the third he sent to his Michigan admirer Calvin H. Greene who had sent Thoreau five dollars, asking that a copy of each of his books be sent to a brother in California and that a daguerreotype be sent to Greene himself. Thoreau accompanied the portrait with $1.70 change and a letter stating in part, "While in Worcester this week I obtained the accompanying daguerreotype—which my friends think is pretty good—though better looking than I." The beard—known as Galway whiskers—had been grown the year before, apparently in an effort to prevent throat colds.

Sanborn, who first met Thoreau in 1855, describes Thoreau in his diary at the time:

"He is a little under size, with a huge Emersonian nose, bluish gray eyes, brown hair, and a ruddy weather-beaten face, which reminds me of some shrewd and honest animal's—some retired philosophical woodchuck or magnanimous fox. He dresses very plainly, wears his collar turned over like Mr. Emerson and often an old dress-coat, broad in the skirts, and by no means a fit. He walks about with a brisk, rustic air, and never seems tired."

[*246*]

formerly candidate for the Presidency, with another particularly white head & beard—Edward Palmer, the anti-money man (for whom communities were made) with [word] ample beard somewhat grayish. Some of them I suspect are very worthy people. Of course you are wondering to what extent all these make one family—to what extent 20. Mrs. [Caroline] Kirkland, and this [a] name only to me, I saw—She just bought a lot here. They all know more about your neighbors & acquaintances than you suspected.

On Sunday evening, I read the moose-story to the children to their satisfaction. Ever since I have been constantly engaged in surveying Eagleswood—through woods ravines marshes & along the shore, dodging the tide—through cat-briar mud & beggar ticks—having no time to look up or think where I am—(it takes 10 or 15 minutes before each meal to pick the beggar ticks out of my clothes—burrs & the rest are left—rents mended at the first convenient opportunity) I shall be engaged perhaps as much longer. Mr Spring wants me to help him about

Walt Whitman in 1856, the year he met Thoreau. "He is a great fellow . . . apparently the greatest democrat the world has seen," Thoreau said.

Leaves

of

Grass.

Brooklyn, New York:
1855.

Title page of the first edition, published at Whitman's own expense. "It is a great primitive poem, an alarum or trumpet-note ringing through the American camp," was Thoreau's response on reading it.

setting out an orchard & vineyard—Mr. Birney asks me to survey a small piece for him, & Mr Alcott who has just come down here for the 3d Sunday—says that Greeley (I left my name for him) invites him & me to go to his home with him next Saturday morning & spend the Sunday.

It seems a twelve-month since I was not here—but I hope to get settled deep into my den again ere long. The hardest thing to find here is solitude & Concord. I am at Mr Spring's house—Both he & she & their family are quite agreeable.

Thoreau stayed on at Eagleswood much longer than he expected. "I am merely Thoreau the surveyor here," he wrote his Worcester friend Blake on November 19. By now he had read three of his old lectures to the Eagleswood group "and unexpectedly, with rare success—i.e., I was aware that what I was saying was silently taken in by their ears." He found time, too, to go over to New York and prowl through two antique bookstores on Fulton Street.

Then came the meeting of the two men whose American classics had been published within a year of one another. Possibly Thoreau had read Whitman's *Leaves of Grass* in Emerson's copy. On Saturday, November 8, he told Blake, he went with Alcott and Greeley,

▶ . . . by invitation of the last, to G.'s farm, thirty-six miles north of New York. The next day A. and I heard Beecher preach; and what was more, we visited Whitman the next morning (A. had already seen him), and were much interested and provoked. He is apparently the greatest democrat the world has seen. Kings and aristocracy go by the board at once, as they have long deserved to. A remarkably strong though coarse nature, of a sweet disposition, and much prized by his friends. Though peculiar and rough in his exterior, his skin (all over (?)) red, he is essentially a gentleman. I am still somewhat in a quandary about him,—feel that he is essentially strange to me, at any rate; but I am surprised by the sight of him. He is very broad, but, as I have said, not fine. He said that I misapprehended him. I am not quite sure that I do. He told us that he loved to ride up and down Broadway all day on an omnibus, sitting beside the driver, listening to the roar of the carts, and sometimes gesticulating and declaiming Homer at the top of his voice. He has long been an editor and writer for the newspapers,—was editor of the "New Orleans Crescent" once; but now has no employment but to read and write in the forenoon, and walk in the afternoon, like all the rest of the scribbling gentry.

On November 25 Thoreau was back home again. "Am glad to get back to New England," the Journal notes, "the dry, sandy, wholesome land, land

of scrub oaks and birches and white pines, now in her russet dress, reminding me of her flaxen-headed children."

He could not stop thinking about Whitman. They had met a second time
on November 10 when, with Alcott, he had found the poet at his mother's
home in Brooklyn. Now, some two weeks after his return to Concord, he
told Blake again of his impressions:

> ▶   That Walt Whitman, of whom I wrote to you, is the most interesting
> fact to me at present. I have just read his 2nd edition (which he gave
> me) and it has done me more good than any reading for a long time.
> Perhaps I remember best the poem of Walt Whitman an American &
> the Sun Down Poem. There are 2 or 3 pieces in the book which are dis-
> agreeable to say the least, simply sensual. He does not celebrate love at
> all. It is as if the beasts spoke. I think that men have not been ashamed
> of themselves without reason. No doubt, there have always been dens
> where such deeds were unblushingly recited, and it is no merit to com-
> pete with their inhabitants. But even on this side, he has spoken more
> truth than any American or modern that I know. I have found his poem
> exhilirating encouraging. As for its sensuality,—& it may turn out to
> be less sensual than it appeared—I do not so much wish that those parts
> were not written, as that men & women were so pure they could read
> them without harm, that is, without understanding them. One woman
> told me that no woman could read it as if a man could read what a
> woman could not. Of course Walt Whitman can communicate to us no

Residence of M. Spring. Esqr   Eagleswood House

The large stone building at Eagleswood that housed Weld's school. At left is
Marcus Spring's home, where Thoreau stayed for a month.

experience, and if we are shocked, whose experience is it that we are reminded of?

On the whole it sounds to me very brave & American after whatever deductions. I do not believe that all the sermons so called that have been preached in this land put together are equal to it for preaching—

We ought to rejoice greatly in him. He occasionally suggests something a little more than human. You cant confound him with the other inhabitants of Brooklyn or New York. How they must shudder when they read him! He is awfully good.

To be sure I sometimes feel a little imposed on. By his heartiness & broad generalities he puts me into a liberal frame of mind prepared to see wonders—as it were sets me upon a hill or in the midst of a plain— stirs me well up, and then—throws in a thousand of brick. Though rude & sometimes ineffectual, it is a great primitive poem,—an alarum or trumpet-note ringing through the American camp. Wonderfully like the Orientals, too, considering that when I asked him if he had read them, he answered, "No: tell me about them."

I did not get far in conversation with him,—two more being present, —and among the few things which I chanced to say, I remember that one was, in answer to him as representing America, that I did not think much of America or of politics, and so on, which may have been somewhat of a damper to him.

Since I have seen him, I find that I am not disturbed by any brag or egoism in his book. He may turn out the least of a braggart of all, having a better right to be confident.

He is a great fellow.

On the day of that letter, December 7, Thoreau took his first skate of the winter, to Fair Haven Pond. His feet needed a few minutes to get used to the skates but soon he was gliding freely over the three-inch ice. "That grand old poem called Winter is round again," he told his Journal.

23

A Plea for
Captain John Brown

"I DO NOT BELIEVE that the North will soon come to blows with the South on this question [of slavery]," Thoreau confided to his journal in April, 1851. He was no peace-at-any-price man trying to reassure himself. On the contrary: "It would be too bright a page to be written in the history of the race at present," he said.

It was the carrying off of Sims to slavery that moved Thoreau to despair of finding men ready to go to war in behalf of another race in their midst. Even the men of the Revolution—the Hancocks, Adamses, Otises—"even they," he said, "if somewhat braver and less corrupt" than the men of 1851, "were not men of that much principle and generosity."

There was a man, however, who measured up to Thoreau's standard. He was John Brown, the Connecticut farmer, surveyor, and wool-grower who, when he heard the news of the passage of the Fugitive Slave Law, organized a band of Gileadites among the fugitive slaves he knew, and urged them to resist the law at all costs.

When the troubles in Kansas broke out, Brown joined his sons there to help defend the Free-Soilers. Almost two years later, he was back East, reporting on his battles with the pro-slavers in Kansas and seeking funds for his secret plans to carry the war into the heart of slavery.

Early in 1857, Brown walked into the Boston office of the New England Emigrant Aid Society, seeking introductions to men who could raise the arms and ammunition to carry out his plans. The society's secretary was young Frank Sanborn, on leave of absence from the Concord Academy.

Soon, with the help of Boston men, he had the guns to arm his force training in Iowa. Early in March he came by the noon train to Concord and had lunch at Mrs. Thoreau's, with the boarders and Henry present. In the afternoon, Emerson dropped by and talked to Brown. That night, a hundred people came to hear Brown speak at the Town House; Emerson was impressed.

One of his good points was [he noted in his Journal] the folly of the peace party in Kansas, who believed that their strength lay in the greatness of their wrongs, and so discountenanced resistance. He wished to know if their wrong was greater than the negro's, and what kind of strength that gave to the negro?

He believes on his own experience that one good, believing, strong-minded man is worth a hundred, nay, twenty thousand men without character, for a settler in a new country; and that the right men will give a permanent direction to the fortunes of a state. For one of these bullying, drinking rowdies,—he seemed to think cholera, smallpox, and consumption were as valuable recruits.

The first man who went into Kansas from Missouri to interfere in the elections, he thought, "had a perfect right to be shot."

A $15 contribution Emerson had made to the Concord Lyceum he now transferred to Brown instead. Thoreau, who had heard Brown talk about his life at the table, had this to say about him:

▶ I should say that he was an old-fashioned man in his respect for the Constitution, and his faith in the permanence of this Union. Slavery he deemed to be wholly opposed to these, and he was its determined foe.

He was by descent and birth a New England farmer, a man of great common sense, deliberate and practical as that class is, and tenfold more so. He was like the best of those who stood at Concord Bridge once, on Lexington Common, and on Bunker Hill, only he was firmer and higher-principled than any that I have chanced to hear of as there. It was no abolition lecturer that converted him. Ethan Allen and Stark, with whom he may in some respects be compared, were rangers in a lower and less important field. They could bravely face their country's foes, but he had the courage to face his country herself when she was in the wrong. A Western writer says, to account for his escape from so many perils, that he was concealed under a "rural exterior;" as if, in that prairie land, a hero should, by good rights, wear a citizen's dress only.

He did not go to the college called Harvard, good old Alma Mater as she is. He was not fed on the pap that is there furnished. As he phrased it, "I know no more of grammar than one of your calves." But he went to the great university of the West, where he sedulously pursued the study of Liberty, for which he had early betrayed a fondness, and having taken many degrees, he finally commenced the public practice of Humanity in Kansas, as you all know. Such were his humanities, and not any study of grammar. He would have left a Greek accent slanting the wrong way, and righted up a falling man.

In John Brown's camp in Kansas, Thoreau heard the Captain say:

▶ . . . he permitted no profanity; no man of loose morals was suffered to remain there, unless, indeed, as a prisoner of war. "I would rather," said he, "have the small-pox, yellow fever, and cholera, all together in my camp, than a man without principle. . . . It is a mistake, sir, that our people make, when they think that bullies are the best fighters, or that they are the fit men to oppose these Southerners. Give me men of good principles,—God-fearing men,—men who respect themselves, and with a dozen of them I will oppose any hundred such men as these Buford ruffians." He said that if one offered himself to be a soldier under him, who was forward to tell what he could or would do if he could only get sight of the enemy, he had but little confidence in him.

He was never able to find more than a score or so of recruits whom he would accept, and only about a dozen, among them his sons, in whom he had perfect faith.

While visiting in Concord, Thoreau continued, Brown

▶ . . . showed to a few a little manuscript book,—his "orderly book" I think he called it,—containing the names of his company in Kansas, and the rules by which they bound themselves; and he stated that several of them had already sealed the contract with their blood. When some one remarked that, with the addition of a chaplain, it would have been a perfect Cromwellian troop, he observed that he would have been glad to add a chaplain to the list, if he could have found one who could fill that office worthily. It is easy enough to find one for the United States Army. I believe that he had prayers in his camp morning and evening, nevertheless.

He was a man of Spartan habits, and at sixty was scrupulous about his diet at your table, excusing himself by saying that he must eat sparingly and fare hard, as became a soldier, or one who was fitting himself for difficult enterprises, a life of exposure.

A man of rare common sense and directness of speech, as of action; a transcendentalist above all, a man of ideas and principles,—that was what distinguished him. Not yielding to a whim or transient impulse, but carrying out the purpose of a life. I noticed that he did not overstate anything, but spoke within bounds. I remember, particularly, how, in his speech here, he referred to what his family had suffered in Kansas, without ever giving the least vent to his pentup fire. It was a volcano with an ordinary chimney-flue. Also referring to the deeds of certain Border Ruffians, he said, rapidly paring away his speech, like an experienced

[254]

soldier keeping a reserve of force and meaning, "They had a perfect right to be hung."

When I expressed surprise that he could live in Kansas at all, with a price set upon his head, and so large a number, including the authorities, exasperated against him, he accounted for it by saying, "It is perfectly well understood that I will not be taken." Much of the time for some years he has had to skulk in swamps, suffering from poverty, and from sickness which was the consequence of exposure, befriended only by Indians and a few whites. But though it might be known that he was lurking in a particular swamp, his foes commonly did not care to go in after him. He could even come out into a town where there were more Border Ruffians than Free State men, and transact some business, without delaying long, and yet not be molested; for, said he, "no little handful of men were willing to undertake it, and a large body could not be got together in season."

Two years later, John Brown was again in Boston, to press the secret committee of his supporters for more money and arms. The antislavery cause, he told one startled businessman, had passed the stage of ballots, and nothing but bayonets and bullets could settle it now. On May 7, 1859, Brown was with Sanborn at Concord, and the next night, Sunday, he spoke at Town Hall. As Bronson Alcott recalled that meeting:

Our people heard him with favor. He impressed me as a person of surpassing sense, courage, and religious earnestness. A man of reserves, yet he inspired confidence in his integrity and good judgment. He seemed superior to any legal traditions, able to do his own thinking; was an idealist, at least in matters of State, if not on all points of his religious faith. He did not conceal his hatred of Slavery, and less his readiness to strike a blow for freedom at the fitting moment. I thought him equal to anything he should dare: the man to do the deed necessary to be done with the patriot's zeal, the martyr's temper and purpose. . . . I am accustomed to divine men's tempers by their voices;—his was vaulting and metallic, suggesting repressed force and indomitable will. . . . Not far from sixty, then, he seemed alert and agile, resolute and ready for any crisis. I thought him the manliest of men and the type of synonym of the just.

On May 9—it was the last birthday he was to celebrate—Brown left Concord and returned to Boston where his backers soon raised the $2000 he needed before he could take to the battlefield.

On Sunday night, October 16, Brown gave the order to his men to strike a blow against slavery at Harpers Ferry.

When the news of the raid was flashed to the country it was as much a surprise to Thoreau as to all. "I subscribed a trifle when he was here three years ago, I had so much confidence in the man,—that he would do right,— but it would seem that he had not confidence enough in me, nor in anybody else that I know, to communicate his plans to us."

That night, he said, "I put a piece of paper and a pencil under my pillow, and when I could not sleep I wrote in the dark."

Thoreau began recording what the newspapers and his neighbors were saying about the sensational event. "It is the best news that America has ever heard," he felt, but he could find few if any who agreed with him in those first days after Brown's capture. "When I reflect to what a cause this man devoted himself, and how religiously, and then reflect to what cause his judges and all who condemn him so angrily and fluently devote themselves, I see that they are as far apart as the heavens and earth are asunder."

The Republican Party and editors, even Garrison, were calling it "a misguided, wild, and apparently insane effort."

The truth about John Brown, the meaning of his act, had to be made clear, Thoreau felt. On October 30 he sent a messenger to tell the villagers he would speak on Brown that night at the Town Hall. This might be premature, one friend warned. "You misunderstood," Thoreau replied; "I did not ask advice."

When the group was gathered, Thoreau began: "I trust that you will pardon me for being here. I do not wish to force my thoughts upon you, but I feel forced myself. Little as I know of Captain Brown, I would fain do my part to correct the tone and the statements of the newspapers, and of my countrymen generally, respecting his character and actions. It costs us nothing to be just. We can at least express our sympathy with, and admiration of, him and his companions, and that is what I now propose to do."

His "Plea for Captain John Brown"—one of the first public defenses— Thoreau wanted to carry as widely as he could. The next day he wrote Harrison Blake in Worcester, offering "to speak to any company who may wish to hear me . . . I think we should express ourselves at once, while Brown is alive. The sooner the better."

On November 1 Thoreau repeated the speech to an audience at the Boston Temple, and on the 3d gave it in Worcester. The *Liberator* printed the text on the 4th. On the 9th Thoreau visited Alcott at Orchard House to find out whether any townspeople would write to Gov. Wise of Virginia to urge clemency for Brown. "He has been the first to speak and celebrate the hero's courage and magnanimity," Alcott's diary noted after that visit: "The men have much in common,—the sturdy manliness, straightforwardness, and independence."

On November 24, replying to an inquiry from Calvin Greene in Michigan, he said his John Brown speech had been reported "after a fashion" in

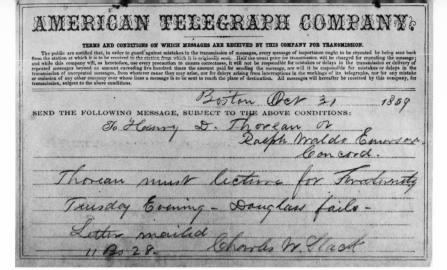

Boston Oct 31 1859

SEND THE FOLLOWING MESSAGE, SUBJECT TO THE ABOVE CONDITIONS:

To Henry D. Thoreau or
Ralph Waldo Emerson.
Concord.

Thoreau must lecture for Fraternity
Tuesday Evening — Douglass fails —
Letter mailed Charles W. Slack
11 Bo 28 —

The day after Thoreau made his "Plea for Captain John Brown" at Concord Town Hall, he received this wire asking him to deliver the speech at Theodore Parker's Temple in Boston, as a last-minute substitute for Frederick Douglass.

A daguerreotype of John Brown made in Boston in the winter of 1856-57, when Brown had just returned from the fighting in Kansas.

FRATERNITY LECTURES.

FIFTH LECTURE THIS (Tuesday) EVENING, at the TREMONT TEMPLE, by

HENRY D. THOREAU.

Subject — "Capt. John Brown, of Ossawottomie.."

Doors open by 6½ o'clock; lecture will commence at 7½ o'clock precisely.

A few single tickets, at 25 cents each, can be had at the Office of the Temple at a quarter past seven o'clock.

nov 1   1t

A Boston paper of November 1859 advertises Thoreau's lecture on John Brown. The next day his 90-minute speech was reported in detail.

John Brown of Ossawottamie.

The fifth lecture of the Fraternity course was delivered last evening in Tremont Temple by Henry D. Thoreau, esq., of Concord, on Capt. John Brown of Ossawottamie.' As usual, a large audience was in attendance.

Prior to the introduction of Mr. Thoreau a few remarks were made by Mr. C. W. Slack, chairman of the lecture committee, explanatory of the non-appearance of Frederick Douglass, previously announced as lecturer for the evening. The committee, he said, had received a communication from Mr. Douglass but a day or two since, from a point not to be named, conveying intelligence that could not be made public. In short it was not safe for a free citizen like Fred. Douglas to venture into our limits. After some further eulogistic comments upon Capt Brown and his recent exploits, Mr. Slack gave way to the lecturer of the evening.

The reason why Douglass was not there, Mr. Thoreau began, was the reason why he was... The...

...all good as his deeds...

Mr. Thoreau continued for some time longer in the same high-wrought vein of eulogy, extolling Brown even above every other man that ever lived. In fact according to his theory he was the only man that ever lived, all others dragged along a mere something not worthy the name of life; even Franklin and Washington, he said, were not exceptions.

His remarks occupied about an hour and a half in delivery.

some half-dozen papers. He had "exerted himself considerably," he added, to get the speech printed and sold for the benefit of Brown's family, "but the publishers are afraid of pamphlets and it is now too late."

As the day set for Brown's execution drew near, some of the Concord townspeople made plans to mark his death.

> I am one of a committee of four, [Thoreau wrote in his Journal] instructed by a meeting of citizens to ask liberty of the selectmen to have the bell of the first parish tolled at the time Captain Brown is being hung, and while we shall be assembled in the town house to express our sym-

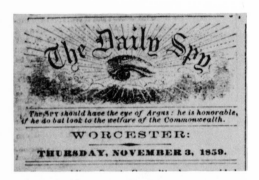

The Worcester *Spy* advises its readers that Thoreau's speech on John Brown "is likely to be worth hearing."

The Daily Spy

The Spy should have the eye of Argus: he is honorable, if he do but look to the welfare of the Commonwealth.

WORCESTER:

THURSDAY, NOVEMBER 3, 1859.

H. D. THOREAU ON JOHN BROWN.—An advertisement in another column announces that Mr. Thoreau of Concord will speak in Worcester, this evening, and that his topic will be John Brown and his doings. The lecture will be delivered in Washburn Hall; and, as Mr. Thoreau never deals in common places,—as he considers Brown a hero,—and as he has been so moved by the Harper's Ferry affair, as to feel compelled to leave his customary seclusion in order to address the public, what he has to say is likely to be worth hearing.

A Concord broadside announcing the memorial services for John Brown on Friday, December 2, 1859, the day of his execution. Thoreau spoke and read verses. Emerson, Alcott, Sanborn, and others took part. The dirge is by Sanborn. The date printed at the bottom is corrected probably in Thoreau's hand, since this copy was used by Thoreau to make notes on the reverse side.

Martyrdom of John Brown.

EXERCISES
—— AT THE ——
TOWN, HALL, IN CONCORD,
On FRIDAY, December 2nd, 1859,
AT 2 O'CLOCK, P. M.

MUSIC.

PRAYER.

HYMN,
"Go to the grave in all thy glorious prime."

READING OF PERTINENT PASSAGES.

SELECTIONS FROM BROWN'S LAST WORDS.

SERVICE FOR THE DEATH OF A MARTYR.

DIRGE;

To-day beside Potomac's wave,
  Beneath Virginia's sky,
They slay the man who loved the slave,
  And dared for him to die.

The Pilgrim Fathers' earnest creed,
  Virginia's ancient faith,
Inspired this hero's noblest deed,
  And his reward is—Death!

Great Washington's indignant shade
  Forever urged him on,—
He heard from Monticello's glade
  The voice of Jefferson.

But chiefly on the Hebrew page
  He read Jehovah's law,
And this from youth to hoary age
  Obeyed with love and awe.

No selfish purpose armed his hand,
  No passion aimed his blow;
How loyally he loved his land
  Impartial Time shall show.

But now the faithful martyr dies,
  His brave heart beats no more,
His soul ascends the equal skies,
  His earthly course is o'er.

For this we mourn, but not for him,
  Like him in God we trust;
And though our eyes with tears are dim,
  We know that God is just.

Concord, Dec. 30, 1859.

pathy with him. I applied to the selectmen yesterday. Their names are George M. Brooks, Barzillai Hudson, and Julius Smith. After various delays they at length answer me to-night that they "are uncertain whether they have any control over the bell, but that, in any case, they will not give their consent to have the bell tolled." Beside their private objections, they are influenced by the remarks of a few individuals. Dr. Bartlett tells me that Rockwood Hoar said he "hoped no such foolish thing would be done," and he also named Stedman Buttrick, John Moore, Cheney (and others added Nathan Brooks, senior, and Francis Wheeler) as strongly opposed to it; said that he had heard "five hundred" (!) damn me for it, and that he had no doubt that if it were done some counterdemonstration would be made, such as firing minute-guns. The doctor himself is more excited than anybody, for he has the minister under his wing. Indeed, a considerable part of Concord are in the condition of Virginia to-day, —afraid of their own shadows.

But the services did take place on December 2, the day Brown was hung in Charlestown, [West] Virginia. Alcott read from the Bible, Emerson from Brown's own words telegraphed from jail around the country. Thoreau's part was to read several poems that he found applicable to the case of Captain Brown. "So universal and widely related is any transcendent moral greatness," he said, "and so nearly identical with greatness everywhere and in every age," that noble verses are the parts of a universal liturgy for "those rare cases of heroes and martyrs for which the ritual of no church has provided."

Then, from Andrew Marvell, Thoreau quoted these lines:

> When the sword glitters o'er the judge's head,
> And fear has coward churchmen silenced,
> Then is the poet's time; 'tis then he draws,
> And single fights forsaken virtue's cause;
> He, when the wheel of empire whirleth back,
> And though the world's disjointed axle crack,
> Sings still of ancient rights and better times,
> Seeks suffering good, arraigns successful crimes.

The day after the memorial services Thoreau helped one of John Brown's men escape to Canada. Twenty-two-year-old Francis Jackson Merriam had evaded capture at Harpers Ferry and, despite a large reward offered for his capture, and his own ill condition, was in Boston where Sanborn was summoned to prevail upon him to flee to Canada for safety. Merriam took the wrong train and wound up in Concord, where he spent the night hidden in Sanborn's house. Sanborn arranged to borrow Emerson's mare and carriage at sunrise, and asked Thoreau to drive the unidentified and strangely acting passenger to South Acton to be put aboard the first Canadian train. Thoreau asked no questions about "X"—neither man knew who the other was—and set out on the mission. In his journal that night he reported what happened:

▶   X was betrayed by his eyes, which had a glaring film over them and no serene depth into which you could look. Inquired particularly the way to Emerson's and the distance, and when I told him, said he knew it as well as if he saw it. Wished to turn and proceed to his house. Told me one or two things which he asked me not to tell S. Said, "I know I am insane,"—

Mr. Sanborn's Case.

WELCOME BY HIS FELLOW CITIZENS OF CONCORD.

Speeches by Mr. Sanborn, Mr. Thoreau, Rev. Mr. Reynolds, Mr. Emerson, Rev. T. W. Higginson and others.

[SPECIAL DISPATCH TO THE BOSTON JOURNAL]

CONCORD, Mass., April 4.

The Town Hall was crowded at 8 o'clock to consider the events of the day and last night. Great enthusiasm was manifested at the decision of the Supreme Court in the case of Mr. F. B. Sanborn.

Mr. Bowers called the meeting to order, and Dr. Josiah Bartlett was chosen Chairman.

After a warm tribute to the two women, who saved the town from the disgrace of the kidnapping of Mr. Sanborn, he introduced Mr. Sanborn to the audience, which received him with shouts of applause. He appeared with the manacles on his hands, which were on them last night; and after expressing his thanks to his townsmen for their prompt action of last night, drew from these late events the lesson of increasing hatred to slavery, whatever disguises it may assume, and whatever persons it may lay claim to.

Rev. Mr. Reynolds followed Mr. Sanborn, and congratulated his townsmen on the result of the day.

Mr. Thoreau next spoke, advocating resistance even to law, when it opposed justice.

He was followed by Mr. A. G. Fay, a dealer in gunpowder, who seemed to think a little of his commodity was needed.

Mr. R. W. Emerson spoke briefly and pointedly against centralization, and in favor of the two women who had behaved so heroically.

Mr. Bowers, Mr. Henry Warren, and E. W. Bull, Esq., also spoke, and finally T. W. Higginson of Worcester, who had come late to the meeting from Boston, spoke of the importance of what had been done, and the necessity of organization to guard against future outrages. The suggestion was accepted by the meeting, and a committee of seven appointed to secure such an organization.

Mr. Sanborn closed the meeting by stating his present position, and his determination to resist the Senate's usurpation to the last. The whole proceedings were full of resolute enthusiasm, and a determination was expressed to defend Sanborn at all hazards.

The following resolutions were adopted:

Resolved, That the fame of old Concord for its spirit of noble daring on the nineteenth of April, 1775, is glorious, and only equaled by the chivalrous rescue of one of our most honored citizens from a band of kidnappers, who had forcibly seized and manacled him, and were hurrying him away from his home and friends, on the third of April, 1860.

Resolved, That the doctrine of the Revolution, that "resistance to tyrants is obedience to God," is our doctrine, and that we proclaim our unswerving determination to resist all attempts to abridge the rights of any citizen to all privileges and guaranties of constitutional liberty.

Resolved, That the attempt of United States officers, by false pretenses, and under cover of darkness, to rob a man of his freedom, is base, mean and cowardly.

On April 3, 1860, federal officers came to Sanborn's house in Concord and attempted to arrest him for refusing to obey a summons to appear before the Senate committee investigating Brown's raid on Harpers Ferry. The neighbors forcibly prevented the arrest, Judge Hoar granted a writ of habeas corpus, and Sanborn was freed. The next night, as this newspaper reported, a crowded Town Hall heard Thoreau speak, "advocating resistance even to law, when it opposed justice."

and I knew it too. Also called it "nervous excitement." At length, when I made a certain remark, he said, "I don't know but you are Emerson; are you? You look somewhat like him." He said as much two or three times, and added once, "But then Emerson wouldn't lie." Finally put his questions to me, of Fate, etc., etc., as if I were Emerson. Getting to the woods, I remarked upon them, and he mentioned my name, but never to the end suspected who his companion was. Then "proceeded to business,"—"since the time was short,"—and put to me the questions he was going to put to Emerson. His insanity exhibited itself chiefly by his incessant excited talk, scarcely allowing me to interrupt him, but once or twice apologizing for his behavior. What he said was for the most part connected and sensible enough.

Merriam leaped off the carriage once but Thoreau somehow—Sanborn suspected forceful persuasion was used—got him back on and saw him safely off on the train. Two years later, in his last illness, Thoreau asked Sanborn who the fugitive was, and Sanborn told him, adding that Merriam was the grandson of Mrs. Thoreau's old friend, Francis Jackson, the treasurer of the Boston Vigilance Committee.

On December 8 Thoreau noted that "Certain persons disgraced themselves by hanging Brown in effigy in this town on the 2nd. I was glad to know that the only four whose names I heard mentioned in connection with it had not been long resident here, and had done nothing to secure the respect of the town."

The body of John Brown was carried to his family's home in North Elba, New York, in the heart of the Adirondacks. Unable to make the trip there for the memorial services on July 4, 1860, Thoreau prepared an address that was read by Richard J. Hinton. "The Last Days of John Brown" concentrated Thoreau's passionate defense of Brown's life as a principled struggle against the evil of slavery:

▶ THE LAST DAYS OF JOHN BROWN

John Brown's career for the last six weeks of his life was meteor-like, flashing through the darkness in which we live. I know of nothing so miraculous in our history.

If any person, in a lecture or conversation at that time, cited any ancient example of heroism, such as Cato or Tell or Winkelried, passing over the recent deeds and words of Brown, it was felt by any intelligent audience of Northern men to be tame and inexcusably far-fetched.

For my own part, I commonly attend more to nature than to man, but any affecting human event may blind our eyes to natural objects. I was so absorbed in him as to be surprised whenever I detected the routine of the natural world surviving still, or met persons going about their affairs indifferent. It appeared strange to me that the "little dipper" should be still diving quietly in the river, as of yore; and it suggested that this bird might continue to dive here when Concord should be no more.

I felt that he, a prisoner in the midst of his enemies and under sentence of death, if consulted as to his next step or resource would answer more wisely than all his countrymen beside. He best understood his position; he contemplated it most calmly. Comparatively, all other men, North and South, were beside themselves. Our thought could not revert to any greater or wiser or better man with whom to contrast him, for he, then and there, was above them all. The man this country was about to hang appeared the greatest and best in it.

Years were not required for a revolution of public opinion; days, nay hours, produced marked changes in this case. Fifty who were ready to say, on going into our meeting in honor of him in Concord, that he ought to be hung, would not say it when they came out. They heard his words read; they saw the earnest faces of the congregation; and perhaps they joined at last in singing the hymn in his praise.

The order of instructors was reversed. I heard that one preacher, who at first was shocked and stood aloof, felt obliged at last, after he was hung, to make him the subject of a sermon, in which, to some extent, he eulogized the man, but said that his act was a failure. An influential class-teacher thought it necessary, after the services, to tell his grown-up pupils that at first he thought as the preacher did then, but now he thought that John Brown was right. But it was understood that his pupils were as much ahead of the teacher as he was ahead of the priest; and I know for a certainty that very little boys at home had already asked their parents, in a tone of surprise, why God did not interfere to save him. In each case, the constituted teachers were only half conscious that they were not leading, but being dragged, with some loss of time and power.

The more conscientious preachers, the Bible men, they who talk about principle, and doing to others as you would that they should do unto you,— how could they fail to recognize him, by far the greatest preacher of them all, with the Bible in his life and in his acts, the embodiment of principle, who actually carried out the golden rule? All whose moral sense had been aroused, who had a calling from on high to preach, sided with him. What confessions he extracted from the cold and conservative! It is remarkable, but on the whole it is well, that it did not prove the occasion for a new sect of Brownites being formed in our midst.

They, whether within the Church or out of it, who adhere to the spirit and let go the letter, and are accordingly called infidel, were as usual foremost to recognize him. Men have been hung in the South before for attempting to rescue slaves, and the North was not much stirred by it.

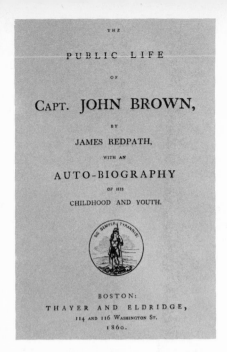

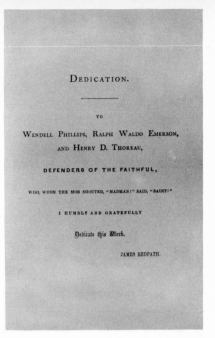

The first book to be published on Brown's life carried a dedication to Thoreau, Emerson, and Phillips.

Whence, then, this wonderful difference? We were not so sure of their devotion to principle. We made a subtle distinction, forgot human laws, and did homage to an idea. The North, I mean the living North, was suddenly all transcendental. It went behind the human law, it went behind the apparent failure, and recognized eternal justice and glory. Commonly, men live according to a formula, and are satisfied if the order of law is observed, but in this instance they, to some extent, returned to original perceptions, and there was a slight revival of old religion. They saw that what was called order was confusion, what was called justice, injustice, and that the best was deemed the worst. This attitude suggested a more intelligent and generous spirit than that which actuated our forefathers, and the possibility, in the course of ages, of a revolution in behalf of another and an oppressed people.

Most Northern men, and a few Southern ones, were wonderfully stirred by Brown's behavior and words. They saw and felt that they were heroic and noble, and that there had been nothing quite equal to them in their kind in this country, or in the recent history of the world. But the minority were unmoved by them. They were only surprised and provoked by the attitude of their neighbors. They saw that Brown was brave, and that he believed that he had done right, but they did not detect any further peculiarity in him. Not being accustomed to make fine distinctions, or to appreciate magnanimity, they read his letters and speeches as if they read

[*263*]

them not. They were not aware when they approached a heroic state-ment,—they did not know when they burned. They did not feel that he spoke with authority, and hence they only remembered that the law must be executed. They remembered the old formula, but did not hear the new revelation. The man who does not recognize in Brown's words a wisdom and nobleness, and therefore an authority, superior to our laws, is a modern Democrat. This is the test by which to discover him. He is not willfully but constitutionally blind on this side, and he is consistent with himself. Such has been his past life; no doubt of it. In like manner he has read history and his Bible, and he accepts, or seems to accept, the last only as an established formula, and not because he has been con-victed by it. You will not find kindred sentiments in his commonplace-book, if he has one.

When a noble deed is done, who is likely to appreciate it? They who are noble themselves. I was not surprised that certain of my neighbors spoke of John Brown as an ordinary felon, for who are they? They have either much flesh, or much office, or much coarseness of some kind. They are not ethereal natures in any sense. The dark qualities predominate in them. Several of them are decidedly pachydermatous. I say it in sorrow, not in anger. How can a man behold the light who has no answering inward light? They are true to their sight, but when they look this way they see nothing, they are blind. For the children of the light to contend with them is as if there should be a contest between eagles and owls. Show me a man who feels bitterly toward John Brown, and let me hear what noble verse he can repeat. He'll be as dumb as if his lips were stone.

It is not every man who can be a Christian, even in a very moderate sense, whatever education you give him. It is a matter of constitution and temperament, after all. He may have to be born again many times. I have known many a man who pretended to be a Christian, in whom it was ridiculous, for he had no genius for it. It is not every man who can be a free man, even.

Editors persevered for a good while in saying that Brown was crazy; but at last they said only that it was "a crazy scheme," and the only evidence brought to prove it was that it cost him his life. I have no doubt that if he had gone with five thousand men, liberated a thousand slaves, killed a hundred or two slaveholders, and had as many more killed on his own side, but not lost his own life, these same editors would have called it by a more respectable name. Yet he has been far more successful than that. He has liberated many thousands of slaves, both North and South. They seem to have known nothing about living or dying for a principle. They all called him crazy then; who calls him crazy now?

All through the excitement occasioned by his remarkable attempt and subsequent behavior the Massachusetts legislature, not taking any steps for the defense of her citizens who were likely to be carried to Virginia as witnesses and exposed to the violence of a slaveholding mob, was wholly absorbed in a liquor-agency question, and indulging in poor jokes on the word "extension." Bad spirits occupied their thoughts. I am sure that no statesman up to the occasion could have attended to that question at all at that time,—a very vulgar question to attend to at any time!

When I looked into a liturgy of the Church of England, printed near the end of the last century, in order to find a service applicable to the case of Brown, I found that the only martyr recognized and provided for by it was King Charles the First, an eminent scamp. Of all the inhabitants of England and of the world, he was the only one, according to this authority, whom that church had made a martyr and saint of; and for more than a century it had celebrated his martyrdom, so called, by an annual service. What a satire on the Church is that!

Look not to legislatures and churches for your guidance, nor to any soulless incorporated bodies, but to inspirited or inspired ones.

What avail all your scholarly accomplishments and learning, compared with wisdom and manhood? To omit his other behavior, see what a work this comparatively unread and unlettered man wrote within six weeks. Where is our professor of belles-lettres, or of logic and rhetoric, who can write so well? He wrote in prison, not a History of the World, like Raleigh, but an American book which I think will live longer than that. I do not know of such words, uttered under such circumstances, and so copiously withal, in Roman or English or any history. What a variety of themes he touched on in that short space! There are words in that letter to his wife, respecting the education of his daughters, which deserve to be framed and hung over every mantelpiece in the land. Compare this earnest wisdom with that of Poor Richard.

The death of Irving, which at any other time would have attracted universal attention, having occurred while these things were transpiring, went almost unobserved. I shall have to read of it in the biography of authors.

Literary gentlemen, editors, and critics think that they know how to

Francis Jackson Merriam, one of John Brown's men at Harpers Ferry, whom Thoreau helped to escape to Canada. Later Merriam served in the Civil War as captain of a Negro infantry company.

write, because they have studied grammar and rhetoric; but they are egregiously mistaken. The art of composition is as simple as the discharge of a bullet from a rifle, and its masterpieces imply an infinitely greater force behind them. This unlettered man's speaking and writing are standard English. Some words and phrases deemed vulgarisms and Americanisms before, he has made standard American; such as "It will pay." It suggests that the one great rule of composition—and if I were a professor of rhetoric I should insist on this—is, to speak the truth. This first, this second, this third; pebbles in your mouth or not. This demands earnestness and manhood chiefly.

We seem to have forgotten that the expression "a liberal education" originally meant among the Romans one worthy of free men; while the learning of trades and professions by which to get your livelihood merely was considered worthy of slaves only. But taking a hint from the word, I would go a step further, and say that it is not the man of wealth and leisure simply, though devoted to art, or science, or literature, who, in a true sense, is liberally educated, but only the earnest and free man. In a slaveholding country like this, there can be no such thing as a liberal education tolerated by the State; and those scholars of Austria and France who, however learned they may be, are contented under their tyrannies have received only a servile education.

Nothing could his enemies do but it redounded to his infinite advantage,—that is, to the advantage of his cause. They did not hang him at once, but reserved him to preach to them. And then there was another great blunder. They did not hang his four followers with him; that scene was still postponed; and so his victory was prolonged and completed. No theatrical manager could have arranged things so wisely to give effect to his behavior and words. And who, think you, was the manager? Who placed the slave-woman and her child, whom he stooped to kiss for a symbol, between his prison and the gallows?

We soon saw, as he saw, that he was not to be pardoned or rescued by men. That would have been to disarm him, to restore to him a material weapon, a Sharp's rifle, when he had taken up the sword of the spirit,— the sword with which he has really won his greatest and most memorable victories. Now he has not laid aside the sword of the spirit, for he is pure spirit himself, and his sword is pure spirit also.

> He nothing common did or mean
> Upon that memorable scene, . . .
> Nor called the gods with vulgar spite,
> To vindicate his helpless right;
> But bowed his comely head
> Down, as upon a bed.

What a transit was that of his horizontal body alone, but just cut down from the gallows-tree! We read that at such a time it passed through Philadelphia, and by Saturday night had reached New York. Thus like a meteor it shot through the Union from the Southern regions toward the North! No such freight had the cars borne since they carried him southward alive.

On the day of his translation, I heard, to be sure, that he was hung, but I did not know what that meant; I felt no sorrow on that account; but not for a day or two did I even hear that he was dead, and not after any number of days shall I believe it. Of all the men who were said to be my contemporaries, it seemed to me that John Brown was the only one who had not died. I never hear of a man named Brown now,—and I hear of them pretty often,—I never hear of any particularly brave and earnest man, but my first thought is of John Brown, and what relation he may be to him. I meet him at every turn. He is more alive than ever he was. He has earned immortality. He is not confined to North Elba nor to Kansas. He is no longer working in secret. He works in public, and in the clearest light that shines on this land.

24

Friend of the Indian

FROM CHILDHOOD ON Thoreau had an absorbing interest in the American
Indian. He and his brother John exchanged long letters addressing each
other by Indian names. When he taught school, he showed his pupils how
to excavate Indian village sites. For many years he planned to write a book
on the Indian and to that end read more than two hundred books on the
subject, filling eleven manuscript volumes with more than half a million
words of notes and quotations in preparation for that work. But illness prevented his carrying out the project and it was abandoned with a tentative
table of contents the only completed portion.

Surprisingly, Indians were still a familiar sight around Concord in
Thoreau's youth. Each year members of the Penobscot tribe camped out
along the banks of the river while they sold their baskets to the townspeople
or came begging to the door. In 1850 he observed:

▶ A squaw came to our door today with two pappooses, and said, "Me
want a pie." Theirs is not common begging. You are merely the rich
Indian who shares his goods with the poor. They merely offer you an
opportunity to be generous and hospitable.

Here and there still you will find a man with Indian blood in his veins,
an eccentric farmer descended from an Indian chief; or you will see a
solitary pure-blooded Indian, looking as wild as ever among the pines,
one of the last of the Massachusetts tribes, stepping into a railroad car
with his gun.

Still here and there an Indian squaw with her dog, her only companion,
lives in some lone house, insulted by school-children, making baskets and
picking berries her employment. You will meet her on the highway, with
few children or none, with melancholy face, history, destiny; stepping
after her race; who had stayed to tuck them up in their long sleep. For
whom berries condescend to grow. I have not seen one on the Musketaquid for many a year, and some who came up in their canoes and camped
on its banks a dozen years ago had to ask me where it came from. A lone

Indian woman without children, accompanied by her dog, wearing the shroud of her race, performing the last offices for her departed race. Not yet absorbed into the elements again; a daughter of the soil; one of the nobility of the land. The white man an imported weed,—burdock and mullein, which displace the ground-nut.

Wherever Thoreau went he found Indian artifacts. So adept was he at finding them that the story has been told over and over again of one of his companions asking him where to look for an arrowhead and Thoreau reached down and picked one up at the man's feet. Thoreau thought that if he could get five cents apiece for each arrowhead he found he could make a comfortable living.

▶ There is scarcely a square rod of sand exposed, in this neighborhood, but you may find on it the stone arrowheads of an extinct race [he noted in 1857]. Far back as that time seems when men went armed with bows and pointed stones here, yet so numerous are the signs of it. The finer particles of sand are blown away and the arrowpoint remains. The race is as clean gone—from here—as this and is clean swept by the wind. Such are our antiquities. These were our predecessors. Why, then, make so great ado about the Roman and the Greek, and neglect the Indian?

Five of the eleven manuscript volumes of notes on the Indian which Thoreau filled with a half-million words. The notebooks are in the Pierpont Morgan Library in New York.

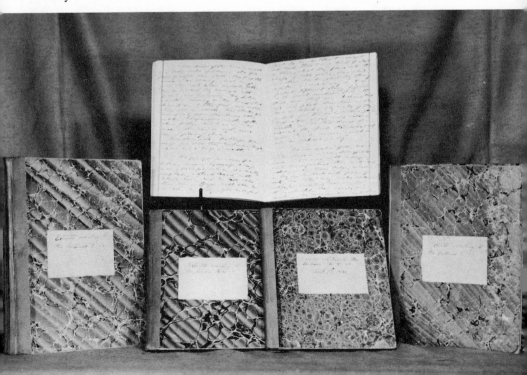

We [need] not wander off with boys in our imaginations to Juan Fernan-
dez, to wonder at footprints in the sand there. Here is a print still more
significant at our doors, the print of a race that has preceded us, and this
the little symbol that Nature has transmitted to us. Yes, this arrow-headed
character is probably more ancient than any other, and to my mind it
has not been deciphered. Men should not go to New Zealand to write or
think of Greece and Rome, nor more to New England. New earths, new
themes expect us. Celebrate not the Garden of Eden, but your own.

When the spring of 1859 came on, he reminded himself:

▶ It is now high time to look for arrowheads, etc. I spend many hours
every spring gathering the crop which the melting snow and rain have
washed bare. When, at length, some island in the meadow or some sandy
field elsewhere has been plowed, perhaps for rye, in the fall, I take note
of it, and do not fail to repair thither as soon as the earth begins to be
dry in the spring. If the spot chances never to have been cultivated
before, I am the first to gather a crop from it. The farmer little thinks
that another reaps a harvest which is the fruit of his toil. As much ground
is turned up in a day by the plow as Indian implements could not have
turned over in a month, and my eyes rest on the evidences of an aboriginal
life which passed here a thousand years ago perchance. Especially if the
knolls in the meadows are washed by a freshet where they have been
plowed the previous fall, the soil will be taken away lower down and the
stones left,—the arrowheads, etc., and soapstone pottery amid them,—
somewhat as gold is washed in a dish or tom. I landed on two spots this
afternoon and picked up a dozen arrowheads. It is one of the regular
pursuits of the spring. As much as sportsmen go in pursuit of ducks,
and gunners of musquash, and scholars of rare books, and travellers of
adventures, and poets of ideas, and all men of money, I go in search of
arrowheads when the proper season comes round again. So I help myself
to live worthily, and loving my life as I should. It is a good collyrium to
look on the bare earth,—to pore over it so much, getting strength to all
your senses, like Antaeus. . . .

I have not decided whether I had better publish my experience in
searching for arrowheads in three volumes, with plates and an index,
or try to compress it into one. These durable implements seem to have
been suggested to the Indian mechanic with a view to my entertainment
in a succeeding period. After all the labor expended on it, the bolt may
have been shot but once perchance, and the shaft which was devoted to
it decayed, and there lay the arrowhead, sinking into the ground, awaiting
me. They lie all over the hills with like expectation, and in due time the
husbandman is sent, and, tempted by the promise of corn or rye, he

Some of the Indian stone implements Thoreau collected. At the top is a bannerstone, below it a sinker, bannerstone, and scraper, and in the bottom row a spearpoint, a spindle-shaped stone, and an axe. This collection is now in the Fruitlands Museum in the town of Harvard, Massachusetts.

plows the land and turns them up to my view. Many as I have found, methinks the last one gives me about the same delight that the first did. Some time or other, you would say, it had rained arrowheads, for they lie all over the surface of America. You may have your peculiar tastes. Certain localities in your town may seem from association unattractive and uninhabitable to you. You may wonder that the land bears any money value there, and pity some poor fellow who is said to survive in that neighborhood. But plow up a new field there, and you will find the omnipresent arrow-points strewn over it, and it will appear that the red man, and other tastes and associations, lived there too. No matter how far from the modern road or meeting-house, no matter how near. They lie in the meeting-house cellar, and they lie in the distant cow-pasture. And some collections which were made a century ago by the curious like myself have been dispersed again, and they are still as good as new. You cannot tell the third-hand ones (for they are all second-hand) from the others, such is their persistent out-of-door durability; for they were chiefly made to be lost. They are sown, like a grain that is slow to germinate, broadcast over the earth. Like the dragon's teeth which bore a crop of soldiers, these bear crops of philosophers and poets, and the same seed is just as good to plant again. It is a stone fruit. Each one yields me a thought. I come nearer to the maker of it than if I found his bones. His bones would not prove any wit that wielded them, such as this work of his bones does. It is humanity inscribed on the face of the earth, patent to my eyes

[*271*]

as soon as the snow goes off, not hidden away in some crypt or grave or under a pyramid. No disgusting mummy, but a clean stone, the best symbol or letter that could have transmitted to me.

At every step I see it, and I can easily supply the "Tahatawan" or "Mantatuket" that might have been written if he had had a clerk. It is no single inscription on a particular rock, but a footprint—rather a mind-print—left everywhere, and altogether illegible. No vandals, however vandalic in their disposition, can be so industrious as to destroy them.

They are not fossil bones, but, as it were, fossil thoughts, forever reminding me of the mind that shaped them. I would fain know that I am treading in the tracks of human game,—that I am on the trail of mind,—and these little reminders never fail to set me right. When I see these signs I know that the subtle spirits that made them are not far off, into whatever form transmitted.

The next summer, heavy rains washed away a nearby bank, and to Thoreau it looked and smelled more mouldy with human relics than ever. He wrote:

▶ I therefore find myself inevitably exploring it. On the edge of the ravine whose beginning I witnessed, one foot beneath the surface and just over a layer some three inches thick of pure shells and ashes,—a gray-white line on the face of the cliff.—I find several pieces of Indian pottery with a rude ornament on it, not much more red than the earth itself. Looking farther, I find more fragments, which have been washed down the sandy slope in a stream, as far as ten feet. I find in all thirty-one pieces, averaging an inch in diameter and about a third of an inch thick. Several of them made part of the upper edge of the vessel, and have a rude ornament encircling them in three rows, as if pricked with a stick in the soft clay, and also another line on the narrow edge itself. At first I thought to match the pieces again, like a geographical puzzle, but I did not find that any I [got] belonged together. The vessel must have been quite large, and I have not got nearly all of it. It appears to have been an impure clay with much sand and gravel in it, and I think a little pounded shell. It is [of] very unequal thickness, some of the unadorned pieces (probably the bottom) being half an inch thick, while near the edge it is not more than a quarter of an inch thick. There was under this spot and under the layer of shells a manifest hollowness in the ground, not yet filled up. I find many small pieces of bone in the soil of this bank, probably of animals the Indians ate.

In another part of the bank, in the midst of a much larger heap of shells which has been exposed, I found a delicate stone tool of this form and size: of a soft slate-stone. It is very thin and sharp on each side edge, and in the middle is not more than an eighth of an inch thick. I suspect that this was used to open clams with.

It is curious that I had expected to find as much as this, and in this very spot too, before I reached it (I mean the pot). Indeed, I never find a remarkable Indian relic—and I find a good many—but I have first divined its existence, and planned the discovery of it. Frequently I have told myself distinctly what it was to be before I found it.

When Thoreau journeyed to the Maine woods, one of his chief aims was to get better acquainted with the Indian in his native habitat and he always hired an Indian guide. He made an agreement with each of his guides: "I would tell him all I knew, and he should tell me all he knew." Joe Polis, the guide on his 1857 trip, made a particularly strong impression on Thoreau, as Emerson pointed out in his funeral address on Thoreau. In *The Maine Woods* Thoreau had this to say of Polis:

▶ I asked him how he guided himself in the woods. "Oh," said he, "I can tell good many ways." When I pressed him further, he answered, "Sometimes I lookum side-hill" and he glanced toward a high hill or mountain on the eastern shore, "great difference between the north and south, see where the sun has shone most. So trees,—the large limbs bend toward south. Sometimes I lookum locks" (rocks). I asked what he saw on the rocks, but he did not describe anything in particular, answering vaguely, in a mysterious or drawling tone, "Bare locks on lake shore,—great difference between north, south, east, west, side,—can tell what the sun has shone on." "Suppose," said I, "that I should take you in a dark night, right up here into the middle of the woods a hundred miles, set you down, and turn you round quickly twenty times, could you steer straight to Oldtown?" "Oh, yer," said he, "have done pretty much same thing. I will tell you. Some years ago I met an old white hunter at Millinocket; very good hunter. He said he could go anywhere in the woods. He wanted to hunt with me that day, so we start. We chase a moose all the forenoon, round and round, till middle of afternoon, when we kill him. Then I said to him, 'Now you go straight to camp. Don't go round and round where we've been, but go straight.' He said, 'I can't do that, I don't know where I am.' 'Where you think camp?' I asked. He pointed so. Then I laugh at him. I take the lead and go right off the other way, cross our tracks many times, straight camp." "How do you do that?" asked I. "Oh, I can't tell you," he replied. "Great difference between me and white man."

It appeared as if the sources of information were so various that he did not give a distinct, conscious attention to any one, and so could not readily refer to any when questioned about it, but he found his way very much as an animal does. Perhaps what is commonly called instinct in the animal, in this case is merely a sharpened and educated sense. Often, when an Indian says, "I don't know," in regard to the route he is to take, he does not mean what a white man would by those words, for his Indian instinct may tell him still as much as the most confident white man knows. He does not carry things in his head, nor remember the route exactly, like a white man, but relies on himself at the moment. Not having experienced the need of the other sort of knowledge, all labeled and arranged, he has not acquired it.

At times Thoreau found himself disappointed and disillusioned with the Indians he knew—their idleness, their vices, their lack of interest in things spiritual. But at his best the idealized Indian of Thoreau's imagination, with his Antaeus-like closeness to Nature and Mother Earth, represented to him man at his best:

▶   The charm of the Indian to me is that he stands free and unconstrained in Nature, is her inhabitant and not her guest, and wears her easily and gracefully. But the civilized man has the habits of the house. His house is a prison, in which he finds himself oppressed and confined, not sheltered and protected. He walks as if he sustained the roof; he carries his arms as if the walls would fall in and crush him, and his feet remember the cellar beneath. His muscles are never relaxed. It is rare that he overcomes the house, and learns to sit at home in it, and roof and floor and walls support themselves, as the sky and trees and earth.

25

Last Years

TUBERCULOSIS WAS THE BANE of nineteenth-century America. Tightly closed windows, overheated rooms, and a lack of understanding of the high contagiousness of the disease all contributed to its rapid spread and its terrible toll.

Henry David Thoreau was an early victim. The illness that forced him out of college for a period was apparently the first attack. Later attacks occurred in 1841, 1843, and 1855. Then in December of 1860 he caught cold while studying tree rings in a snowstorm. Because he insisted on fulfilling a lecture engagement in Waterbury, Connecticut, against doctor's orders, the cold developed into bronchitis, and the bronchitis opened the old tubercular lesions in his lungs. Bronson Alcott, visiting him on January 28, 1861, reported:

> Channing writes tenderly of Thoreau's confinement, and I see him this morning and find his hoarseness forbids his going out as usual. 'Tis a serious thing to one who has been less a house-keeper than any man in town, has lived out of doors for the best part of his life, has harvested more wind and storm, sun and sky, and has more weather in him, than any—night and day abroad with his leash of keen senses, hounding any game stirring, and running it down for certain, to be spread on the dresser of his page before he sleeps and served as a feast of wild meats to all sound intelligence like his. If any can make game for his confinement it must be himself, and for solace, if sauce of the sort is desired by one so healthy as he has seemed hitherto. We have been accustomed to consider him the salt of things so long that we are loath to believe it has lost savor; since if it has, then "Pan is dead" and Nature ails throughout.
>
> I find him in spirits—busied, he tells me, with his Journals, and, bating his out-of-doors, in his usual working trim. Fair weather and spring time, I trust, are to prove his best physicians, and the woods and fields know their old friend again presently.

By spring Thoreau had failed so rapidly that doctors despaired of his life and told him that his only hope for recovery was to try a different climate. He thought first of going to the West Indies, but then decided upon Minnesota—perhaps because there he might have an opportunity to further his favorite studies of both the American Indian and the flora and fauna of his native land. It was obvious that he would need assistance on the long journey, and he first decided upon Ellery Channing, who had been his companion on many earlier journeys. But Channing, always notoriously undependable, hemmed and hawed until Thoreau in desperation turned to another old friend, Harrison Grey Otis Blake of Worcester, Massachusetts. Blake could not leave on such short notice and Thoreau finally turned to Horace Mann, Jr., the son of the famed educator. Although in 1861 Mann was only seventeen years old, he was already an accomplished naturalist, and he and Thoreau had been consulting each other, chiefly on the identification of birds and plants and various small mammals, for many months.

Young Mann quickly accepted the invitation and on May 10, 1861, they purchased railroad tickets to Chicago, with stopover privileges at Niagara

Horace Mann, Jr., a young botanist, who was Thoreau's companion on a trip to Minnesota in 1861. He died of tuberculosis at the age of 24.

The steamboat *Frank Steele*, at right, tied up at the St. Paul dock. Thoreau sailed on it some 300 miles up the Minnesota River with a party of 200, to visit Indian villages.

Falls and Detroit. They spent five days in the falls area, hoping that Ellery Channing might change his mind and catch up with them. By the 21st they were in Chicago, and on the 23d took the train to Dunleith (now East Dubuque, Illinois), where the next morning they started up the Mississippi River by boat. They spent nearly a month in the St. Paul area, with time out for a journey up the Minnesota River to see the annual government payment of the Indians at Redwood. But it was obvious that Thoreau's health was growing worse rather than better. They returned down the Mississippi to Prairie du Chien, by railroad to Milwaukee, then by steamboat to Goderich, Ontario, returning to Concord via Toronto, by train.

Thoreau's notes taken on the journey are only fragmentary. His best account is a letter written to his Concord friend F. B. Sanborn from Redwing, Minnesota, on June 25, 1861:

▶ I was very glad to find awaiting me, on my arrival here on Sunday afternoon, a letter from you. I have performed this journey in a very dead and alive manner, but nothing has come so near waking me up as the receipt of letters from Concord. I read yours, and one from my sister (and Horace Mann, his four) near the top of a remarkable isolated bluff here, called Barn Bluff or the Grange, or Redwing Bluff, some 450 feet high and half a mile long—a bit of the main bluff or bank standing alone.

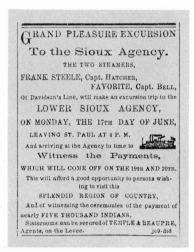

Advertisement for the "grand pleasure excursion" to the Sioux country on the *Frank Steele,* which Thoreau probably saw in the St. Paul *Pioneer and Democrat* on June 15, 1861.

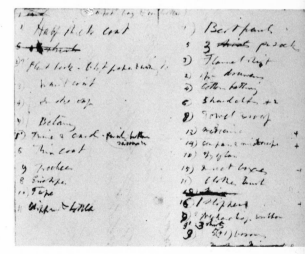

The clothing and equipment Thoreau planned to take on his Minnesota trip. Carpet-bag and umbrella top his list.

A WEEK ON THE FRONTIER

STEAMER FRANK STEELE,
Minnesota River, June 22.

MR. EDITOR:—With an excursion party of about 200 Minnesotians, I am just returning from a visit to see the Sioux tribe of Indians at their annual council at Red Wood, a trading post on the head waters of the Minnesota. I want to tell your readers something of our trip.

RESOLVES.

—Some of the solemn wags aboard have just held an enthusiastic meeting on the hurricane deck and adopted, with numerous "hi! hi!s," the following:

Resolved, That we have had a high old time.

Resolved, That it is 'a big thing' and we can 'see it.'

Resolved, That Capt. J. R. Hatcher is a brick of the first water, and is hereby tendered the freedom of the river.

Resolved, That Gov. Monger, Chief of the Gra Twoston Band, is a 'gay and festive cuss'tomer, and we joyfully recommend him and his followers to the favor of everybody and his wife and children.

Resolved, That judging from our experience, the Minnesota river is always on a bender. Long may she Wave!

Resolved, That while admiring the beauty, we also commiserate the condition, of "Lowe—the poor Indian" whom we have heard so much about, and his whole family, and that we will send them each a pair of suspenders, a standing collar and a green cotton umbrella.

—*Quantum suf!*—"not any more, I thank you."

—But I am certain that this is the sentiment of the party in the rough.

THE PARTY.

We had a very choice and select company, among whom were Gov. and Mrs. Ramsey, District Att'y Nourse, Speaker Benson, U S. Marshal Buck, Commissioner Cox, Deputies Brackett and Cleveland, Horace Mann, Jun., son of the lamented statesman, Samuel May, Esq., Henry D. Thoreau, Esq. the celebrated abolitionist, &c.—there being about 25 or 30 ladies. It is very rarely that an excursion party is assembled combining such a degree of sociability, refinement, intelligence and culture as this. It was, in fact, composed mainly of the *creme de la creme*—the rich yellow skim from the mottled milk of frontier society. In all the trip, I heard hardly one profane or boisterous word, and did not see one rude loafer, nor one tipsy man. Vanity Fair and the sickish social pictures of Howadji were dimly

A vivid contemporary account of the steamer voyage appeared in this Minneapolis newspaper on July 3, 1861. "Henry D. Thoreau, Esq., the celebrated abolitionist," was listed among the "very choice and select company."

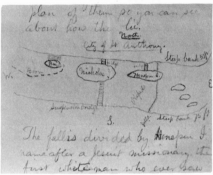

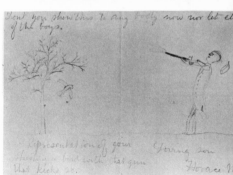

Drawings made by young Horace Mann, Jr., in letters home describing his trip with Thoreau. The Barn Bluff at Red Wing and the Metropolitan Hotel are at top; the falls at St. Anthony are at center; at bottom he pokes fun at the way he handled a kicking rifle.

The top, as you know, rises to the general level of the surrounding country, the river having eaten out so much. Yet the valley just above & below this (we are at the head of Lake Pepin) must be 3 or 4 miles wide.

The grand feature hereabouts is, of course, the Mississippi River. Too much can hardly be said of its grandeur, & of the beauty of this portion of it—(from Dunleith, and prob. from Rock Island to this place.) St. Paul is a dozen miles below the Falls of St. Anthony, or near the head of uninterrupted navigation on the main stream about 2000 miles from its mouth. There is not a "rip" below that, & the river is almost as wide in the upper as the lower part of its course. Steamers go up to the Sauk Rapids, above the Falls, near a hundred miles farther, & then you are fairly in the pine woods and lumbering country. Thus it flows from the pine to the palm.

The lumber, as you know, is sawed chiefly at the Falls of St. Anthony (what is not rafted in the log to ports far below) having given rise to the towns of St. Anthony, Minneapolis, &c &c. In coming up the river from Dunleith you meet with great rafts of sawed lumber and of logs— 20 rods or more in length, by 5 or 6 wide, floating down, all from the pine region above the Falls. An old Maine lumberer, who has followed the same business here, tells me that the sources of the Mississippi were comparatively free from rocks and rapids, making easy work for them, but he thought that the timber was more knotty here than in Maine.

It has chanced that about half the men whom I have spoken with in Minnesota, whether travelers or settlers, were from Massachusetts.

After spending some three weeks in and about St. Paul, St. Anthony, and Minneapolis, we made an excursion in a steamer some 300 or more miles up the Minnesota (St. Peter's) River, to Redwood, or the Lower Sioux Agency, in order to see the plains & the Sioux, who were to receive their annual payment there. This is eminently the river of Minnesota, for she shares the Mississippi with Wisconsin, and it is of incalculable value to her. It flows through a very fertile country, destined to be famous for its wheat; but it is a remarkably winding stream, so that Redwood is only half as far from its mouth by land as by water. There was not a straight reach a mile in length as far as we went,—generally you could not see a quarter of a mile of water, & the boat was steadily turning this way or that. At the greater bends, as the Traverse des Sioux, some of the passengers were landed & walked across to be taken in on the other side. Two or three times you could have thrown a stone across the neck of the isthmus while it was from one to three miles around it. It was a very novel kind of navigation to me. The boat was perhaps the largest that had been up so high, & the water was rather low (it had been about 15 feet higher). In making a short turn, we repeatedly and designedly ran square into the steep and soft bank, taking in a cart-load of earth, this

The house on Main Street, where Thoreau died at 9 o'clock, Tuesday morning, May 6, 1862.

The family clock of the Thoreaus.

The inkstand and quill pen, the last Thoreau wrote with.

being more effectual than the rudder to fetch us about again; or the deeper water was so narrow & close to the shore, that we were obliged to run into & break down at least 50 trees which overhung the water, when we did not cut them off, repeatedly losing a part of our outworks, though the most exposed had been taken in. I could pluck almost any plant on the bank from the boat. We very frequently got aground and then drew ourselves along with a windlass & a cable fastened to a tree, or we swung around in the current, and completely blocked up & blockaded the river, one end of the boat resting on each shore. And yet we would haul ourselves round again with the windlass & cable in an hour or 2, though the boat was about 160 feet long & drew some 3 feet of water, or, often, water and sand. It was one consolation to know that in such a case we were all the while damming the river & so raising it. We once ran fairly on to a concealed rock, with a shock that aroused all the passengers, & rested there, & the mate went below with a lamp expecting to find a hole, but he did not. Snags & sawyers were so common that I forgot to mention them. The sound of the boat rumbling over one was the ordinary music. However, as long as the boiler did not burst, we knew that no serious accident was likely to happen. Yet this was a singularly navigable river, more so than the Mississippi above the Falls, & it is owing to its very crookedness. Ditch it straight, & it would not only be very swift, but soon run out. It was from 10 to 15 rods wide near the mouth & from 8 to 10 or 12 at Redwood. Though the current was swift, I did not see a "rip" on it, & only 3 or 4 rocks. For 3 months in the year I am told that it can be navigated by small steamers about twice as far as we went, or to its source in Big Stone Lake, & a former Indian agent told me that at high water it was thought that such a steamer might pass into the Red River.

THE FUNERAL OF THOREAU, which took place in Concord yesterday, drawing together a large company of his towns-people, with some votive pilgrims from parts beyond, was an occasion more impressive and memorable, by much, than is the wont of such scenes. It derived uncommon interest from the remarkable character of the man whose earthly life was ended, and from the weight and worth of the tributary words so fitly, so tenderly spoken there by friendly and illustrious lips. As that fading image of pathetic clay, strewn with wild flowers and forest sprigs, lay awaiting interment, thoughts of its former occupant seemed blent with all the local landscapes. And though the church-bell—after the affecting old custom—tolled the forty-four years he had numbered, we could not deem that he was dead whose ideas and sentiments were so vividly alive in our souls.

Selections from the Bible were read by the minister. A brief ode, written for the purpose by William Ellery Channing, was plaintively sung. Mr. Emerson read an address of considerable length, marked by all his felicity of conception and diction—an exquisite appreciation of the salient and subtle traits of his friend's genius—a high strain of sanative thoughts, full of beauty and cheerfulness, chastened by the gentle sorrow of the hour. Referring to the Alpine flower adelweiss, or noble purity, which the young Switzers sometimes lose their lives in plucking from its perilous heights, Mr. Emerson said, "Could we pierce to where he is we should see him wearing profuse chaplets of it; for it belonged to him. Where there is knowledge, where there is virtue, where there is beauty, where there is progress, there is now his home."

Mr. Alcot read some very appropriate passages from the writings of the deceased, and the service closed with a prayer by the Rev. Mr. Reynolds. A long procession was then formed to follow the body to the grave. The hands of friends reverently lowered it into the bosom of the earth, on the pleasant hillside of his native village, whose prospects will long wait to unfurl themselves to another observer so competent to discriminate their features, and so attuned to their moods. And now that it is too late for any further boon amidst his darling haunts below,

There will yet his mother yield
A pillow in her greenest field,
Nor the June flowers scorn to cover
The clay of their departed lover.

PERSONAL.

—Henry D. Thoreau, the genial writer on the natural scenery of New-England, died at Concord, Mass., on Tuesday, May 6, after a protracted illness of more than eighteen months. He was a native of Boston, but removed with his family at the age of five years to Concord, where he has since resided. He graduated at Harvard College in 1837, and was nearly forty-five years old at the time of his death. His writings include A Week on the Concord and Merrimack Rivers; Walden, or Life in the Woods; and various contributions to the periodical literature of the day. They are remarkable for their freedom and originality of thought, their quaint humor, and their warm sympathy with all the manifold aspects of nature. His disease was consumption, and, as we are informed, " his humor and cheerful courage did not forsake him during his sickness, and he met death as gayly as Theramenes in Xenophon's story." Mr. Thoreau, in spite of the racy individuality of his character, was much beloved and respected by his townsmen, and his writings have numerous admirers. He was honored with a public funeral from the Town Hall of Concord, on Friday, the 9th inst.

The Boston *Transcript* of May 10 (left) described the funeral. On the same day Greeley's *Tribune* (above) ran this obituary notice.

STANZAS:

Friday, May 9th, 1862.

———

Hearest thou the sobbing breeze complain
How faint the sunbeams light the shore,—
His heart more fixed than earth or main,
Henry! that faithful heart is o'er.

O weep not thou thus vast a soul,
O do not mourn this lordly man,
As long as Walden's waters roll,
And Concord river fills a span.

For thoughtful minds in Henry's page
Large welcome find and bless his verse,
Drawn from the poet's heritage,
From wells of right and nature's source.

Fountains of hope and faith! inspire
Most stricken hearts to lift this cross,
His perfect trust shall keep the fire,
His glorious peace disarm all loss!

Wm. E. Channing

At the funeral on May 9, stanzas written by Ellery Channing were sung. This circular, printed for distribution at the church, is signed by Channing.

In short this river proved so very long and navigable, that I was reminded of the last letter or two in the Voyages of the Baron la Hontan (written near the end of the 17 century, I think) in which he states that after reaching the Mississippi (by the Illinois or Wisconsin), the limit of previous exploration westward, he voyaged up it with his Indians, & at length turned up a great river coming in from the west which he called "La Riviere Longue" & he relates various improbable things about the country & its inhabitants, so that this letter has been regarded as pure fiction—or more properly speaking a lie. But I am somewhat inclined now to reconsider the matter.

The Governor of Minnesota, (Ramsay)—the superintendent of Ind. Affairs in this quarter,—& the newly appointed Ind. agent were on board; also a German band from St. Paul, a small cannon for salutes, & the money for the Indians (aye and the gamblers, it was said, who were to bring it back in another boat). There were about 100 passengers chiefly from St. Paul, and more or less recently from the N. Eastern states; also half a dozen young educated Englishmen. Chancing to speak with one who sat next to me, when the voyage was nearly half over, I found that he was a son of the Rev. Samuel [No; Joseph] May, & a classmate of yours, & had been looking for us at St. Anthony.

The last of the little settlements on the river, was New Ulm, about 100 miles this side of Redwood. It consists wholly of Germans. We left them 100 barrels of salt, which will be worth something more when the water is lowest, than at present.

Redwood is a mere locality, scarcely an Indian village—where there is a store & some houses have been built for them. We were now fairly on the great plains, and looking south, and after walking that way 3 miles, could see no tree in that horizon. The buffalo was said to be feeding within 25 or 30 miles.

A regular council was held with the Indians, who had come in on their ponies, and speeches were made on both sides thro' an interpreter, quite in the described mode; the Indians, as usual, having the advantage in point of truth and earnestness, and therefore of eloquence. The most prominent chief was named Little Crow. They were quite dissatisfied with the white man's treatment of them & probably have reason to be so. This council was to be continued for 2 or 3 days—the payment to be made the 2d day—and another payment to other bands a little higher up the Yellow Medicine (a tributary of the Minnesota) a few days thereafter.

In the afternoon the half naked Indians performed a dance, at the request of the Governor, for our amusement & their own benefit & then we took leave of them & of the officials who had come to treat with them.

Excuse these pencil marks but my ink stand is unscrewable & I can only direct my letter at the bar. I could tell you more and perhaps more interesting things, if I had time. I am considerably better than when I left home, but still far from well.

Our faces are already set toward home. Will you please let my sister know that we shall probably start for Milwaukee & Mackinaw in a day or 2 (or as soon as we hear from home) via Prairie du Chien & not La Crosse.

Shortly after his return to Concord, Thoreau wrote Ricketson:

▶ When your last letter was written I was away in the far North-West, in search of health. My cold turned to bronchitis which made me a close prisoner almost up to the moment of my starting on that journey, early in May. As I had an incessant cough, my doctor told me that I must "clear out"—to the West Indies or elsewhere, so I selected Minnesota. I returned a few weeks ago, after a good deal of steady travelling, considerably, yet not essentially better, my cough still continuing. If I do not mend very quickly I shall be obliged to go to another climate again very soon.

My ordinary pursuits, both indoor and out, have been for the most part omitted, or seriously interrupted—walking, boating, scribbling, &c.

A small granite stone, marked "Henry," stands over Thoreau's grave in Concord's Sleepy Hollow Cemetery. It is on the ridge where many writers lie. The Thoreau family plot is opposite the Hawthorne plot and next to the Alcotts'. Farther along the ridge is Emerson's grave.

Indeed I have been sick so long that I have almost forgotten what it is to be well, yet I feel that it all respects only my envelope.

By mid-autumn he thought briefly he was better and that there might be some chance of his recovery. He wrote Ricketson:

▶ I think that, on the whole, my health is better than when you were here; & my faith in the doctors has not increased.

I thank you all for your invitation to come to New Bedford, but I suspect that it must still be warmer here than there, that, indeed, New Bedford is warmer than Concord only in the winter, & so I abide by Concord.

September was pleasanter & much better for me than August, and October thus far has been quite tolerable. Instead of riding on horseback, I take a ride in a wagon about every other day. My neighbor, Mr [E. R.] Hoar, has two horses, & he being away for the most part this fall has generously offered me the use of one of them, and, as I notice, the dog throws himself in, and does scouting duty.

I am glad to hear that you no longer chew, but eschew, sugar plums. One of the worst effects of sickness even is that it may get one into the habit of taking a little something, his bitters or sweets, as if for his bodily good, from time to time, when he does not need it. However, there is no danger of this if you do not dose even when you are sick.

It is easy to talk, but hard to write.

But soon his health had relapsed. By mid-winter it was obvious that all hope must be abandoned. Feeling, as he told a Concord friend, that he must leave behind some estate for his widowed mother and unmarried sister Sophia, he set to work to edit as many of his unpublished manuscripts as he could before the end. Alcott, visiting him on New Year's Day, 1862, recorded:

To Thoreau, and spend the evening, sad to find failing and feeble. He is talkative, however; is interested in books and men, in our civil troubles especially, and speaks impatiently of what he calls the temporizing policy

This is the obituary notice Emerson wrote for the Boston *Daily Advertiser*. It is the germ of his remarks at Thoreau's funeral. Later, he enlarged upon it for the *Atlantic Monthly*.

Henry D. Thoreau.

Died at Concord, on Tuesday, 9 May, Henry D Thoreau, aged 44 years.

The premature death of Mr. Thoreau is a bitter disappointment to many friends who had set no limit to their confidence in his power and future performance. He is known to the public as the author of two remarkable books, "A Week on the Concord and Merrimack Rivers," published in 1849, and "Walden, or Life in the Woods," published in 1854. These books have never had a wide circulation, but are well known to the best readers, and have exerted a powerful influence on an important class of earnest and contemplative persons.

Mr. Thoreau was born in Concord, in 1817; was graduated at Harvard University, in 1837. Resisting the example of his companions, and the advice of friends, he declined entering either of the learned professions, and for a long time pursued his studies as his genius led him, without apparent method. But being a good mathematician and with an early and controlling love of nature, he afterwards came by imperceptible steps into active employment as a land-surveyor,—whose art he had first learned in the satisfaction of his private questions,—a profession which gave him lucrative work, and not too much of it, and in the running of town lines and the boundaries of farms and woodlands, carried him precisely where he wished to go,- to the homes of new plants, and of swamp and forest birds, as well as to wild landscape, and Indian relics. A man of simple tastes, hardy habits, and of preternatural powers of observation, he became a patient and successful student of nature in every aspect, and obtained an acquaintance with the history of the river on whose banks he lived, and with the habits of plants and animals, which made him known and valued by naturalists. He gathered a private museum of natural curiosities, and has left a large collection of manuscript records of his varied experiments and observations, which are much more than scientific value. His latest studies were in forest trees, the succession of forest growths, and the annual increment of wood. He knew the literature of natural history, from Aristotle and Pliny, down to the English writers on his favorite departments.

But his study as a naturalist, which went on increasing, and had no vacations, was less remarkable than the power of his mind and the strength of his character. He was a man of stoic temperament, highly intellectual, of a perfect probity, full of practical skill, an expert woodsman and boatman, acquainted with the use of tools, a good planter and cultivator, when he saw fit to plant, but without any taste for luxury, without the least ambition to be rich, or to be popular, and almost without sympathy in any of the common motives of men around him. He led the life of a philosopher, subordinating all other pursuits and so-called duties to his pursuit of knowledge and to his own estimate of duty. He was a man of firm mind and direct dealing, never disconcerted, and not to be bent by any inducement from his own course. He had a penetrating insight into men with whom he conversed, and was not to be deceived or used by any party, and did not conceal his disgust at any duplicity. As he was incapable of any the least dishonesty or untruth, he had nothing to hide, and kept his haughty independence to the end. And when we now look back at the solitude of this erect and spotless person, we lament that he did not live long enough for all men to know him.

E.

of our rulers; blames the people too for their indifference to the true issues of national honor and justice. Even Seward's letter to Earl Grey respecting Mason's and Liddell's case, comforting as it is to the country and serving as a foil to any hostile designs of England for the time at least, excites his displeasure as seeming to be humiliating to us, and dishonorable.

We talk of Pliny, whose books he is reading with delight. Also of Evelyn and the rural authors. If not a writer of verse, Thoreau is a poet in spirit, and has come as near to the writing of pastorals as any poet of his time. Were his days not numbered, and his adventures in the wild world once off his hands, then he might come to orchards and gardens, perhaps treat these in manner as masterly, uniting the spirit of naturalist and poet in his page. But the most he may hope for is to prepare his manuscripts for others' editing, and take his leave of them and us. I fear he has not many months to abide here, and the spring's summons must come for him soon to partake of "Syrian peace, immortal leisure."

By February, too weak to hold a pencil in his hands, he was dictating his revisions and his correspondence to his sister. James T. Fields, editor of the *Atlantic Monthly,* wrote to ask for papers for his journal, and Thoreau replied:

▶ Only extreme illness has prevented my answering your note earlier. I have no objection to having the papers you refer to printed in your monthly—if my feeble health will permit me to prepare them for the printer. What will you give me for them? They are, or have been used as, lectures of the usual length,—taking about an hour to read & I dont see how they can be divided without injury—How many pages can you print at once?—Of course, I should expect that no sentiment or sentence be altered or omitted without my consent, & to retain the copyright of the paper after you had used it in your monthly.—Is your monthly copyrighted?

On March 21, 1862, he wrote what has been erroneously termed his "last letter" (actually there were several business communications to James T. Fields after that date). Myron Benton, a young poet of the Hudson River Valley, had written expressing his admiration of Thoreau's books, and Thoreau replied:

▶ I thank you for your very kind letter, which, ever since I received it, I have intended to answer before I died, however briefly. I am encouraged to know, that, so far as you are concerned, I have not written my books in vain. I was particularly gratified, some years ago, when one of my

In August of 1861, after his return from Minnesota, Thoreau visited his old friend Daniel Ricketson in New Bedford and was there persuaded to pose for an ambrotype by E. S. Dunshee. Thoreau's family did not know of the existence of this portrait until after his death, when Ricketson sent a copy to Thoreau's sister Sophia, saying, "We all consider it very lifelike and one of the most successful likenesses we ever saw. What is rather remarkable is that it shows scarcely at all Henry's loss of health, suffering deeply as he was at the time it was taken, from his disease." Sophia however thought she could "discover a slight shade about the eyes expressive of weariness." And young Walton Ricketson, Daniel's son, said years later, "For all that it is one of the best of Thoreau, still it lacks the 'clear-eyed courage and directness,' qualities so dominant in his personality."

friends and neighbors said, "I wish you would write another book,—write it for me." He is actually more familiar with what I have written than I am myself.

The verses you refer to in Conway's "Dial," were written by F. B. Sanborn of this town. I never wrote for that journal.

I am pleased when you say that in "The Week" you like especially "those little snatches of poetry interspersed through the book," for these, I suppose, are the least attractive to most readers. I have not been engaged in any particular work on Botany, or the like, though, if I were to live, I should have much to report on Natural History generally.

You ask particularly after my health. I suppose that I have not many months to live; but, of course, I know nothing about it. I may add that I am enjoying existence as much as ever, and regret nothing.

Although it was obvious even to himself that Thoreau was sinking fast, he kept his spirits to the end. When Parker Pillsbury, the Quaker abolitionist, called a few days before Thoreau's death and inquired, "You seem so near the brink of the dark river, that I almost wonder how the opposite shore may appear to you," Thoreau replied, "One world at a time." When his aunt inquired if he had made his peace with God, he answered, "I did not know we had ever quarrelled."

The end came on May 6, 1862, when Thoreau was only forty-four. His sister Sophia described the last few days in a letter to Daniel Ricketson:

You ask for some particulars relating to Henry's illness. I feel like saying that Henry was never affected, never reached by it. I never before saw such a manifestation of the power of spirit over matter. Very often I have heard him tell his visitors that he enjoyed existence as well as ever. He remarked to me that there was as much comfort in perfect disease as in perfect health, the mind always conforming to the condition of the body. The thought of death, he said, could not begin to trouble him. His thoughts entertained him all his life, and did still.

When he had wakeful nights, he would ask me to arrange the furniture so as to make fantastic shadows on the wall, and he wished his bed was in the form of a shell that he might curl up in it. He considered occupation as necessary for the sick as for those in health, and has accomplished a vast amount of labor during the past few months in preparing some papers for the press. He did not cease to call for his manuscripts till the last day of his life.

During his long illness I never heard a murmur escape him, or the slightest wish expressed to remain with us; his perfect contentment was truly wonderful. None of his friends seemed to realize how very ill he was, so full of life and good cheer did he seem. One friend, as if by way

Perhaps the best indication that Henry David Thoreau has at long last achieved "official" recognition as one of America's great men is the fact that in 1962 his bust was finally placed in the Hall of Fame on the campus of New York University. Comparatively little-known people such as James Buchanan Eads won election in 1920; William Morton, in 1945; George Peabody and Joseph Story in 1900. But Thoreau was not elected to the Hall of Fame until 1960. As a result a bust by famed sculptor Malvina Hoffman was dedicated on the centennial of his death, May 6, 1962, inevitably recalling Thoreau's comment in his Journal for September 18, 1859:

"Dr. Bartlett handed me a paper to-day, desiring me to subscribe for a statue to Horace Mann. I declined, and said that I thought a man ought not any more to take up room in the world after he was dead. We shall lose one advantage of a man's dying if we are to have a statue of him forthwith. This is probably meant to be an opposition statue to that of Webster. At this rate they will crowd the streets with them. A man will have to add a clause to his will, 'No statue to be made of me.' It is very offensive to my imagination to see the dying stiffen into statues at this rate. We should wait till their bones begin to crumble—and then avoid too near a likeness to the living."

of consolation, said to him, "Well, Mr. Thoreau, we must all go." Henry replied, "When I was a very little boy I learned that I must die, and I sat that down, so of course I am not disappointed now. Death is as near to you as it is to me."

There is very much that I should like to write you about my precious brother, had I time and strength. I wish you to know how very gentle, lovely, and submissive he was in all his ways. His little study bed was brought down into our front parlor, when he could no longer walk with our assistance, and every arrangement pleased him. The devotion of his friends was most rare and touching; his room was made fragrant by the gift of flowers from young and old; fruit of every kind which the season afforded, and game of all sorts was sent him. It was really pathetic, the way in which the town was moved to minister to his comfort. Total strangers sent grateful messages, remembering the good he had done them. All this attention was fully appreciated and very gratifying to Henry; he would sometimes say, "I should be ashamed to stay in this world after so much had been done for me, I could never repay my friends." And they so remembered him to the last. Only about two hours before he left us, Judge Hoar called with a bouquet of hyacinths fresh from his garden, which Henry smelled and said he liked, and a few minutes after he was gone, another friend came with a dish of his favorite jelly.

I can never be grateful enough for the gentle, easy exit which was granted him. At seven o'clock Tuesday morning he became restless and desired to be moved; dear mother, Aunt Louisa, and myself were with him; his self-possession did not forsake him. A little after eight he asked to be raised quite up, his breathing grew fainter and fainter, and without the slightest struggle, he left us at nine o'clock.

A funeral was held in the First Parish Church in Concord, with Emerson reading his eulogy. Concord schools were dismissed so that the school children he had always loved might follow the funeral procession to the grave, strewing wild flowers along the path. As Emerson turned away from the newly filled grave, he turned to a friend and whispered, "He had a beautiful soul."

Thoreau Chronology

1812 John Thoreau marries Cynthia Dunbar at Concord, Mass.

1812 Helen Thoreau, sister, born at Concord.

1815 John Thoreau, Jr., brother, born at Concord.

1817 Henry David Thoreau born July 12 at Concord.

1818 Family moves to Chelmsford, Mass.

1819 Sophia Thoreau, sister, born at Chelmsford.

1821 Family moves to Boston.

1823 Family moves back to Concord.

1824 Father begins making pencils.

1827 Earliest essay, "The Seasons."

1828 Enters Concord Academy.

1833 Enters Harvard College.

1834 Ralph Waldo Emerson moves to Concord.

1835 On leave from Harvard, teaches school at Canton, Mass. Studies German with Orestes Brownson.

1836 Goes to New York with father, peddling pencils.

1837 Is graduated from Harvard. Begins Journal. Teaches briefly in Concord public school.

1838 Makes first trip to Maine. Opens private school in home. Moves school to Concord Academy; brother John becomes preceptor. Delivers his first lecture at Concord Lyceum.

1839 Takes excursion on Concord and Merrimack Rivers with brother John. Ellen Sewall visits Concord.

1840   Publishes first essay, "Aulus Persius Flaccus," and first poem, "Sympathy," in *The Dial*. Continues contributing to it until final volume in 1844. Writes "The Service."

1841   Goes to live at Emerson house for two years. With brother John, takes affirmative in debate at Concord Lyceum on "Is It Ever Proper to Offer Forcible Resistance?"

1842   Brother John dies Jan. 11. Hawthorne moves to Concord.

1843   From now on, lectures almost annually at Concord Lyceum. Helps Emerson edit *The Dial*. Begins to contribute to other magazines. From May to December tutors William Emerson's children on Staten Island.

1844   Accidentally sets fire to Concord woods in April. Builds Texas House with his father.

1845   Begins building Walden cabin in March. Moves in on July 4. Publishes article on Wendell Phillips in the *Liberator*.

1846   In July, is arrested and put in jail overnight for nonpayment of taxes. Makes trip to Maine woods.

1847   Leaves Walden Pond in September to spend year in Emerson's house while latter lectures in England. Does first professional surveying. Begins collecting natural history specimens for Louis Agassiz at Harvard.

1848   Lectures on January 26 before Concord Lyceum on "The Rights and Duties of the Individual in Relation to Government" ("Civil Disobedience"). Lectures for first time outside Concord, at Salem, on November 22. "Ktaadn and the Maine Woods" appears in *Union Magazine*. Returns from Emerson's to live in father's house.

1849   Sister Helen dies June 14. Publishes *A Week on the Concord and Merrimack Rivers*. Meets H. G. O. Blake. "Resistance to Civil Government" ("Civil Disobedience") appears in *Aesthetic Papers*. In October makes first trip to Cape Cod with Ellery Channing. Lectures in Salem, Portland, Worcester.

1850   Moves to Yellow House on Main Street, where he lives until death. In June makes second trip to Cape Cod. In July visits Fire Island to search for body of Margaret Fuller Ossoli. In September spends week in Canada with Ellery Channing. Lectures at Danvers, Worcester, Newburyport.

1851   Lectures at Clinton, Medford, Worcester. Helps fugitive slave escape to Canada.

1852   Lectures at Lincoln, Plymouth, Boston.

1853   Makes second trip to Maine woods. Publishes "A Yankee in Canada" in *Putnam's Magazine*. Family pencil business supplanted by preparation of plumbago for electrotyping.

1854   Makes speech on "Slavery in Massachusetts" at July 4 abolitionist meeting in Framingham. Publishes *Walden* in August. Meets Daniel Ricketson at New Bedford, Thomas Cholmondeley at Concord. Lectures in Plymouth, Philadelphia, Providence, New Bedford, Nantucket.

1855   Receives gift of Oriental books from Thomas Cholmondeley. Visits Cape Cod. Publishes part of *Cape Cod* in *Putnam's Magazine.* Lectures in Worcester.

1856   Makes botanical trip to Brattleboro. Does surveying and lecturing at "Eagleswood," Perth Amboy, N. J. Meets Walt Whitman in Brooklyn. Lectures in Philadelphia and Amherst, N. H.

1857   Meets Captain John Brown in Concord. Walks the length of Cape Cod. With Edward Hoar makes last trip to Maine woods. Lectures in Fitchburg and Worcester.

1858   Publishes "Chesuncook" in *Atlantic Monthly.* Visits the White Mountains and Mount Monadnock. Lectures in Lynn.

1859   Father dies February 3. After John Brown's capture at Harpers Ferry, delivers "A Plea for Captain John Brown" at Concord, Boston, and Worcester, and (when Brown is executed) "After the Death of John Brown" on December 2 in Concord.

1860   Camps out on Mount Monadnock with Ellery Channing. "A Plea for Captain John Brown" appears in *Echoes of Harper's Ferry;* "The Last Days of John Brown" in the *Liberator.* Lectures on "The Succession of Forest Trees" at the Middlesex Cattle Show. Lectures also in Lowell and Waterbury. Catches cold that brings on his final illness.

1861   Makes trip to Minnesota with Horace Mann, Jr., May 11 to July 10. Revises many of his manuscripts.

1862   Dies on May 6, at 9 A.M., aged 44 years, 9 months, 24 days. Buried in New Burying Ground. Years later, his body was moved to Sleepy Hollow Cemetery.

A Thoreau Reading List

The standard edition of Thoreau's works is the twenty-volume Walden (or Manuscript) Edition published by Houghton Mifflin of Boston in 1906. It includes the fourteen volumes of Thoreau's journals that were republished separately by Houghton Mifflin in 1949. The *Collected Poems* (Chicago, 1943) have been edited by Carl Bode, and the *Correspondence of Henry David Thoreau* (New York, 1958), by Carl Bode and Walter Harding. There are many editions of *Walden* available, ranging from paperback to limited editions. The only fully annotated edition is the *Variorum Walden* (New York; Twayne, 1962). Two useful anthologies of his works are the Modern Library *Walden and Other Writings* (1937) and the Viking *Portable Thoreau* (1947)—both of these editions have been re-issued as paperbacks.

The best biography of Thoreau to date is Henry Salt's *Life of Henry D. Thoreau* (London, 1890). Henry Seidel Canby's *Thoreau* (Boston, 1939) is more up to date, but carelessly written and often questionable in its interpretations. Ellery Channing's *Thoreau, the Poet-Naturalist* (Boston, 1873) and F. B. Sanborn's *Henry D. Thoreau* (Boston, 1882; completely rewritten as *The Life of Henry David Thoreau,* Boston, 1917) have the benefit of firsthand acquaintance of the authors with Thoreau, but both are unnecessarily perverse in following generally accepted standards of organization. Walter Harding's *Thoreau: Man of Concord* (New York, 1960) anthologizes the reminiscences of nearly a hundred friends and acquaintances of Thoreau.

The best critical evaluations of Thoreau's work are Sherman Paul's *The Shores of America* (Urbana, 1958), Joseph Wood Krutch's *Henry David Thoreau* (New York, 1948), and Reginald L. Cook's *Passage to Walden* (Boston, 1949). Walter Harding's *Thoreau: A Century of Criticism* (Dallas, 1954) anthologizes twenty-four of the best-known critical articles on Thoreau. Sherman Paul's *Thoreau: A Collection of Critical Essays* (Englewood Cliffs, 1962) confines itself to twentieth-century opinion.

A Chronological List
of First Editions
# of Thoreau's Works

A Week on the Concord and Merrimack Rivers. Boston: James Munroe & Co., 1849.

Walden; or, Life in the Woods. Boston: Ticknor & Fields, 1854.

Excursions. Boston: Ticknor & Fields, 1863.

The Maine Woods. Boston: Ticknor & Fields, 1864.

Cape Cod. Boston: Ticknor & Fields, 1864 [1865].

Letters to Various Persons. Boston: Ticknor & Fields, 1865.

A Yankee in Canada, with Anti-Slavery and Reform Papers. Boston: Ticknor & Fields, 1866.

Early Spring in Massachusetts. Boston: Houghton, Mifflin & Co., 1881.

Summer. Boston: Houghton, Mifflin & Co., 1884.

Winter. Boston: Houghton, Mifflin & Co., 1888 [1887].

Autumn. Boston: Houghton, Mifflin & Co., 1892.

Familiar Letters of Henry David Thoreau. Boston: Houghton, Mifflin & Co., 1894.

Poems of Nature. Boston: Houghton, Mifflin & Co., 1895.

The Service. Boston: Charles E. Goodspeed, 1902.

The First and Last Journeys of Thoreau. Boston: The Bibliophile Society, 1905.

Sir Walter Raleigh. Boston: The Bibliophile Society, 1905.

Journal. Boston: Houghton, Mifflin & Co., 1906.

The Moon. Boston: Houghton, Mifflin & Co., 1927.

The Transmigration of the Seven Brahmans. New York: William Edwin Rudge, 1932.

Collected Poems of Henry Thoreau. Chicago: Packard & Co., 1943.

The Correspondence of Henry David Thoreau. New York: New York University Press, 1958.

[*295*]

Thoreau
Collections

Outside of Concord there are five major collections of Thoreau manuscripts and books that are open to the public.

The Houghton Library at Harvard University in Cambridge, Massachusetts, has a large collection of Thoreau manuscripts including many letters, rough drafts of some of his essays such as "Life without Principle" and "Walking," the manuscript of "The Transmigration of the Seven Brahmans," portions of Sophia Thoreau's journal, and many manuscript fragments. Harvard also has the manuscript classbooks and other records of Thoreau's college class of 1837. Thoreau's herbarium is in the Agassiz Museum at Harvard. A catalog of the Thoreau manuscripts at Harvard will be found in *Thoreau Society Bulletins* 43 (Spring, 1953) and 53 (Fall, 1955).

The Abernethy Library at Middlebury College in Middlebury, Vermont, has numerous Thoreau manuscripts including letters, poems, some of the college essays, and various fragments. It also has numerous volumes from Thoreau's personal library, including his annotated copy of *Walden,* some of Helen Thoreau's scrapbooks, Thoreau pencils, and other Thoreau relics, and a large collection of books by and about Thoreau, including many translations of his works. A catalog of the Abernethy collection will be found in Viola C. White, *A Check List: Abernethy Library of American Literature* (Middlebury College Press, 1940).

The Henry W. and Albert A. Berg Collection of the New York Public Library in New York City has the largest collection of manuscripts of Thoreau letters and also many unpublished manuscripts of nature notes and charts. It has the unpublished manuscript of Thoreau's journal for his 1846 trip to the Maine woods. Its collection also includes many first editions of Thoreau's works, including a number of autographed presentation copies from Thoreau to his friends and distinguished contemporaries. The Berg Collection Thoreau manuscripts are catalogued in *Thoreau Society Bulletin* 43 (Spring, 1953).

The Pierpont Morgan Library in New York City has not only the manuscript of roughly 95 per cent of Thoreau's journal, but also his unpublished Indian and Canadian notebooks and the manuscripts of many of his poems, letters, and miscellaneous manuscripts. The Morgan Library Thoreau manuscripts are catalogued in *Thoreau Society Bulletin* 19 (April, 1947).

The Henry E. Huntington Library in San Marino, California, houses the manuscripts of many of Thoreau's poems and letters, fragments from his journal, the rough drafts of early versions of *Walden*, the Minnesota journal, the corrected page proofs of *A Week on the Concord and Merrimack Rivers*, and many other important manuscripts. They are catalogued in *Thoreau Society Bulletin* 43 (Spring, 1953).

All the above institutions occasionally conduct exhibitions of their Thoreau holdings. Qualified students are usually permitted to examine materials not on exhibition upon application in advance to the curators or directors of the institutions.

Visiting Concord

Concord, Massachusetts, is located about twenty miles northwest of Boston, just off Route Two. The turn in to Concord is clearly marked on both the western and eastern approaches. Trains to Concord may be taken from North Station in Boston, and buses from Harvard Square in Cambridge.

The main business street of Concord, where most of the shops are located, is known as the Mill Dam. At the northern end of Mill Dam is Monument Square where the Concord Chamber of Commerce maintains a tourist information booth.

TOUR ONE.   From Monument Square, proceed east on Lexington Road. *The First Parish Church* from which Thoreau was buried in 1862 is the large white steepled church on the right. *Emerson's House* is the large white house on the right at the intersection of Lexington Road and Cambridge Turnpike. It is open to the public at a nominal admission charge and is still furnished much as it was in Emerson's day. Thoreau, when he lived with the Emersons, used the small bedroom at the head of the stairs. The *Concord Antiquarian Society* is located in the fork between Lexington Road and Cambridge Turnpike. It is open to the public (except in the winter months) at a nominal fee. It contains Thoreau's Walden furniture among many other Concord relics. A quarter mile further east, on the left-hand side of Lexington Road is the *Orchard House,* also open to the public, where Thoreau often visited the Alcott family. Just beyond it is the *Wayside,* owned successively by the Alcotts and the Hawthornes, where Thoreau again frequently visited. The house is open to the public. Thoreau is also supposed to have helped Alcott with the landscaping and terracing of the grounds. At Merriam's Corner, a quarter mile further east, turn left and then right at the first corner. This is Virginia Road. *Thoreau Farm,* a quarter mile down the road on the left, is the site of Thoreau's birthplace. The house in which he was born has been moved. It is the next farmhouse on the left. Both of these farms are now privately owned.

TOUR TWO.   From Monument Square proceed north on Bedford Street. *Sleepy Hollow Cemetery* is in the second block on the left. Signs at the northern gates direct one to Author's Ridge in the northwestern corner of the cemetery. There

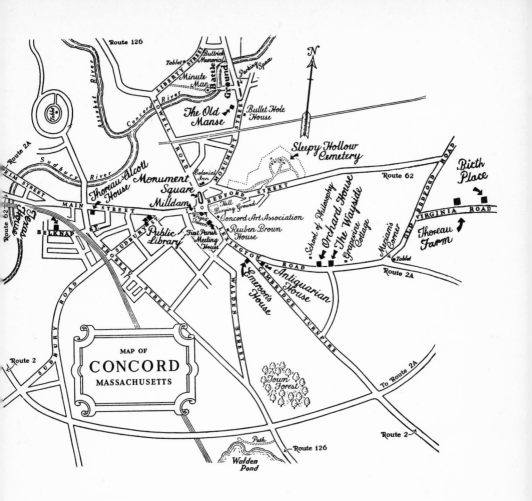

one will find the graves of Thoreau, Hawthorne, Emerson, and the Alcotts all in close proximity. Returning along Bedford Street, take the street on the right just beyond the cemetery, and the first right again on to Monument Street. The *Old Manse,* where Emerson wrote *Nature* and where Hawthorne spent the first years of his marriage, sits back from the road on the left beyond the railroad tracks. It is open to the public at a nominal fee. Just beyond the Old Manse is the Old North Bridge and the Concord Battleground. Thoreau sang in a choir at the dedication of the monument at the nearer end of the bridge.

TOUR THREE.   From Monument Square proceed south on Mill Dam to the *Concord Free Public Library* at the intersection of Main Street and Sudbury Road. Here one will find the original crayon portrait of Thoreau by Rowse, the bust of Thoreau by Walton Ricketson, Thoreau's surveying instruments, and many books from his personal library. The Alfred Hosmer Collection of books by and about Thoreau is housed in a special alcove. Proceed south on Main Street. The *Thoreau-Alcott House,* where Thoreau lived the last twelve years of his life and died, is a large white house on the left, at 73 Main Street. It is privately owned and not open to the public, but is marked with a bronze tablet. Turn left on Thoreau Street and just short of the railroad station, turn right on Belknap Street. The site of the *Texas House,* which Thoreau and his father built in 1844, is on the right marked by a tablet. The house was destroyed by fire and hurricane in the 1930's.

TOUR FOUR. From Monument Square proceed south on Mill Dam and left at the first intersection on Walden Street. Just beyond the intersection with Route Two (a little over a mile from town) will be found *Walden Pond State Reservation.* A pair of granite posts on the right mark the footpath in to the site of *Thoreau's cabin,* which is marked by a bronze plaque, a cairn of stones (to which traditionally each visitor adds a stone), and granite posts indicating the exact location of the cabin. The Indian path, which Thoreau mentions in *Walden,* is still plainly visible at the edge of the pond and may be followed completely around the pond.

A Note on Thoreau Portraits

All known portraits of Thoreau taken from life have been included in the text of this volume. There are in addition a number of other portraits that should at least be mentioned.

Walton Ricketson, the son of Thoreau's New Bedford friend Daniel Ricketson, who as a boy had known Thoreau as a frequent visitor in his home, years later made a bust of Thoreau, the original of which is now in the Concord Free Public Library. It is obviously based on the Rowse crayon portrait of Thoreau. The sculptor once said of the bust, "I feel the value as a likeness is largely due to the friendly interest shown in the work (as it progressed) by Mr. Emerson [Edward Emerson, Ralph Waldo's son], to whose suggestions I attribute much of its success."

Of the work in a former letter he writes—

"Let me say at once that I like it better than even before. It cannot be exactly like even if that were desirable, but it is sufficiently like and tells the story of clear-eyed courage and directness, a suggestion of Nature[']s ruggedness with Nature[']s refinement and wholesomeness, and a hint too of the tenderness and faith that make him poet as well as naturalist. It is a happy face as it should be."

Ricketson also made a profile medallion of Thoreau of which F. B. Sanborn has said, it "is less known than it should be,—for it alone of the four likenesses extant shows the aquiline features as his comrades of the wood and mountain saw them,—not weakened by any effort to bring him to the standard of other men in garb or expression."

In 1917 one of Houghton Mifflin's editors happened upon what was apparently a new portrait of Thoreau. Edward Emerson said that it brought back to him the Thoreau he had known when a child as no other portrait did. But it was later discovered to be a drawing made in the early 1900's by a Henry K. Hannah, based on a now unknown sketch supposedly made by Sophia Thoreau supplemented by a study of the other authenticated portraits of Thoreau.

Edward Emerson himself once made a sketch of Thoreau from memory. He was a competent amateur artist—indeed he held a lectureship in art-anatomy at the Boston Museum of Fine Arts for many years—and apparently thought of creating his own portrait of Thoreau as a frontispiece for his 1917 memoir of Thoreau. This plan was abandoned and he used the Hannah drawing instead. A photograph of the Walton Ricketson bust is shown here.

A NOTE ON THOREAU PORTRAITS

There has long existed a legend that Thoreau's sister Sophia painted a portrait of Henry as a companion to her portrait of her brother John that is now in the Concord Antiquarian Society. According to legend she gave the portrait of Henry to a neighbor with the stipulation that it never be published. Unfortunately the legend does not name the neighbor. In the early 1920's, George S. Hellman, the New York book dealer, turned up a portrait in Bangor, Maine (where Sophia Thoreau had spent the last years of her life), which he thought to be either the missing portrait retouched by a professional artist or a hitherto unknown portrait of Thoreau done in the late 1830's. That portrait is now owned by the Concord Antiquarian Society, but few if any of the recognized Thoreau scholars accept it as genuine and the Antiquarian Society has removed it from public display.

According to Bronson Alcott's journal, Henry Kirk Browne, who did the equestrian statue of George Washington in Union Square, New York City, visited Concord on October 30, 1854, and made a sketch of Thoreau and his Canadian woodchopper friend Therien. Whether that sketch is still extant is not known.

Picture

Credits

Key to picture position: t-top; c-center; b-bottom; l-left; r-right; combinations: tl-top left, etc.

The following are abbreviations used for picture sources:

AAS	American Antiquarian Society	HBH	Mrs. Herbert B. Hosmer
AC	Authors' Collection	HCL	Harvard College Library
AL	Abernethy Library	LK	Leonard Kleinfeld
BC,NYPL	Berg Collection, New York Public Library	LOC	Library of Congress
CAS	Concord Antiquarian Society	MHS	Minnesota Historical Society
CFPL	Concord Free Public Library	ML	Pierpont Morgan Library
CHW	Mrs. Caleb H. Wheeler	NYHS	New-York Historical Society
ESQ	Emerson Society Quarterly	NYPL	New York Public Library
		PC,NYPL	Picture Collection, New York Public Library
		RWR	Roland W. Robbins

PICTURE CREDITS

Index

INDEX

Salem, 1, 136
Salem Lyceum, 124
Salem Observer, 124, 125
Salt, Henry, 238, 294
Sanborn, Franklin B., 40, 95, 96, 101, 252, 255, 258, 259, 260, 265, 277, 288, 294, 301; description of Thoreau, 247
Sartain's Union Magazine, 72, 73, 231, 233, 292
Scituate, Mass., 58
"Service, The," 292
Sewall, Edmund, 40-43
Sewall, Ellen, 40, 58-60, 291
Shadrach, 196
Shanley, J. Lyndon, 233
Shattuck, Daniel, 8
"Sic Vita," 62-64
Sims, Thomas, 197, 202, 204, 206, 252
"Slavery in Massachusetts," 293
Sleepy Hollow Cemetery, 293, 298
Smith, Julius, 259
Spring, Marcus, 118, 174, 245-249
Staples, Samuel, 18, 158, 159, 162, 172
Staten Island, 64, 66, 76-88, 157, 292
Stuart, Gilbert, 32
"Succession of Forest Trees," 293
Sumner, Charles, 118
Surveying, 168-174, 292
"Sympathy," 292

Taunton, Mass., 38
Teaching, 36-46, 268
Teale, Edwin Way, 212
"Texas House," 15, 292, 300
Thatcher, George, 7?, 182
Thatcher, Rebecca, 182
Thoreau birthplace, 14
Thoreau houses, 7-9
Thoreau pencils, 136-139
Thoreau sketches, 213
Thoreau, Cynthia Dunbar (mother), 1-2, 6, 21, 44, 58, 84, 85, 112, 114, 252, 261, 290, 291
Thoreau, Helen (sister), 4, 6, 23, 45, 81, 82, 85, 191, 291, 292, 296
Thoreau, Henry David, birth, 1; childhood, 5, 7; education, 21-35; as teacher, 36-46; trip on Concord and Merrimack Rivers, 47-50; friendship with Emerson, 51-57; relations with women, 58-67; on writing, 68-75; on Staten Island, 76-88; on Concord neighbors, 89-110; on reform movements, 111-117; as lecturer, 124-135; Furness sketch of, 133; pencil-making, 136-139; inventiveness, 139; at Walden Pond, 140-157; and farming, 147-151; "Civil

Disobedience," 158-167; and surveying, 168-174; *A Week on the Concord and Merrimack Rivers,* 175-180; as traveller, 181-190; and abolitionism, 190-211 (*see also* Negro slavery); as naturalist, 212-221; publication of *Walden,* 230-237; Rowse portrait of, 236; disciples of, 238-244; Ricketson sketch of, 239; Maxham daguerreotype of, 247; meeting with Walt Whitman, 249-251; defense of John Brown, 252-267; on Indians, 268-274; last years and death, 275-290; grave, 284; Dunshee ambrotype of, 287; Hoffman bust of, 289; chronology, 291-293; reading list, 294; first editions, 295; collections of manuscripts and books, 296-297; sites to visit, 298-300; other portraits of, 301-302
Thoreau, Jane (aunt), 4, 6
Thoreau, John (brother), 4, 38, 39, 43, 45, 47, 49, 51, 53, 58, 60, 141, 169, 175, 268, 291, 292, 302
Thoreau, John (father), 1, 2, 3, 4, 8, 14, 19, 85, 136, 291, 292, 293
Thoreau, John (grandfather), 3, 8
Thoreau, Maria (aunt), 6, 162, 191
Thoreau, Sophia (sister), 4, 6, 49, 85, 139, 145, 187, 236, 240, 245, 285, 287; describes death of Thoreau, 288-290, 291, 301, 302
Thoreau: The Poet-Naturalist, 66
Ticknor & Fields, 177, 179, 180, 233, 237
Tomlinson, H. M., 175
"To the Maiden in the East," 60-62
Transcendentalism, 113
Travelling, 181-190

Very, Jones, 30, 123

Walden, 6, 102, 140, 157, 169, 177, 180, 195, 239, 240; quoted, 142-157; published and reviewed, 230-237; foreign editions, 235; 293, 294, 295, 296, 300
Walden Pond, 30, 73, 140-157, 172, 175, 216, 230; map of, 146, 292, 300
"Walking," 126
"Walk to Wachusett, A," 85
Ward, Mrs. Joseph, 6, 191
Ward, Prudence, 6, 79, 191
Warren, Henry, 40
Watson, Marston, 62
Wayside, 298
Webster, Daniel, 86, 162
Week on the Concord and Merrimack Rivers, A, 50, 141, 157, 162, 230, 237, 288; published and reviewed, 175-180, 292

INDEX

Weiss, John, 27, 30
Weld, Theodore, 245-246, 250
Westminster Review, 237
Wheeler, Charles Stearns, 30, 140
Wheeler, Francis, 259
White, Deacon John, 8
White Mountains. *See* New Hampshire
Whitman, Walt, 245, 249-251
Whittier, John Greenleaf, 176, 177
Wiley, B. B., 243
Williams, Henry, 199

Women, 58-67
Worcester, 130, 238, 240, 247, 256, 276
Worcester *Palladium*, 129
Worcester *Spy*, 258
Wright, H. C., 112, 122
Wright, Henry G., 122
Writing, 68-75

Yankee in Canada, A, 163, 190
"Yellow House," 15, 280, 292
Yeoman's Gazette, 41, 73